▼ FOCUS ON

Academic Skills for

IELTS

PEARSON
Longman

MORGAN TERRY JUDITH WILSON

SERIES EDITOR SUE O'CONNELL

Map of the book

Reading	Writing	Listening	Speaking	Language review
MODULE A ▶The feel-good factor page 8 *(Focus on IELTS* Units 1 and 2)				
Changes in eating habits True/False/Not Given Summary (with bank)	1 The language of change *(increase, decrease,* etc.) 2 Interpreting information from diagrams Describing the data (Task 1: graphs)	Sports centre job (Section 1) Note completion	Describing habits (Part 1) Understanding the questions Extending your answers Fluency markers	1 Topic vocabulary 2 General words 3 Describing graphs 4 Word formation: language of change
MODULE B ▶City page 20 *(Focus on IELTS* Units 3 and 4)				
Light years ahead Sentence completion (with bank) Matching	Interpreting and comparing data (Task 1: bar charts) Writing and organising the description	Wind-powered school (Section 2) Multiple choice Labelling a map	Comparing and contrasting (Parts 1 and 3) Organising responses Modifying expressions	1 Topic vocabulary 2 Parallel phrases 3 Describing qualities and quantities 4 Topic vocabulary: money and natural resources
PROGRESS CHECK 1 page 32				
MODULE C ▶Rush page 34 *(Focus on IELTS* Units 5 and 6)				
Clocking cultures Matching headings Multiple choice Summary (no bank)	Presenting arguments (Task 2: argument-led approach) Analysing the question Anaysing a sample answer	Sharing a flat (Section 1) Table completion	Describing people (Part 2) Analysing a sample answer Organising your talk	1 Topic vocabulary 2 Sentence rewriting 3 Speaking – using colloquial language 4 Writing: reference links
MODULE D ▶The cultural scene page 46 *(Focus on IELTS* Units 7 and 8)				
Fighting the dust Sentence completion (no bank) Multiple choice with multiple answers	Problems and solutions (Task 2: problem and solution) Presenting and justifying solutions (Modal verbs/ conditionals)	1 Music course (Section 3) Multiple choice with multiple answers Short answers/lists 2 Art in Bali (Section 4) Table completion Note completion	Answering different question types (Part 1) Question forms Extending answers	1 Topic vocabulary 2 Parallel expressions: avoiding repetition 3 Problems and solutions 4 Linking expressions 5 Describing research
PROGRESS CHECK 2 page 58				
MODULE E ▶Natural forces page 60 *(Focus on IELTS* Units 9 and 10)				
Eating up the **Titanic** True/False/Not Given Table completion Multiple choice with multiple answers	Describing diagrams showing natural processes (Task 1: diagram) Understanding the diagram Linking ideas	Rotorua, New Zealand (Section 2) Labelling a map Table completion	1 Describing a place (Part 2) Dealing with rounding off questions 2 Describing problems and solutions (Part 3) Developing the topic	Topic vocabulary
MODULE F ▶Brainpower page 72 *(Focus on IELTS* Units 11 and 12)				
The knowledge society Multiple choice Yes/No/Not Given	Presenting an opinion (Task 2: thesis-led approach) Developing and supporting ideas Analysing a sample answer	Survey on computer facilities (Section 3) Multiple choice Matching	1 Describing a past event (Part 2) Explaining 2 Giving opinions (Part 3) Justifying opinions	1 Topic vocabulary 2 Word formation: adjective endings 3 Language of research: research methods 4 Linking ideas: concession and contrast
PROGRESS CHECK 3 page 84				

3

▶ Introduction

What is *Focus on Academic Skills for IELTS*?

Focus on Academic Skills for IELTS offers systematic preparation for students wishing to take the IELTS exam. It provides training for students taking the Listening, Speaking, Academic Writing and Academic Reading modules.

Focus on Academic Skills for IELTS offers:

- detailed information about the four modules of the exam, including all task types.
- guided practice for all four skills in every module.
- language input for the different parts of the Speaking and Writing modules.
- hints and tips to help with special areas of difficulty.
- intensive work on academic English, including collocations, useful phrases and the language of research as well as key language for specific academic topics.
- a Language review section at the end of each module which pulls together key vocabulary and concepts.
- five Progress tests which recycle key language and skills in new contexts.
- examples of answers to writing tasks at higher and lower band levels with guidance on assessing your writing.
- ideas for speaking and writing on IELTS-related topics where students can apply and extend ideas from the reading and listening texts.
- preparation tips for all four skills in a special section at the end.

How can *Focus on Academic Skills for IELTS* be used?

1 To accompany the coursebook *Focus on IELTS*
Focus on Academic Skills for IELTS reflects the structure and organisation of *Focus on IELTS,* and can be used to accompany the coursebook either in class or for homework activities. Each of the modules A–J in *Focus on Academic Skills for IELTS* relates to a pair of units in *Focus on IELTS,* covering the same general topic area and reinforcing and extending the skills and language work and the examination training provided there. Cross references are supplied for key

activities and language points to help teachers and students use the two books together.

2 As a short intensive course to help students to prepare for the exam
Focus on Academic Skills for IELTS can also be used on its own as a short intensive course for students who only have a limited amount of time to prepare for the exam. It may also be used by students who have already used *Focus on IELTS* but who wish to do more preparation for the exam. The book offers a full introduction to all the tasks the students will meet in the IELTS exam, together with the key language and skills needed. Used in this way, the book could be completed in about 30–40 hours.

3 For students to use to prepare for the exam on their own
Students can use *Focus on Academic Skills for IELTS* on their own at home or in a self-access centre. The book provides clear guidance and useful tips on all tasks, and full answer keys and tapescripts are provided. Training is given on self-assessment of writing and speaking, and students are encouraged to record themselves for speaking activities wherever possible.

Recommended procedure

- Work through the units in the order they are in the book. Although all the tasks are at the level candidates will meet in the exam, the exam preparation is graded, as more support is provided at the beginning.
- Work though the different sections of each module in order. Earlier sections will provide language and ideas for the later parts of the module.
- Don't use a dictionary while doing reading tasks. However, once a task has been completed, go back over the text to highlight and record useful phrases – including new collocations of words that are already known. (The same procedure should be followed with Listening. After the task has been completed, listen again – with or without the tapescript – and note useful words and phrases.)
- Students should evaluate their own work critically and use the answer keys appropriately.

4

▶ The IELTS exam

What is IELTS and where can I take it?

IELTS stands for International English Language Testing Service. The IELTS examination is taken by students who want to live, study or work in an English-speaking country, and especially by those who are going to follow academic courses at a university or similar institution, or more general training courses. It can be taken at Test Centres world-wide on fixed days throughout the year.

Exam overview

The examination tests all four language skills: Listening, Reading, Writing and Speaking. There are separate Reading and Writing Modules for those requiring qualifications in academic skills or more general skills. This book focuses on Academic Reading and Academic Writing skills.

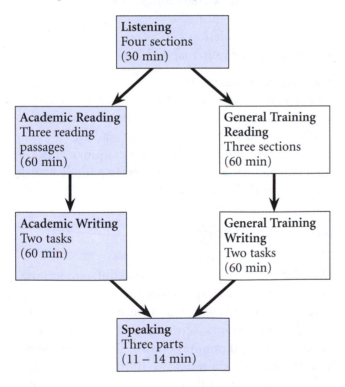

Listening
Four sections
(30 min)

Academic Reading
Three reading passages
(60 min)

General Training Reading
Three sections
(60 min)

Academic Writing
Two tasks
(60 min)

General Training Writing
Two tasks
(60 min)

Speaking
Three parts
(11 – 14 min)

Results

You will get your IELTS results within two weeks of taking the exam. You will not be given a pass or a fail grade, but instead you will receive a Test Report Form giving you a band score for each of the four skills, and a final overall band which is an average of these. These band scores are expressed on a range of 0 to 9 and cover the whole range of language ability. For more information, look on the IELTS website www.ielts.org.

THE IELTS NINE-BAND SCALE

Band 9 – Expert User

Has fully operational command of the language: appropriate, accurate and fluent with complete understanding.

Band 8 – Very Good User

Has fully operational command of the language with only occasional unsystematic inaccuracies and inappropriacies. Misunderstandings may occur in unfamiliar situations. Handles complex detailed argumentation well.

Band 7 – Good User

Has operational command of the language, though with occasional inaccuracies, inappropriacies and misunderstandings in some situations. Generally handles complex language well and understands detailed reasoning.

Band 6 – Competent User

Has generally effective command of the language despite some inaccuracies, inappropriacies and misunderstandings. Can use and understand fairly complex language, particularly in familiar situations.

Band 5 – Modest User

Has partial command of the language, coping with overall meaning in most situations, though is likely to make many mistakes. Should be able to handle basic communication in own field.

Band 4 – Limited User

Basic competence is limited to familiar situations. Has frequent problems in understanding and expression. Is not able to use complex language.

Band 3 – Extremely Limited User

Conveys and understands only general meaning in very familiar situations. Frequent breakdowns in communication occur.

Band 2 – Intermittent User

No real communication is possible except for the most basic information using isolated words or short formulae in familiar situations and to meet immediate needs. Has great difficulty in understanding spoken and written English.

Band 1 – Non User

Essentially has no ability to use the language beyond possibly a few isolated words.

Band 0 – Did not attempt the test

No assessable information provided.

Listening

Time and organisation

The Listening Module has four sections of increasing difficulty, with a total of 40 questions, and takes about 30 minutes. Each section has 10 questions and is heard **once only**. You have time to look through the questions before you listen, and also time to check your answers after each section. You write your answers on the question paper as you listen, and you then have ten minutes at the end to transfer your answers to a separate answer sheet.

Content and task types

Sections 1 and 2 develop the listening skills needed for survival in an English-speaking country, in situations such as shopping, accommodation, etc. Sections 3 and 4 have a more academic context – for example, they may be a recording of part of a tutorial, seminar or lecture. You will hear a variety of accents including British, North American and Australian English.

The following task types may be included:

- multiple choice
- matching
- classification
- short-answer questions and lists
- note / table / flow chart completion
- sentence completion
- summary completion
- labelling a diagram, map or plan

Marking and assessment

All the answers have one mark. Any answer which is above the word limit specified for that task will not receive a mark, so it is important to read the instructions carefully. Spelling and grammar must be correct. The final score is converted to a whole or half band on the IELTS band scale.

Academic Reading

Time and organisation

The Academic Reading Module has three reading passages, and a total of 40 questions to be answered in one hour. The first two reading passages have 13 questions each, and the last one has 14 questions. The total length of the three passages is between 2,000 and 2,750 words. All your answers must be written on a separate Answer Sheet **during the exam**. No extra time is allowed for this at the end of the exam.

Content and task types

The reading passages will be on academic topics of general interest. You don't need to have specialised knowledge of the topic, as any specialised vocabulary needed for the task will be explained in the text or in a glossary. However, you need to have a good understanding of more general academic terms in order to cope with the tasks successfully in the time given, and it will help you if you have some awareness of the types of general issues covered in the modules of this book.

The following task types may be included:

- multiple choice
- matching lists or phrases
- matching headings to sections/paragraphs
- classification
- identification of information – True/False/ Not Given
- identification of writer's views – Yes/No/Not Given
- locating information in sections/paragraphs
- short-answer questions and lists
- note / table / flow chart completion
- sentence completion
- summary completion
- labelling a diagram, map or plan

Marking and assessment

All the answers have one mark. Any answer which is above the word limit specified for that task will not receive a mark, so it is important to read the instructions carefully. Spelling and grammar must be correct. The final score is converted to a whole or half band on the IELTS band scale.

Academic Writing

Time and organisation

The Writing Module consists of two different writing tasks and the whole paper takes one hour. You do not have any choice of tasks. Task 1 must be a minimum of 150 words and it is recommended that you spend no longer than 20 minutes on this. Task 2 must be at least 250 words and carries two thirds of the marks, so it is recommended that you spend 40 minutes on this. Underlength answers lose marks.

Content and task types

The Task 1 prompt is always a type of diagram. You have to write about the information shown, describing the main features, trends or differences. You have to refer closely to the diagram and, where relevant, illustrate your main points with figures. You are **not** required to give any explanation for the data, but have to describe only the information given in the task.

Task types may involve describing information from
- a graph, chart or table
- a flow chart or process diagram
- a plan or map
- a diagram showing how something works
- a diagram showing or comparing objects
- a set of small diagrams

In Task 2 you are required to discuss an issue, question or opinion of general interest, and to give your own point of view. The topics do not require you to have specialist knowledge, but you have to be able to present ideas on general issues. The prompt is usually a background statement introducing the topic, followed by an instruction to the candidate. This instruction tells you how you should approach the topic and it is very important that you spend time analysing exactly what you are expected to write about.

Instruction types include:
- giving and justifying opinions
- comparing opposing opinions
- evaluating advantages and disadvantages
- comparing arguments for and against
- analysing problems and suggesting solutions
- answering direct questions on an issue

For Task 2 you are expected to write in a formal style, appropriate for an academic exam.

Marking and assessment
Task 2 carries more marks than Task 1, so you should take care to spend a full 40 minutes on Task 2.

Task 1 is assessed in terms of:

Task fulfilment: how well you have reported and illustrated the main points of the information.
Coherence and cohesion: how well you have organised the information across your answer and how you have linked the ideas within and between sentences.
Vocabulary and sentence structure: how appropriately and accurately you have used a range of language.

Task 2 is assessed in terms of:

Arguments, ideas and evidence: how well you have been able to present relevant ideas and opinions and develop these into a well-supported argument or point of view.
Communicative quality: how well you have organised and linked your points and ideas.
Vocabulary and sentence structure: how appropriately and accurately you have used a range of language.

Your scores on these criteria are combined to give you a Task Band for each task. These are then combined to give you a Final Band for Writing. There are no half bands for this module.

Speaking

Time and organisation
In the Speaking Module, each candidate has a face-to-face interview with an examiner. The interview consists of three parts and takes between 11 and 14 minutes. The examiner records the interview.

Content and task type
Part 1 lasts for 4 to 5 minutes and begins with introductions. The examiner then asks you a series of questions on two or three different topics connected to your life, your interests or what you do.

Part 2 lasts 3 to 4 minutes and is based on the candidate giving a short talk. You are given a card with a familiar topic and several prompts. You then have one minute to make notes on what you want to say before speaking for two minutes on the topic given. You do not have a choice of topic but the topics are based on your own experience, such as a person or place you know, or an event or activity you have experienced.

The examiner may ask you a brief question at the end of your talk.

Part 3 lasts for 4 to 5 minutes. Here the examiner asks you more abstract questions related to your topic and develops a more general discussion.

Marking and assessment
Candidates are assessed on all parts of the interview. Remember that if you give very short answers, the examiner has very little language to assess.

The criteria are:

Fluency and coherence: how well you are able to maintain the flow of conversation, and how clearly you can express and link ideas.
Lexical resource: how appropriately and accurately you use a range of vocabulary.
Grammatical range and accuracy: how appropriately and accurately you use a range of structures.
Pronunciation: how clearly you speak and how well you use the different features of English pronunciation.

The scores on these criteria are combined to give the Final Band for Speaking. There are no half bands for this module.

▶ THE FEEL-GOOD FACTOR

Focus on reading *General strategies; True/False/Not Given; summary*

FORMING A GENERAL PICTURE
▶ *Focus on IELTS page 12*

1 Before you look at the questions for each part of the IELTS Reading Module, you should spend a couple of minutes getting a general idea of what the text is about. This will help you to tackle the tasks.

a Read the titles and the first two or three sentences of Texts 1 and 2 to identify the topics. Spend no more than 20 seconds on this.

1 Which text is about eating habits? Text ......
2 Which is about a physical problem? Text ......

b Before you read the rest of each text, think about these questions to prepare yourself.

1 How are people's eating habits changing in your country?
2 What are the results of these changes on a) people's health b) social relationships?

c Look through both texts quickly and compare the information given with your ideas in b.

DEALING WITH UNKNOWN VOCABULARY

2 IELTS Reading texts may contain specialist words and expressions, but you will not need to understand all of these to answer the questions. Specialist words which are important for the meaning are often explained for you in the text.

a Look at the three underlined words and phrases in Texts 1 and 2. Decide which **two** of them are important in each text. Find and underline a phrase in the same sentence or the following sentence which helps you understand their meanings.

b One of the three underlined words in each text is less important. You don't need to know this word to understand the general message. In each text, what general things can you guess about the meaning of this word from the context?

Text 1

Childhood obesity goes global

A Childhood <u>obesity</u> is rapidly becoming a global epidemic. The US continues to lead the way, with as many as 37% of its children and adolescents carrying around too much fat. But other countries are rapidly catching up. According to statistics presented at the European Congress on Obesity in Finland, more than 20% of European youngsters between the ages of 5 and 17 are either overweight or obese. Asia lags behind the US and Europe in its obesity statistics, but Thailand, Malaysia, Japan and the Philippines have all reported troubling increases in recent years. Up to 10% of China's 290 million children are already believed to be overweight or obese, and that percentage is expected to have doubled a decade from now. So across Asia too, childhood obesity is on the rise, and a less marked trend has been documented even in urbanised areas of sub-Saharan Africa.

B Why do children become obese? One important factor is <u>insulin</u>, a hormone which enables the body to store extra calories as fat. Physical exercise helps control insulin levels, while ingesting fat combined with starches and sugar can cause surges in insulin levels. A child who sits in front of the TV for hours on end, eating potato chips and <u>doughnuts</u>, is an ideal fat-storage machine.

C What is urgently needed is for schools, health professionals, parents and children to work together. Encouragingly, changing a family's lifestyle in healthy ways does not appear to be all that difficult: it involves regular exercise, slightly smaller portions and slightly different foods. And this, say health officials, is a message that badly needs to get out.

Text 2

Dinner time then and now

A Patterns of food consumption in Britain are changing rapidly. A major survey by research group Mintel shows that, for the first time, convenience meals account for the largest slice of all consumer spending on food – 30.1 per cent of the market. Over the past decade, pizza sales have risen by 98 per cent. Sales of pasta products have enjoyed a similar increase.

B But the trend has resulted in profound changes to eating habits. The proportion of adults who say they regularly eat a traditional Sunday dinner, with <u>roast</u> meat and vegetables, has fallen by ten per cent over the same period. Now less than half say they usually have a roast each week. Meat and fish account for a fifth of the UK's total food market, but the sector has shown no growth over the past decade. Spending on

fruit and vegetables, meanwhile, has gone up by only six per cent – despite a huge government education campaign to get people eating more healthily.

C However, the Mintel survey found that 40 per cent of the population still consider themselves as 'traditionalist' diners. In contrast, 27 per cent are '<u>convenience seekers</u>', who are happy heating up meals in the microwave. A growing proportion of consumers – 31 per cent – are classed as '<u>casual diners</u>', people who skip breakfast and eat out most nights, not for pleasure but because they can't be bothered to cook.

D It is predicted that more people will become casual diners as changes in society see the size of households declining. This development, added to the increasing number of childless households, means that the pressure to cook a balanced meal has declined, Mintel suggests.

TRUE/FALSE/NOT GIVEN

▶ *Focus on IELTS* page 14

3 In this task, you have to decide whether the information given in a statement is *true* or *false* according to the text or *not given* in the text. The statements focus on facts. They are in the same order as the information in the text.

LOCATING THE ANSWERS

a Look at True/False/Not Given statements 1–6 below and underline the key words.

HELP

To help you this time, the key words in the text are all the same as in the statements and you only have two choices for each question.

b Quickly find which paragraph in Text 1 contains the information relevant to each statement. Write the paragraph letter (A, B or C) next to each statement. Don't try to answer the questions yet.

c Read the relevant part of the text carefully and decide whether each statement (1–6) agrees with the information given.

Questions 1–6

Do the following statements agree with the information given in Text 1?

Write

TRUE	if the statement agrees with the information
FALSE	if the statement contradicts the information
NOT GIVEN	if there is no information on this

1 Just over one third of the total population of the US is overweight. (T or NG?)

2 Asia and Europe have an equal proportion of obese children. (T or F?)

3 It is forecast that the proportion of overweight or obese children in China will reach 20% in ten years' time. (T or NG?)

4 There is a downward trend in childhood obesity in some African towns and cities. (T or F?)

5 Insulin levels rise sharply when foods with high levels of starch, sugar and fat are eaten. (T or F?)

6 Parents play the most important role in improving eating habits. (F or NG?)

SUMMARY

4 In one type of summary task, you have to complete a gapped summary of part or all of the text using words from a box. The information in the summary may be in a different order from the text. There may be several words that fit the gaps grammatically, so to identify the correct one you have to read the text carefully.

a Read through the summary in the exam task below for general understanding.

b Read the sentence with the first gap carefully. Think about the possible form and meaning of the missing word.

    1 What part of speech is needed for question 7? a) an infinitive b) a past participle c) an adjective

    2 What type of information is most likely? a) an amount b) a change

c Look at the words and expressions in the box. Which three have the correct form to fit question 7?

d Find the correct information in Text 2 for question 7.

    1 What does the text tell us about fruit and vegetables?

    2 Which phrase in the text has a similar meaning to *consumption*?

    Use this information to help you choose the correct answer for question 7.

e Now look at questions 8–14. Which of these need a) a past participle, b) an infinitive, c) an adjective, d) another type of word? Think about what type of information is most likely, then do the task.

> **TIP** Underline key words in the summary. Look in the text for the same words or for paraphrases to help you locate the information you need.

Questions 7–14

Complete the summary of Text 2 below using words from the box.

In Britain, convenience meals are now the most popular type of food. Fruit and vegetable consumption has **7** ...., and consumption of meat and fish has **8** ...., but the traditional Sunday dinner is eaten by **9** .... people. Despite this, almost **10** .... the population are 'traditionalists' in their food habits. Just over **11** .... are 'convenience seekers', while almost **12** .... are 'casual diners'. The number of causal diners is likely to **13** .... as households become **14** ....

smaller	risen
more	remained constant
older	decrease
fewer	fluctuate
a third	healthier
half	larger
fallen	a quarter
increase	

IDEAS FOR SPEAKING AND WRITING

5 Thinking about topics such as the ones in these reading texts will help you prepare for other modules in the IELTS exam.

Answer these questions orally or in writing.

1 How important a problem is childhood obesity in your country?
    Example: *Childhood obesity is a serious problem in my country. Children don't take enough exercise, and eat too much junk food.*

2 How far is the situation described in Text 2 true in your country?

3 Which of the three categories of eater described in Text 2 do you think you are?

Focus on writing 1 *The language of change*

Task I
▶ *Focus on IELTS* pages 19–20

For Task 1, you may be asked to describe a graph which shows changes over a period of time. To do this you need to use **language expressing change** and **appropriate tenses.**

USING LANGUAGE OF CHANGE

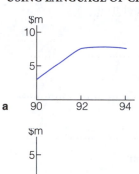

a

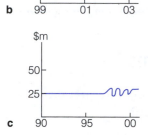

b

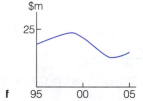

c

1 Underline the verb or verb phrase in each of the following sentences. Then match each sentence to a graph. You can use a graph more than once. Use a dictionary to help you if necessary.

1 Sales <u>started</u> at $3 million in 1990. ..*a*..

2 From 1997 to 2000, sales fluctuated. ......

3 Sales reached a peak of 3 million in 2001. ......

4 Sales increased for two years then levelled off. ......

5 Sales declined between 1999 and 2003. ......

6 Sales dipped briefly in 2002, then recovered. ......

7 In 1990, sales stood at $25 million. ......

8 Sales overtook costs in 2003. ......

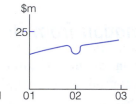

d

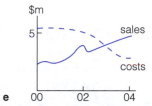

e

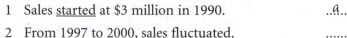

f

2 Add the verb phrases from Exercise 1 to the correct category in the table below. Can you add some more verbs with the help of your dictionary?

Movement upwards	Movement downwards	More than one movement	No movement
increase	decline	reach a peak	start

3 Complete these sentences with a preposition from the box. Use a dictionary to help you if necessary.

at (x2) *between* *by* *of* *to*

1 Profits rose from 2 billion dollars .... 5 billion last quarter.

2 Since 1985, the price of houses has increased .... 200%.

3 Road accidents reached a peak .... 50,000 in November.

4 Car sales remained constant .... around 75 per month for the rest of the period.

5 During the summer, temperatures fluctuate .... 20 and 30 degrees.

6 By close of business, the value of the company's shares stood .... $25.

11

4 Two common patterns used when describing changes in academic English are:

noun + verb + adverb
There + *be* + adjective + noun + *in* + noun

Rewrite these sentences, using one of these patterns.

Example: The consumption of fruit has risen steadily.
There *has been a steady rise in the consumption of fruit.*

1 Meat consumption has fallen sharply.
There ....

2 There was a brief dip in share prices at the start of the year.
Share prices ....

3 Her fitness level improved dramatically.
There was ....

4 There will be a rapid recovery in share prices next year.
Share prices ....

5 The use of GM foods has grown steadily in some countries.
There ....

Focus on writing 2 *Interpreting information from diagrams*

Task 1: Graphs
UNDERSTANDING THE DATA

1 To answer a Task 1 question, you need to understand and interpret the data correctly as well as using appropriate language to describe it.

Read the instructions for the Writing task below. Then look at the graph to find the answers to these questions.

1 What period of time does the horizontal axis show?
2 What information does the vertical axis show?
3 What do the three lines represent? (*look at the key in the box*)
4 What tense do you need to use in order to describe this information?
5 What main changes does the graph illustrate?

WRITING TASK 1

You should spend about 20 minutes on this task.

The graph shows the rates of participation in three different activities in a UK sports club between 1983 and 2003.

Write a report for a university lecturer describing the information.

Write at least 150 words.

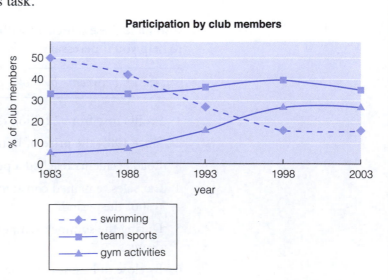

DESCRIBING THE DATA

2 Complete the sample answer below with the correct expression according to the information in the graph.

> This graph shows changes in the popularity of three different activities in a UK sports club over a period of 20 years.
>
> In 1983 around 50% of club members participated in swimming, so this was clearly the most popular activity. However, this figure **1** dipped/decreased steadily to 15% in 1998 and **2** remained constant/levelled off at this rate until 2003.
>
> In contrast, 32% of members did team sports in 1983, and this rate **3** stood at/reached a peak of 40% in 1998 before **4** dropping/growing to its former level. Participation rates for team sports **5** increased/overtook those for swimming and became the highest for all activities from 1993 to 2003.
>
> Finally, participation in gym activities **6** finished at/stood at only 5% in 1983, but this figure **7** fell/grew rapidly from 1988 to 1998, eventually **8** levelling off at/reaching a peak of around 25%, making gym the second most popular activity.
>
> Overall, participation in swimming **9** fluctuated/dropped considerably during the period. Team sports, however, remained popular, while participation in gym activities **10** declined/rose significantly over the period.

ORGANISING THE DESCRIPTION

3 Analyse the way the sample answer is organised by answering these questions.

1 How many paragraphs are used?

2 What information does each paragraph give?
Paragraph 1: Introduction
Paragraph 2: ....
Paragraph 3: ....
Paragraph 4: ....
Paragraph 5: Summary of ....

3 Underline the words that are used to link the paragraphs.

EDITING FOR LANGUAGE

4 In the exam, make sure you leave time to edit your written answer. You will lose marks if you make too many mistakes in grammar and vocabulary use.

a Read this extract from a student's response. Find ten mistakes in the extract and match them to the list of common mistakes.

> The graph show changes in participation of different activities at a sports club.
> Firstly, participation in swimming was decreased for 1983 to 2003. In 1983 50% of club members do swimming but only 15% participate in this in 2003. Secondly, the percentage who do team sports have been remained constant during that period.
> Participation reached peak in 1998. Finally, gym activities grew up from 1983 to 2003.

Common mistakes
1 Wrong tense
2 Active/passive verb confused
3 Agreement: single subject with plural verb
4 Preposition error
5 Article (*a*, *the*) missing

TIP When you write your own answers, try to make a note of the most common types of mistake you make so that you can focus your editing on these in the future.

b Now correct the mistakes.

Focus on listening   *Note completion*

Section I
▶ *Focus on IELTS* page 22

Before each section of the Listening Module, you hear a short introduction. This tells you who is speaking and what the situation is. It also tells you how many questions you have to answer before the next break in the recording. Listen carefully, as this information is not given on the exam paper. You are then given some time to look at the questions. There is a short break in the middle of the recording in Sections 1, 2 and 3, and you are given time to look at the remaining questions for that section.

In Section 1 of the Listening Module, you listen to a conversation about an everyday topic.

IDENTIFYING THE CONTEXT

1 🎧 **Listen to the introduction to the task opposite and answer these questions.**

1   Who are the two speakers?
2   Are they face to face or on the phone?
3   What are they talking about?
4   How many questions will you have to answer before the break in the recording?

NOTE COMPLETION
▶ *Focus on IELTS* page 23

2 Note completion is a common task in Section 1. Read the instructions and notes carefully in the time you are given and try to predict the information you need.

a   Look at the instructions for the task. What is the maximum number of words you should write for each answer?

PREDICTING POSSIBLE
ANSWERS

b   Look at the notes for questions 1–10. Which questions will probably need a) a number? b) a time? c) days of the week?

LISTENING FOR PARALLEL
EXPRESSIONS

TIP In IELTS Listening, the numbered items are always in the same order as you hear them in the recording.

3 To help you identify the information required for each gap as you listen, you need to match the headings in the notes with expressions you hear.

Match each of the following expressions from the recording to one heading on the form in the exam task.

Example: Can I just check on where you are?   *Address of Sports Centre*

1   Can I choose which days?   ....
2   You'd mainly be responsible for …   ....
3   You can get through to me directly on …   ....
4   have your …. with you when you come   ....
5   At present we're looking for …   ....

4 🎧 Now listen to the conversation and complete the notes as you listen.

Questions 1–10

Complete the notes below.

Write *NO MORE THAN THREE WORDS AND/OR A NUMBER* for each answer.

White Water Sports Centre

Example	Answer
Manager's name	*Steve Thompson*............

Job available: **1** .... (part-time)

Job responsibilities:
– supervising swimmers
– care of **2** .... for beginners' classes
– carrying out **3** .... regularly

Days: Two per week (**4** .... and ....)

Working hours: **5** .... to ....

Maximum pay: **6** .... per hour

Interview: Friday at 2 p.m.

Address of Sports Centre: **7** 23–27 ...., East Gate

Steve's direct line: **8** ....

Remember to bring: **9** ....

10 ....

CHECKING YOUR WORK

5 Make sure that:

- the information you have given makes sense in the gap.
- you have spelled the words correctly.
- you haven't written more than three words. (Often, you only need one word.)
- you haven't written words that are already included in the notes (possibly in another form, e.g. *regularly* in question 3).

TIP When you transfer your answers to the answer sheet in the exam, copy **only** the words you have actually written yourself. Do not copy words or symbols printed on the question paper.

Focus on speaking *Describing habits*

Part 1 Interview
▶ *Focus on IELTS* pages 8–9

Part 1 of the Speaking Module lasts for four to five minutes and the examiner will ask you questions about yourself, your life and your habits. Make sure you understand the questions and give relevant answers. Try to extend your answers rather than giving short responses.

UNDERSTANDING THE QUESTIONS

> **TIP** If you don't hear the question, ask the examiner to repeat it.

1 a 🎧 Listen and complete the four questions you hear. They are all about habits.

1 What do you ....?

2 What do you ....?

3 What do you ....?

4 What kind of ....?

GIVING RELEVANT ANSWERS

b 🎧 Now listen to speakers A–D answering the questions above. Match each speaker to the correct question.

Speaker A ......   Speaker B ......   Speaker C ......   Speaker D ......

EXTENDING YOUR ANSWERS

2 🎧 The speakers extended their answers by contrasting their present habits with past habits. Listen again to the first two speakers and complete the extracts below.

Speaker A

1 .... I don't actually do much cooking.

2 I .... eat in the student canteen.

3 I .... cook for myself ....

4 But when I was living at home, I .... my mother with the cooking.

5 I .... make the salad and cook the pasta and so on.

Speaker B

1 Nothing special ....

2 I mean, when I was younger I .... quite a lot of running and things.

3 .... I did a bit of sport.

USEFUL LANGUAGE: FLUENCY MARKERS

3 The use of expressions called *fluency markers* helped the speakers sound fluent and natural.

a Read the following quotes and match the fluency markers in bold to their uses (a–f).

1 '**To be honest** I don't like cooking much at all. **I'm afraid** I'm not very good at it. Though I do quite like making snacks and sandwiches **and so on**.'

2 'Well, **actually**, I don't get much time for exercise these days. **I mean**, I work long hours most days and I just don't get the chance, really.'

3 '**Well, I suppose** I like documentaries best, but they have to be on interesting topics, of course.'

16

a) used to tell someone politely something that may annoy or disappoint them
b) used when explaining or giving an example of something
c) used to say what really happens or is really true
d) used to tell someone what you **really** think
e) used after a list to show there are other similar things that could be mentioned
f) used to say you think something is true, although you are uncertain about it

b Complete the response below with appropriate fluency markers from a. Use each expression once only.

What do you do to keep fit?

Not much, 1 .... I don't really like doing any kind of exercise, 2 .... Of course, I had to do some when I was at school, and I used to be quite good at football, 3 .... But these days, I'd rather spend my time studying or reading 4 ....

c 🎧 Listen and check your answers.

EXAM PRACTICE

4 a Using the language in the box below, and fluency markers, write responses to the questions in Exercise 1a.

Nowadays These days	I	always sometimes hardly ever	cook watch wear
When I was …			used to go …

b Now practise giving extended answers to the following questions. Record yourself speaking if possible.

1 Which sports do you enjoy watching on TV?
2 Do you prefer to watch or play sports?
3 What kind of physical activities did you do when you were at school?
4 What are the most popular sports in your country? Has this changed in recent years?

1 Topic vocabulary overview

The three main topics covered in Module A (*Focus on IELTS* Units 1 and 2) were exercise, nutrition and health. You may need to recognise and use words and phrases connected with these topics in IELTS Reading, Writing, Listening and Speaking Modules.

a Complete each phrase below by choosing the best word from the boxes. Use each word once only. (All the phrases are found in *Focus on IELTS* Units 1 and 2 and/or Module A.)

Exercise

centre   exercise   expenditure
programme   sports

1 sports ....
2 energy ....
3 physical ....
4 training ....
5 competitive ....

Nutrition

consumption   fat and sugar   habits
diet   products

6 intake of ....
7 a balanced ....
8 dairy ....
9 fruit and vegetable ....
10 sensible eating ....

Health and health problems

benefits   disease   epidemic   levels   obesity

11 a global ....
12 long-term ....
13 insulin ....
14 childhood ....
15 heart ....

b Now complete these extracts with appropriate phrases from Exercise 1a.

Speaking Part 1: Keeping healthy

Examiner: What do you do to keep healthy?
Candidate: Well, I think it's important to have regular exercise; I try to do some sort of intense 1 .... every day, so I go to the 2 .... , where I have quite a demanding 3 .... And I quite like 4 .... , so I play football every weekend.

Listening Section 2: Healthy eating

Young people sometimes find it hard to maintain 5 .... once they've left home. In order to stay healthy, you need to eat the right food to have a 6 .... In particular:
- eat fresh food rather than convenience foods
- limit intake of 7 ....
- increase 8 .... (at least five portions daily)
- eat 9 .... such as cheese and milk in moderation.

Reading: The role of insulin

Each time we eat starch or sweet food, insulin is released into the blood. This removes the sugar and stores it so that it can be used when energy is required. However, high 10 .... can lead to 11 .... and other medical problems. Nowadays, with decreasing levels of exercise and an increase in 12 .... , we could be seeing the beginning of a 13 .... of insulin-related problems.

2 General words

Some words do not relate to specific topics, but can be used in a wide variety of general and academic contexts. Often these words are used in texts to introduce or refer back to more specific words and examples. They are therefore useful for linking ideas. You will find these words useful for both Tasks 1 and 2 of the Writing Module.

Complete the sentences using a general word from the box. Then underline the specific examples given in the sentence for each general word.

activities   benefits   developments   events
factors   functions   products   responsibilities
sectors   trends

1 You can buy and sell tickets for sporting .... such as football matches and horse races on the Internet.
2 The main .... of a receptionist are answering the phone and dealing with customer queries.
3 Doing housework, gardening and similar everyday .... is a good way of keeping fit.

4 Exercise and diet are the two main ....
which contribute to obesity.

5 The move towards ready-made meals and the
increasing popularity of snack foods are
growing .... which are affecting the
health of the population.

6 Bodily .... such as breathing and
digestion, use up quite a lot of energy.

7 A sensible programme of exercise can bring
many .... , including physical fitness
and social contacts.

8 In the last hundred years, technical and
economic .... such as changes in
transport and the nature of work, have
profoundly affected people's energy
requirements.

9 Consumer .... such as televisions and
cars, have contributed to the rise of obesity in the
West.

10 Eating out is now the UK's favourite leisure time
pursuit, and this has led to growth in all
.... of the food industry, especially fast
food and specialist foods.

3 Describing graphs

In Module A pages 11–13, you looked at how to
organise and write a description of a line graph.

a Look at the sentences below and number them in
the best order to describe this graph. The first
and last ones have been done for you.

Changes in food consumption in Great Britain

grams per person per week

1975 1980 1985 1990 1995 2000

―■― fresh fruit   ---△--- sugar   ―○― ice cream

☐ Although it dipped in 1985, it then rose
steadily and reached 750 grams in 2000.

☐ By 2000 it was at the same level as the
consumption of sugar.

☐ In 1975, the consumption of fresh fruit stood
at 500 grams, then increased to 600 grams in
1980.

☐ However, this gradually increased
throughout the period.

[1] The graph shows changes in the amount of
fresh fruit, sugar and ice-cream eaten per
person per week in Britain between 1975
and 2000.

[11] In addition, the consumption of ice-cream,
while at a relatively low level, rose significantly
during this period.

☐ In contrast, there was a consistent drop in
sugar consumption.

☐ From the graph we can see that overall, the
consumption of fruit rose, while the
consumption of sugar fell.

☐ People consumed more fresh fruit than
either sugar or ice-cream throughout the
period.

☐ The amount consumed decreased steadily
from almost 400 grams per person to only
100 grams by 2000.

☐ The amount of ice-cream consumed weekly
started at about 50 grams.

b Write out the sentences as a complete report,
dividing them up into paragraphs.

c Rewrite the following sentences from Exercise 3a
as shown, using a noun form rather than a verb.

1 Although it dipped in 1985, it then rose
steadily and reached 750 grams in 2000.
Although there was a .... ,
this was followed by .... to
750 grams in 2000.

2 However, this gradually increased …
However, there was then ....

3 Overall, the consumption of fruit rose, while
the consumption of sugar fell.
Overall, there was .... ,
while the consumption of sugar fell.

4 The amount consumed decreased steadily
from almost 400 grams per person to only
100 grams by 2000.
There was a ....
per person to only 100 grams by 2000.

4 Word formation: language of change

Tick the verbs in the list below which are unchanged
in the noun form. Where the noun is different, write
it next to the verb.

1 to decline   6 to decrease
2 to dip   7 to fluctuate
3 to increase   8 to recover
4 to grow   9 to drop
5 to fall   10 to rise

 **CITY**

Focus on reading *Sentence completion; matching*

FORMING A GENERAL
PICTURE

1 **a** Read the title and subheading of the text opposite. Without reading the rest of the text, answer the following questions.

1 What general problem is the text about?
2 Where does the problem exist?
3 What could be a possible solution?
4 What is one drawback to this solution?

b Now read the first and last paragraphs of the text to check your answers.

c **You can often get a general picture of a text quickly by looking for proper nouns.**

Look through the whole text quickly and underline or highlight all the proper nouns which refer to people or institutions. What does that part of the text tell you about the role of each of these? Spend no more than two minutes on this.

Example: (para B) *Fred Kajubi — Ugandan electrician — belongs to Uganda Change Agents Association*

SENTENCE COMPLETION
► *Focus on IELTS* page 33

2 **In one type of sentence completion task, you have to complete sentences using words from a box.**

LOCATING THE ANSWERS

a Look through the sentence beginnings 1–6 below. Some key words have been underlined. The same words are in the text. Look for these words to help you locate the paragraphs which contain the information you need.

b Read the paragraphs you have marked carefully, and complete the task below.

HELP
The answers all occur in just **three** paragraphs of the text

---

Questions 1–6
*Complete each sentence with the correct ending **A–J** from the box.*

1 Graham Knight believes that for some purposes, it may be better to use solar power rather than energy from

2 Sunshine Solutions' solar panels are cheap because they use

3 At present, the majority of Ugandans use batteries and kerosene as sources of power, rather than

4 In the long term, solar panels are a cheaper source of power for radios than

5 It has been shown that in some places, small-scale projects for energy production are more successful than

6 Fossil fuels cause more damage to the environment than

A ambitious enterprises
B amorphous silicon
C batteries
D cheap technology
E clockwork mechanisms
F crystalline silicon
G mains electricity
H energy from renewable sources
I in the past
J local solutions

Light years ahead

Charlotte Denny in Kampala

Cheap solar panels could be the answer to Uganda's power shortage, but they are proving to be a hard sell

A Uganda may be one of the world's poorest countries, but it has been blessed with a climate that is almost perfect. With sunshine going spare, one Ugandan electrician believes he has the solution to the country's power shortage – low-tech solar panels that can run anything from a radio to a mobile phone.

B The electrician, Fred Kajubi, belongs to an organisation known as the Uganda Change Agents Association, which helps local people learn skills that can make a difference to their lives and their communities. Members of the organisation, who are known as Change Agents, run credit unions, set up self-help groups in villages, become active in local politics and, in Mr Kajubi's case, promote the use of solar power. He has set up his own small company, Sunshine Solutions, which offers customers a solar panel to meet their every need.

C The materials for the solar panels come from a company in Britain called BioDesign, set up five years ago by a retired inventor, Graham Knight. After seeing a TV programme on the invention of a radio powered by clockwork, Mr Knight decided that in some parts of the world, solar power would be a more effective energy resource for radios and similar everyday equipment. He set up a firm to make the components for low-cost solar panels for use in Africa and South America. These are sent out in kit form, together with instructions on how to assemble them. Graham Knight's panels, which use amorphous silicon, are ten times cheaper than the crystalline silicon panels more commonly used for large-scale solar power production. Sunshine Solutions can therefore sell solar panels that are much less expensive than the ones available in the shops.

D Only a small minority of Ugandans currently have access to mains electricity, which leaves most families reliant on batteries to power their radios and on kerosene lamps to light their houses. But for just 15,000 shillings ($8.50), the same price as two months' supply of batteries, one of the solar panels sold by Sunshine Solutions can run a radio for several years. In spite of this, it's proving a struggle for the company to persuade people to invest in their solar panels. Although the solar panels work out cheaper than batteries in the long term, the initial cost is more than many people can afford.

E Uganda plans to bring power to poor villages over the next five years, with the building of a big dam on the Nile. But even if the ambitious plans for rural electrification succeed, there will still be sections of the population that cannot afford to hook up to the national grid. 'The experience of the last couple of decades in developing countries is that ambitious schemes are not effective in getting power to the poorest people,' says Andrew Simms, an expert from the New Economics Foundation in London. 'Small-scale enterprises have a better track record at getting energy to the people who need it.' Better still, solar and other renewable energy sources allow countries to avoid the effects of pollution caused by heavy reliance on fossil fuels, Mr Simms says.

F Even the World Bank, often criticised for being obsessed with large-scale power projects, recognises that there is place for solar power. According to a World Bank representative, solar power can be an effective complement to grid-based electricity, which is often too costly for sparsely settled and remote areas.

G But even cheap technology is hard to sell in a country where half the population lives below the poverty line and there are few effective marketing and distribution channels. Mr Simms believes that the only solution to spreading solar energy more widely is government subsidies, because the initial costs of the solar power panels are beyond most household budgets.

H In the meantime, Mr Kajubi is pinning his hopes on the spread of micro-credit schemes that will loan money to families to help them raise the cash for his products. His company has yet to make a profit, although he says sales are picking up. He is planning another trip into the countryside to demonstrate his solar panels as well as a new solar cooker. Asked if he ever gets downhearted, he points to the motto on his workshop wall: Never give up, it says.

PARALLEL EXPRESSIONS

3 To do Exercise 2, you had to find related phrases in the questions and the text. Which phrases from the questions relate to the following from the text?

1 more effective   ....

2 less expensive   ....

3 only a small minority (*look for the* **opposite** *meaning*) ....

4 over several years   ....

5 large-scale schemes (*look for the* **opposite** *meaning*)   ....

6 schemes   ....

7 have a better track record   ....

8 pollution   ....

MATCHING

► *Focus on IELTS* page 32

4 This task involves matching two sets of information. One set will be names of people or things from the text. The second set will be statements, opinions, theories, etc. The order of the numbered items (1, 2, 3, etc.) will not be the same as in the text.

> **TIP** The name may not be given in exactly the same form in all places (e.g. Fred Kajubi / Mr Kajubi).

a Look through the text quickly. In which paragraphs will you find information about the people A–D in the box below?

b Now complete the task below. To help you, the key words in the statements have been underlined.

Questions 7–13

Look at the following descriptions (Questions 7–13) and the list of people below.
Match each person with the description which relates to them.

7 He has <u>set up a business selling</u> <u>solar</u> panels.

8 He believes that <u>small-scale projects</u> are the <u>most effective</u> way of providing people with power.

9 He believes he can <u>solve a problem</u> affecting his country.

10 He says that solar power is more suitable than <u>electricity</u> for <u>far-off places where very few people live</u>.

11 He uses a <u>very inexpensive</u> method to produce the components for solar panels.

12 He thinks that the <u>government</u> should help people <u>by paying part of the cost of</u> solar power products.

13 He supports the idea of <u>lending money</u> to people to help them buy solar panels.

> **List of People**
> **A** Fred Kajubi
> **B** Graham Knight
> **C** Andrew Simms
> **D** a World Bank representative

► Ideas for speaking and writing page 141

Focus on listening *Multiple choice (single answer); labelling a map*

Section 2

In Section 2 of the Listening Module, you listen to someone giving information about an everyday topic. It could be a speech, a radio broadcast or a recorded message.

MULTIPLE-CHOICE QUESTIONS

1 Multiple-choice questions like the ones below are quite common throughout all sections of the Listening Module. The questions will be in the same order as the information you hear.

PREDICTING POSSIBLE ANSWERS

Before you listen, look at questions 1–5 and underline key words in each sentence beginning. This will give you an idea of what to listen for.

LISTENING FOR PARALLEL EXPRESSIONS

2 To help you identify the information you need as you listen, look at the sentence beginnings and listen for related words (these may be parallel expressions or the same words).

Match phrases in questions 1–5 to the following extracts from the recording.

1 was originally established
2 the number of students in the school is just 90, compared to almost 200 in 1983
3 powered by
4 school lunches
5 special

EXAM PRACTICE

3 ∩ Now listen to the first part of the recording and do the task.

Questions 1–5
Choose the correct letter, A, B or C.

1 Cranley Hill Primary School first opened in

   A 1830.   **B** 1899.   **C** 1983.

2 There are fewer pupils in the school now than in the past because

   A there are not enough teachers.

   B students have transport problems.

   C the local population has declined.

3 The head teacher is proud that the school is provided with energy from

   A wind power from their own turbine.

   B coal from the local mines.

   C electricity supplied by nearby villages.

4 The head teacher believes that primary pupils should study problems which

   A are regional rather than global.

   B can be solved locally.

   C may have no clear answer.

5 The children's meals at school are unusual because

   A they include food grown by the children.

   B they are provided by local people.

   C the children are involved in cooking the food.

TIP If you are not sure, mark the answer you think is most likely. Remember you will **not** hear the recording a second time.

LABELLING A MAP

4 In Section 2, you may have to label a map. You may be given the words you need in a box. The numbers on the map will be in the same order as the information you hear. Some information will already be shown there. You need to look at the numbered items and think about where they are.

ORIENTING YOURSELF

> **TIP** As you listen, pay attention to expressions of direction. If you sometimes confuse left and right, write these words on your answer sheet before you listen.
>
> ← left   right →

Look at the plan below. You are here * facing the front of the school.

1 In which direction are you facing, north or south? ....
2 What is on the left of the school building? Number ....
3 What is at the far end of the car park? Number ....
4 What is immediately behind the school? The ....
5 What is in the bottom corner of the secret garden? The ....
6 What is in the middle of the secret garden? Number ....
7 What is at the top end of the garden? The ....

EXAM PRACTICE

5 🎧 Listen to the continuation of the recording and label the map. Write the correct letter from the box in each space. Do not copy the whole word.

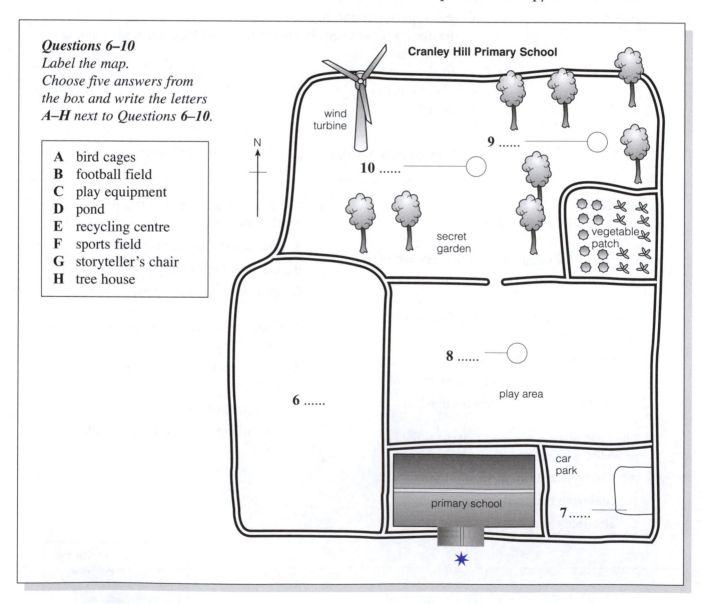

Questions 6–10
Label the map.
Choose five answers from the box and write the letters A–H next to Questions 6–10.

A	bird cages
B	football field
C	play equipment
D	pond
E	recycling centre
F	sports field
G	storyteller's chair
H	tree house

Cranley Hill Primary School

wind turbine

N

9 ......

10 ......

secret garden

vegetable patch

8 ......

6 ......

play area

primary school

car park

7 ......

▶ Ideas for speaking and writing page 141

Focus on writing *Interpreting and comparing data*

Bar charts

▶ *Focus on IELTS* pages 19 and 39

UNDERSTANDING THE DATA

1 In Task 1 you have to think about both the meaning of the data in the task and the language you need to describe it.

Read the Writing task below and look at the bar chart. Answer these questions.

1 What information does the horizontal axis show? How many sectors are there? What does each bar represent?

2 What information does the vertical axis show?

3 Does the diagram show changes or differences? (Look back at Module A page 11 to compare.)

4 Can you use language like *increase* and *decrease* when reporting the data?

5 What are the main similarities and differences between the countries?

6 What grammatical structures do you need to use in your description?

WRITING TASK 1

You should spend about 20 minutes on this task.

The bar chart gives information about the percentage of workers in different sectors of employment in three countries at different stages of economic development.

Write a report for a university lecturer describing the information shown.

Write at least 150 words.

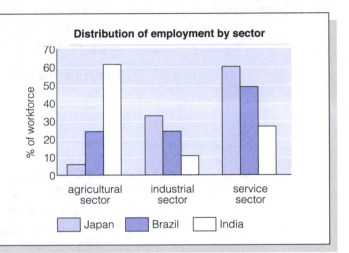

COMPARING DATA

2 Use the information in the Writing task to fill the gaps with words from the box. Use each expression once only.

as	*as many*	*fewer*	*largest*	*highest*	*a larger percentage*
lowest proportion		*majority*	*more developed*	*most*	*more*

1 In Japan the .... proportion of the workforce is in the service sector.

2 India has many .... people employed in the agricultural sector than either Japan or Brazil, but it has .... workers in the industrial sector.

3 Brazil has .... workers in the agricultural sector .... it has in the industrial sector.

4 In India, ... people work in the agricultural sector.

5 The .... of workers in Brazil are in the service sector.

6 The .... of Japanese workers are employed in the agricultural sector.

7 Of the three countries, Japan has the .... percentage of employees in the industrial sector.

8 Countries which have .... economies seem to have .... of the workforce in the service sector.

**USING PARALLEL
EXPRESSIONS**

3 In Writing Task 1, you need to take special care to avoid repetition of words and phrases.

Match the expressions below with parallel expressions from the box.

the majority of   the same number of   the largest percentage of   the fewest
the lowest percentage of   the workforce   the working population

1 the highest proportion of / the largest percentage of

2 people employed .... /......................................

3 an equal number of ....

4 the smallest proportion of .... / ....

**REWORDING
THE INTRODUCTION**

4 If you simply copy your introduction directly from the Writing task on the question paper, this will not be considered as part of your writing. Instead you need to reword – or paraphrase – the information. This is an important academic skill.

Underline the most appropriate words to rewrite the introduction from the task.

> The chart **1** gives information about / compares / presents the **2** percentage of workers / majority of workers / proportion of the workforce *employed* in **3** different sectors of employment / agriculture, industry and service sectors / different industrial sectors in **4** three countries / Japan, Brazil and India / three economically different countries.

WRITING THE DESCRIPTION

5 Now complete the main body of the description by filling in the gaps with appropriate expressions. Use two words for each answer.

> First of all, we can see that both Japan and Brazil have the **1** .... of the workforce in the service sector (61% and 50% respectively). But while Japan has **2** .... people employed in the agricultural sector with only 7% of the working population, an **3** .... of Brazilians work in the agriculture and industry sectors (25% in each).
>
> In contrast, we can see that **4** .... of the Indian workforce, amounting to 61%, is employed in the agricultural sector, the **5** .... of employees work in industry and the remaining 27% are in the service sector.

ENDING THE DESCRIPTION

6 In Writing Task 1, it is a good idea to end your answer by summarising the main information shown by the diagram. You are not required to explain this information.

Which of the two conclusions below is a better ending for the description in Exercise 5?

A Overall, the data indicates that countries with more developed economies have a higher proportion of workers in the industrial and service sectors than in the agricultural sector.

B In conclusion, we can see that Japan and Brazil have more workers in the industrial and service sectors. This is because they have more industrialised economies and so the workers have more disposable incomes and require more services, which makes the service sector grow. In contrast, agriculture in these countries is more mechanised so that fewer workers are needed.

LOGICAL LINKS

7 Underline the logical links that are used to help organise the description in Exercises 5 and 6.

Example: *First of all*

CHECKING YOUR WORK

8 There are five things you should check your answer for, before you edit the language. Complete these questions.

1 Have you reworded the ...., and not just copied it?
2 Have you focused on the main .... and used figures as examples?
3 Have you used appropriate verb .... to describe the data?
4 Have you ended with a .... statement, not an explanation?
5 Have you written at least .... words?

USING FIGURES

9 a Read the description in Exercise 5 again. Why are some of the figures in brackets and others not?

b Now read the sentences below and correct them.

1 Brazil has the same proportion of workers in the agricultural and industrial sectors, 25% in each.
2 In Brazil and Japan the majority of workers 50% and 61% respectively work in the service sector.
3 Japan has the most workers in the industrial sector and the fewest in the agricultural sector, 32% and 7%.
4 India has the fewest workers in the service sector at 27%.
5 The lowest proportion of Indian workers 11% are in the industrial sector.

EDITING FOR LANGUAGE 10 a Read these extracts from students' responses. Find five common mistakes and match them to the list below.

India has highest proportion of workers in the agricultural sector and Brazil has more workers in this sector as Japan.

India has the fewest workers in the industrial sector. While Japan has the most.

61% of Japanese workers employed in the service sector. Brazil has fewer employees in this sector, and the proportion in India is lowest of all three countries.

Common mistakes
1 Misuse of comparative/superlative forms
2 Active/passive verb confused
3 Incorrect punctuation

b Now correct the mistakes.

Focus on speaking *Comparing and contrasting*

**COMPARING ADVANTAGES
AND DISADVANTAGES**
► *Focus on IELTS* pages 214–215

Part 1

1 In Parts 1 and 3 of the Speaking Module, you may be asked questions that require you to compare things, or to discuss the relative advantages or disadvantages of different things.

a Look at the question below.

> 1 Would you prefer to live in a city or a village? Why?

b Write down three advantages of each type of place. You can use phrases with adjectives (e.g. *quieter*) or nouns (e.g. *fewer cars*) or adverbs (e.g. *live more comfortably*).

City	Village
more interesting	quieter

c Now write down three disadvantages of each type of place.

City	Village
less peaceful	fewer shops

SAMPLE ANSWER

2 a 🎧 Listen to a student answering question 1 above and tick the comparative expressions he uses from the list below.

1 (it's) much more exciting
2 (they're) exactly the same
3 (there are) more shops
4 (the streets are) busier
5 (there's) too much traffic
6 (there's) more to do (in the evenings)
7 (you can have) much more fun
8 (there are) far fewer skyscrapers
9 (living in a village) … much healthier
10 (there's) less pollution
11 (life is) much quieter
12 (it's) a lot less crowded

ORGANISING YOUR RESPONSES

b Look at the words the speaker used to organise his response. What order did he say them in?

☐	because
☐	on the other hand
☐	well, I'd prefer to

3 **a** Make notes on questions 2–4, similar to the ones you made in Exercise 1.

2 Do you think it's better to live in a modern flat or an old house? Why?

3 Would you rather live in a modern town or an historic city? Why?

4 Would you prefer to live in the city centre or in the suburbs? Why?

b Answer questions 1–4 using expressions from Exercises 1 and 2, and your notes. Record yourself if you can.

Part 3
COMPARING THE PRESENT
WITH THE PAST

4 In Part 3, you may be asked to compare a current situation with a past situation. You need to be careful with tenses in order to describe past and present habits and situations.

SAMPLE ANSWER

⌒ Read the question, then listen to a student's response and fill the gaps with words that you hear.

Do you think modern homes are different from homes your grandparents had?

Yes, they're **1** .... People in the past used to live in **2** .... houses because **3** .... people lived together then. They weren't **4** .... buildings are now, of course, and they were **5** .... comfortable to live in. Nowadays people tend to live in flats which are **6** .... , but they're **7** .... with central heating and running water and so on …

USEFUL LANGUAGE:
MODIFYING EXPRESSIONS

5 The speaker in Exercise 4 doesn't just say 'homes are different now'. He says they are 'completely different'. When speaking, it is very natural to stress the difference by using modifying expressions.

a Look at the phrases below and cross out the incorrect modifying expression in each one.
1 *a lot / more or less* the same
2 *a great deal / completely* newer
3 *much / totally* darker
4 *far/ really* polluted
5 *very / much* different
6 *very / far* higher
7 *totally / a lot* new

SAMPLE ANSWER

b ⌒ Now listen to a speaker talking about question 1 below and check your answers to Exercise 5a.
1 Are city buildings very different from those in your grandparents' day?
2 Do you think modern homes are different from homes your grandparents had?
3 Do you think cities are the same today as they were 50 years ago?
4 Do you think people know more or less about the world than they did in the past?

EXAM PRACTICE

6 Now use expressions from Exercise 5a in response to questions 1–4 above. Record yourself if you can.

1 Topic vocabulary overview
Module B (*Focus on IELTS* Units 3 and 4) covered a range of topics connected with the way people live together and their share of the world's resources.

a Complete the mindmaps below using words from the box.

> agriculture birth congestion crops densely developed developing expectancy facilities financial irrigation land literacy poverty prosperity rural standard ~~urban~~ wages

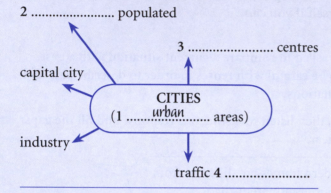

2 .... populated

3 .... centres

capital city

CITIES
(1 .... areas)
urban

industry

traffic 4 ....

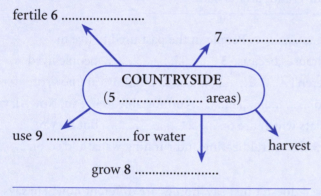

fertile 6 ....

7 ....

COUNTRYSIDE
(5 .... areas)

use 9 .... for water

harvest

grow 8 ....

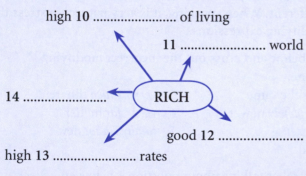

high 10 .... of living

11 .... world

14 ....

RICH

good 12 ....

high 13 .... rates

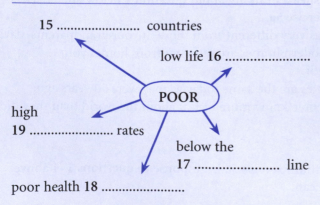

15 .... countries

low life 16 ....

POOR

high 19 .... rates

below the 17 .... line

poor health 18 ....

b Now complete these extracts using words and expressions from the completed mindmaps.

Listening Section 3: Growing rice in Vietnam

> **Student:** Next, we looked at rural areas of Vietnam. Here, most people make their living through 1 .... as there is little industry. One of the main 2 .... grown is rice. This needs 3 .... and plenty of water. Usually, the rice plants are provided with water through 4 ....

Writing Task 2: The advantages of city life

> For the first time in human history, over 50% of the world's population lives in cities. In many ways, it makes sense to live in a 5 .... area, rather than in remote areas in the countryside where the population is more scattered. Those living in 6 .... such as towns or cities have easy access to services such as electricity and water. They are able to earn 7 .... and so they have a higher standard of 8 .... than those in rural areas, together with improved rates of 9 .... and a higher life 10 ....

c Look back through the units and add more words to the diagrams.

2 Parallel phrases
In many IELTS Reading and Listening tasks, you have to be able to recognise words and phrases with similar or parallel meanings. The ability to use a wide range of vocabulary is also assessed in the Speaking and Writing Modules.

For each sentence, find two more words or phrases from the box with a similar meaning to the word in italics.

> abandon associations built desert enterprises a high proportion of low-tech the majority of obstacles organisations schemes stumbling blocks unambitious constructed

1 Governments could provide subsidies to encourage local *projects* / .... / .... using alternative energy sources.
2 In some countries, large dams have been *made* / .... / .... to provide power, but these sometimes have harmful effects on the environment.

3 Unfortunately there are many *problems* / ....
.... / .... in the way of
developing an efficient recycling system.

4 Often, *small-scale* / .... / ....
.... projects are more efficient than large-
scale plans.

5 Local and national *groups* / .... / ..
.... need to be formed to address
the problems of poverty and unemployment.

6 Many people are having to *leave* / .... /
.... their homes in the rural areas in
order to seek work in the cities.

7 In many parts of the world, *most* / .... /
.... people live in urban areas.

3 Describing qualities and quantities

For Writing Task 1, you often have to describe
qualities and quantities. (See Module B pages
25–26.)

a Read through the following sentences and choose
the expression in italics which best completes
each of them. Both expressions are grammatically
correct; you must think about the meaning and
decide which one gives correct information.

1 A *much lower* / *far higher* **quantity** of waste is
produced by households in the USA than in
China.

2 Lack of electricity is a *much more* / *far less*
serious **problem** in Uganda than in North
America.

3 Surprisingly, world population **figures** in 1700
AD were *more or less the same as* / *a great deal
higher than* in 1200 AD.

4 Burying rubbish underground is probably a
much less / *slightly more* effective **solution**
than burning it, as burning produces harmful
chemicals.

5 A *significantly greater* / *slightly lower*
proportion of households in Berlin have
running water, compared with Ho Chi Minh
City.

6 It appears that population growth may be a
rather less / *far more* urgent **issue** now than 20
years ago, as the increase shows signs of
slowing down.

7 In the future, hydrogen could be a *much less* /
far more important energy **resource** than oil.

8 One fifth of the world's population consumes
a *far larger* / *much smaller* **amount** of the
world's resources than the remaining four-
fifths put together.

9 A *significantly higher* / *considerably lower*
percentage of people travel to work by public

transport in Moscow than in Los Angeles.

10 Many environmentalists believe that
developing small community projects is a
far worse / *rather better* **idea** than investing in
large-scale international schemes.

b Look at the words in bold in the sentences above.
Which five words always refer to quantities or
numbers?

4 Topic vocabulary: money and natural resources

Module B (*Focus on IELTS* Units 3 and 4) included
vocabulary related to financial matters and to
natural resources. These are important topics for the
IELTS exam.

a Put the expressions in the box under the
appropriate heading below.

> *budget clockwork coal costs distribution trade
> fossil fuels investment gas loan marketing oil
> renewable sales solar power subsidies electricity
> wind power profit cash*

Money and business	Energy and resources
budget	

b Use words from Exercise 4a to complete these
sentences.

1 In other cases, institutions such as banks may
be prepared to give .... which can be
repaid once the business is making a
....

2 Gas, ... and other ....
are examples of
non-renewable resources; at present, they
contribute about 80% of the world's energy.

3 The main problem for individuals beginning
their own small businesses is raising the
.... to cover the initial .... of
setting up the business.

4 There are two types of energy resources,
non-renewable and ....

5 In some cases, the government may provide
.... to help with some of the costs.

6 Renewable energy resources include ....
.... and .... as well as
water power.

c Now re-order the sentences into two separate
paragraphs and write them out in your notebook.
One paragraph should be about setting up a
business and the other about energy resources.

1 Vocabulary

Read the pairs of sentences below and put a tick (✓) if they mean the same thing and a cross (✗) if they are different. Underline any phrases which make the meanings different.

1. a) We are fully staffed at present.
    b) We don't have any vacancies just now.
2. a) The prices fluctuated slightly in June.
    b) There was a slight dip in prices in June.
3. a) Births recovered to 6 million in 1986.
    b) Births reached a peak at 6 million in 1986.
4. a) There was a slight decrease in sales figures.
    b) Sales figures fell marginally.
5. a) There was a steady upward trend in spending during the period.
    b) Overall, spending rose steadily during the period.
6. a) In New York City, 40 per cent of children live below the poverty line.
    b) Over half the children in New York City are very poor.
7. a) The initial cost of setting up a solar power system is quite low.
    b) It does not cost much to run a solar power system.
8. a) A low intensity exercise programme would probably be best for you.
    b) You should probably follow a programme of vigorous exercise.
9. a) We used to live in a small apartment at the edge of the town when I was a child
    b) When I was young, we lived in a little flat on the outskirts of the town.
10. a) The job will involve supervising the children's meals.
    b) The person doing this job will be responsible for cooking the children's meals.

2 Reading: True/False/Not Given

Farming comes to town to feed the world

What is one of the biggest industries in most of the world's cities? Surprisingly, it is farming. On roadside verges and balconies, alongside railway lines and by airports, city-dwellers are growing crops. A study of urban farming in 100 cities in 30 countries, released in Istanbul by the United Nations, concludes that one in three of the world's urban residents grows food, either for their own consumption or to sell for profit.

Urban agriculture provides an estimated 15 per cent of the world's food, says the report. Calcutta raises a quarter of its fish supply in tanks within the city. In Moscow, two-thirds of families now grow food.

'Planners used to believe that cities were for industry and countryside was for farming. But this is very outdated,' said the report's author, Jac Smit. Urban farming is making a nonsense of the boundaries between town and country, he said. In Bangkok, for instance, 60 per cent of the land is devoted to farming.

'Urban farms are recycling vital resources and producing high crop yields,' said Anders Wijkman, who headed the UNDP delegation in Istanbul. 'They are a life-saver for millions of urban dwellers worldwide.'

a Do the following statements agree with the information given in the reading passage? Write *True, False* or *Not Given*.

1. The results of research about urban farming have been made public by the United Nations.
2. The majority of people who grow food in cities sell it in order to make money.
3. Over one quarter of the world's food comes from farms in urban areas.
4. Urban farming used to be confined to areas near city boundaries.
5. Bangkok has a higher percentage of land used for farming than any other city.
6. According to Anders Wijkman, urban farms tend to have disappointing harvests.

b Use the context to help you choose the best meaning for these words in the text.

1. verges (paragraph 1)
    a) the edge of a road   b) the surface of a road
2. tanks (paragraph 2)
    a) military vehicles   b) large water containers
3. devoted to (paragraph 3)
    a) liking very much   b) used for
4. dwellers (paragraph 4)
    a) residents   b) researchers

3 Writing: Task 1

Complete the answer to the Writing task below by choosing the correct word from the box.

but	compared with	higher (x2)	In contrast
main	indicates	lower	Overall	smallest
than	while			

The pie charts below show average household expenditure in Hong Kong and Britain in the year 2000.

Write a report for a university lecturer describing the information below.

Household expenditure in Britain 2000

Clothing 7%
Housing 18%
Transport 17%
Food 22%
Other goods and services 36%

Household expenditure in Hong Kong 2000

Clothing 4%
Housing 32%
Transport 9%
Food 27%
Other goods and services 28%

The pie charts show the proportion of money spent on various household expenses in Hong Kong and Britain in 2000.

We can see that in Hong Kong the greatest proportion of expenditure (32%) was on housing, 1 .... in Britain housing accounted for just 17% of the total.
2 ...., in Britain the greatest single expense was other goods and services at 36%,
3 .... 28% in Hong Kong. Food came in second place in Britain, at 22%, while in Hong Kong the actual proportion was
4 .... (27%). In Britain another major expense was transport, at 17%, but this was much 5 .... in Hong Kong (9%). In both countries the 6 .... percentage of expenditure was on clothing.

7 ...., the data 8 .... that in both cases food, housing and other goods and services were the 9 .... expenses,
10 .... that in Britain, transport and other goods and services took up a
11 .... proportion of total expenditure
12 .... in Hong Kong.

---

4 Speaking: Part 3

Read the question and a candidate's response. Complete the candidate's response using phrases and sentences from the list a–d on the right.

Examiner: Do you think the way people eat now is different from the way they ate in your grandparents' day?

Candidate: Yes, I think it's changed a great deal. For example, my grandparents always used to have their main meal in the middle of the day, 1 .... And they ate a big breakfast, a cooked breakfast,
2 .... And my grandparents just ate the same sort of food every day 3 .... But I suppose the main difference is that in my grandparents' day, they say everyone used to sit down and eat together round the table, every meal. 4 .... It's a pity really.

a) We don't often do that, at least not during the week, because we all get home at different times.

b) but we have much more variety ... a lot of our food is imported from other countries.

c) but nowadays we're all at work then, so we have it in the evening.

d) but we don't usually do that – actually to be honest, lots of the time I don't have anything to eat at all, just a coffee.

 **RUSH**

Focus on reading *Matching headings; multiple choice (single answer); summary*

FORMING A GENERAL PICTURE

1 a Read the title, subheading and first paragraph of the text on page 35. Think of some more countries which might have different attitudes to time. What effects might these differences have on daily life?

b Read the first sentence of paragraphs B–F. Is the information in the text organised according to

  a) researchers and their findings?   b) countries?

c Scan the text for a list of countries where one piece of research was done. Read that part and compare your ideas in Exercise 1a.

IDENTIFYING MAIN IDEAS

2 In academic texts, each paragraph usually has one main idea supported by details, examples or evidence. Identifying the main idea of each paragraph will help you understand the text better. In IELTS, this skill is tested in the heading-matching task.

a Read paragraphs A and B. Decide which sentence below, 1 or 2, reflects the main idea and which is a detail, example or piece of evidence.

Paragraph A
1 You should not be late for meetings in New York.
2 Attitudes to time vary between cultures and give us information about those cultures.

Paragraph B
1 Variations in attitudes to time can lead to misunderstandings.
2 Ambassadors need to know the social rules of the countries they live in.

b Now read the remaining paragraphs and think about the main idea of each. Underline the parts that tell you.

MATCHING HEADINGS
▶ *Focus on IELTS* page 50

3 In this task, you have to choose the best heading to summarise the main idea of a paragraph or section of the text. There may be an example or examples already done for you. To check that you have selected the heading that matches the main idea, look for words with parallel meanings in the text and the heading.

a Read paragraph A and look at the example (heading x) in questions 1–6 of the exam task opposite. Use the underlined key words in the heading to help you answer these questions.

  1 Which linking word in paragraph A suggests a **difference**?

  2 Which words or phrases in the last sentence of the paragraph have parallel meanings to these?

    a) (is) an indication of   b) individual

b Now do the exam task.

Questions 1–6

The reading passage has seven paragraphs A–G.
Choose the correct heading for each paragraph from the list of headings below.

List of Headings

i	Time and technological development
ii	A problem for those researching attitudes to time
iii	Learning the laws of time for intercultural understanding
iv	Time and individual psychology
v	Comparing the value of time for different groups of workers
vi	Research and conclusions on the speed different nationalities live at
vii	The history of time measurement
viii	Attitudes to time and authority – a cross-cultural relationship
ix	Variation in theoretical views of time
x	Attitude to time as an <u>indication</u> of cultural and <u>individual differences</u>

Example	Paragraph **A**	*Answer*	x
1	Paragraph **B**	....	
2	Paragraph **C**	....	
3	Paragraph **D**	....	
4	Paragraph **E**	....	
5	Paragraph **F**	....	
6	Paragraph **G**	....	

TIP The headings are numbered with Roman letters (**i**, **ii**, etc.).
Be careful to copy these accurately when you transfer them to your answer sheet in the exam.

CLOCKING CULTURES

What is time? The answer varies from society to society

A If you show up a bit late for a meeting in Brazil, no one will be too worried. But if you keep someone in New York City waiting for ten or fifteen minutes, you may have some explaining to do. Time is seen as relatively flexible in some cultures but is viewed more rigidly in others. Indeed, the way members of a culture perceive and use time tells us about their society's priorities, and even their own personal view of the world.

B Back in the 1950s, anthropologist Edward T Hall described how the social rules of time are like a 'silent language' for a given culture. These rules might not always be made explicit, he stated, but 'they exist in the air'. He described how variations in the perception of time can lead to misunderstandings between people from separate cultures. 'An ambassador who has been kept waiting by a foreign visitor needs to understand that if his visitor "just mutters an apology", this is not necessarily an insult,' Hall wrote. 'You must know the social rules of the country to know at what point apologies are really due.'

C Social psychologist Robert V Levine says 'One of the beauties of studying time is that it's a wonderful window on culture. You get answers on what cultures value and believe in.' Levine and his colleagues have conducted so-called pace-of-life studies in 31 countries. In *A Geography of Time*, published in 1997, Levine describes how he ranked the countries by measuring three things: walking speed on urban sidewalks, how quickly postal clerks could fulfill a request for a common stamp, and the accuracy of public clocks. From the data he collected, he concluded that the five fastest-paced countries are Switzerland, Ireland, Germany, Japan and Italy; the five slowest are Syria, El Salvador, Brazil, Indonesia and Mexico.

D Kevin Birth, an anthropologist, has examined time perceptions in Trinidad. In that country, Birth observes, 'if you are meeting friends at 6.00 at night, people show up at 6.45 or 7.00 and say, "any time is Trinidad time".' When it comes to business, however, that loose approach works only for the people with power. A boss can show up late and just say 'any time is Trinidad time', but those under him are expected to be on time. Birth adds that the connection between power and waiting time is true for many other cultures as well.

E The complex nature of time makes it hard for anthropologists and social psychologists to investigate. 'You can't simply go into a society, walk up to someone and say, "Tell me about your concept of time",' Birth says. 'People don't really have an answer to that. You have to come up with other ways to find out.'

F Birth attempted to get at how Trinidadians regard time by exploring how closely their society links time and money. He surveyed rural residents and found that farmers – whose days are dictated by natural events, such as sunrise – did not recognise the phrases *time is money*, *budget your time* or *time management* even though they had satellite TV and were familiar with Western popular culture. But tailors in the same areas were aware of such notions. Birth concluded that wage work altered the tailors' views of time. 'The ideas of associating time with money are not found globally,' he says, 'but are attached to your job and the people you work with.'

G In addition to cultural variations in how people deal with time at a practical level, there may be differences in how they visualise it from a more theoretical perspective. The Western idea of time has been compared to that of an arrow in flight towards the future; a one-way view of the future which often includes the expectation that life should get better as time passes. Some cultures see time as closely connected with space: the Australian Aborigines' concept of the 'Dreamtime' combines a myth of how the world began with stories of sacred sites and orientation points that enable the nomadic Aborigines to find their way across the huge Australian landscape. For other cultures, time may be seen as a pattern incorporating the past, present and future, or a wheel in which past, present and future revolve endlessly. But theory and practice do not necessarily go together. 'There's often considerable variation between how a culture views the mythology of time and how they think about time in their daily lives,' Birth asserts.

MULTIPLE CHOICE (SINGLE ANSWER)

▶ *Focus on IELTS* pages 52–53

> **TIP** Wherever possible, use proper nouns to help you locate the information needed for a task.

> **TIP** To help you choose the correct answer, look for parallel expressions in the text and options.

4 To do this type of task, you can:
- read the question stem only, then read the information in the text. Then look back at the options and choose the best one, OR
- read the question stem and options, then look at the text.

a Quickly look for the following names in the text and underline them.

1 Edward Hall
2 Robert Levine
3 Kevin Birth
4 Trinidad

b The following pairs of expressions occur in the text and the multiple-choice options. Decide if the meaning of each pair is parallel or different.

1 different views of time/variations in the perception of time
2 answer a question/fulfil a request
3 his employees/the people under him
4 on time/punctual
5 observing people's behaviour/surveying people
6 their attitudes to time/how they think about time

c Now do the multiple-choice task below.

Questions 7–11
Choose the correct letter, A, B, C or D

7 Edward Hall used the example of the ambassador to show that

A people in power are easily insulted.

B rules of time are different now from in the past.

C problems can be caused by different views of time.

D misunderstandings over time cannot be avoided.

> **HELP**
> A word in an option may also be in the text, but the phrase may have a different meaning.

8 In his research, Robert Levine measured the speed at which postal workers

    A delivered letters.

    B performed a task.

    C learned a new skill.

    D answered a question.

> **HELP**
> One of the options is partly true, but does not summarise the aim of the research.

9 Kevin Birth found out that in Trinidad

    A expectations of punctuality vary according to relationships.

    B time is regarded differently from anywhere else.

    C employees as well as bosses may be late for work.

    D people who are punctual eventually become more powerful.

> **HELP**
> The text describes three groups of people. Find the option which reflects this.

10 Birth studied Trinidadian attitudes to time by

    A asking questions connected with language.

    B asking people how they felt about time.

    C observing how people behaved in different settings.

    D collecting phrases to do with time.

> **HELP**
> Find the phrase *he surveyed rural residents* in the text. Read carefully to find out how he did this.

11 Birth finds there is often a difference between

    A what cultures believe about time and what individuals believe.

    B people's practical and theoretical attitudes to time.

    C what people believe about time and what they say.

    D people's past and present attitudes to time.

> **HELP**
> Look for another quotation from Birth later in the text.

SUMMARY
▶ *Focus on IELTS* page 53–54
▶ Module A page 10

> **TIP** You should not make any change to the form of the word you choose from the text.

5 In Module A, you completed a summary using a bank of answers. You may also have to complete a summary using words from the text. Often, the summary relates to just one part of the text, so you have to scan the text to find this first. Your answers must fit grammatically.

Read the summary below. Then scan to find the part of the text which has the relevant information, using the capitalised name *Australian Aborigines* to help you. Now read that section of the text carefully to find the answers.

Questions 12–14
Complete the summary below.
*Choose **NO MORE THAN TWO WORDS** from the passage for each answer.*

Different cultures have different theories of time. In the West, time is sometimes said to be like an **12** .... 'Dreamtime' for Australian Aborigines involves a special relationship between time and space. In other cultures, time may be compared to a **13** .... or a **14** ....

▶ Ideas for speaking and writing page 141

Focus on listening *Table completion*

Section 1
UNDERSTANDING SPELLINGS
AND CORRECTIONS

1 In the Listening Module, you may have to write down words which are spelled out for you. You may also have to understand and record information when the speaker changes or corrects the information that is given.

🎧 Listen to ten short extracts and complete the notes. Write **no more than three words and/or a number** for each answer.

1   Address: ..19,.. *Street*.....

2   Street: .... *Drive*......

3   E-mail: ....

4   Address: ....

5   Name: .... *Jones*.....

6   Company address: ....

7   Name: ....

8   Cost: .....$..

9   Tel: ....

10 Arrival date: ..*Tuesday*...

TABLE COMPLETION
▶ *Focus on IELTS* pages 41–42
▶ Module A page 14

2 You have already done a Section 1 note completion task. Table completion is similar to note completion but the information is more clearly organised for you. The headings of the table will tell you what to listen for. There may also be a title explaining what the table shows.

UNDERSTANDING THE TASK

a   Read the instructions for the exam task opposite. What is the maximum number of words you can write for each answer in questions 1–8?

b   Look at the table to find the answers to these questions.

1   What is the main topic of the table?
2   How many people does the table give information about?
3   Will the description in the recording give information row by row (horizontally) or column by column (vertically)? (*look at the order of the question numbers*)

LISTENING FOR
LANGUAGE SIGNALS

c   As you write in the answers, you need to be careful to put the information in the correct column. Listen for signals that tell you what information you are about to hear.

Match the following phrases from the recording to the correct column of the table (Name, Job, Description, Special requirements).

Example: he was called …   *Name*..

1   he sounded …   ....

2   he says he needs …   ....

3   he struck me as …   ....

4   I got the impression he was …   ....

5   he wants to …   ....

6   he's a/an …   ....

EXAM PRACTICE

3 ∩ Now listen to the recording and complete the exam task.

Questions 1–8
Complete the table below.
Write **NO MORE THAN THREE WORDS** *for each answer.*

People interested in sharing the flat

Name	Job	Description	Special requirements
Example Phil Parrott	**1** .... teacher	• **2** .... • too health-conscious?	**3** .... (because of equipment)
David **4**	lawyer	• older • quiet • **5**	to pay less for gas and electricity
Leo Norris	**6**	• funny • lazy? • not **7** .... or .... • outdoor type	somewhere to keep his **8** ....

Questions 9–10
Complete the notes below.
Write **NO MORE THAN THREE WORDS AND/OR A NUMBER** *for each answer.*

Leo's phone number (mobile) **9** ....

Leo would like to move in on **10** ....

USEFUL VOCABULARY

4 What qualities would be most important for you in a flatmate? Choose three from the box or use your own ideas.

athletic   creative   adventurous   sociable   tidy   intelligent   patient

▶ Ideas for speaking and writing page 141

Focus on speaking *Describing people*

Part 2 Long turn
▶ *Focus on IELTS* page 61

In Part 2 of the Speaking Module, you have to talk about a topic for one to two minutes, using prompts on a task card given to you by the examiner. This is called the 'long turn'. You may be asked to describe **one of the following: a person, a place, an event, an activity or an object.**

DESCRIBING PEOPLE

1 a Complete each sentence below with an adjective from the box that is opposite in meaning to the adjective underlined.

supportive   calm   funny   hardworking   noisy   selfish   shy   warm

1 She's not very <u>sociable</u>, in fact she's a bit ....

2 He gives the impression of being very <u>serious</u>, but actually he's got a great sense of humour and can be really ....

3 Her mother gets rather <u>stressed</u> and finds it difficult to stay ....

4 She's not at all .... She's very <u>caring</u> and <u>considerate</u>, always thinking about others.

5 His parents used to think he was a little <u>lazy</u>, but at school he was really ....

6 She was rather <u>competitive</u> in class, but always .... if you asked her for help.

7 Teachers thought he was too .... and excitable, but one-to-one he was very <u>quiet</u>.

8 People often think she is a bit <u>unfriendly</u> at first, but when you get to know her, she is really ....

b **Put the adjectives into the correct category.**

Adjectives with positive meanings	Adjectives with negative meanings
caring	stressed

c **Complete this information with examples from the sentences above.**

1 Negative adjectives are often softened by adding *a bit*, ... or ....

2 Positive adjectives are often emphasised by adding *very* or ....

d **Write sentences to describe these people, using the language in Exercise 1.**

1 a member of your family
2 a neighbour
3 a friend
4 a celebrity you don't like

ANALYSING THE TASK

2 The candidate task card always asks you to **describe** something and to **explain** something. The prompts give you sufficient material to talk about for two minutes.

TIP Every task has the same number of prompts, but these are not numbered on the task card.

Read the candidate task card below and answer these questions.

1 What do you have to describe and explain?
2 How many prompts are given in addition to the 'describe' and 'explain' instructions?
3 What tense will you use for each of the prompts?
4 Who would you choose to talk about?

Describe someone you know who is popular in your neighbourhood.

    You should say:

        (1) who this person is
        (2) when you first met this person
        (3) what sort of person he/she is

    and explain (4) why you think this person is popular.

**ANALYSING A SAMPLE
ANSWER**

3 **a** 🎧 Listen to a candidate talking about this topic and complete the notes below.

Prompt 1	Prompt 2	Prompt 3	Prompt 4
Local doctor	Met him ...	Calm; quiet, gentle way of speaking	Good doctor

b 🎧 Listen again and answer these questions.

1 Did the speaker use all the prompts?
2 Did you learn much about the person she described and their relationship?
3 Did the speaker describe the person's physical appearance in detail?
4 Did she speak for at least two minutes?
5 Was it clear when the speaker moved from describing to explaining?
6 Did the speaker use the same tense for each prompt?

ORGANISING YOUR TALK

4 Look at the 'signals' which the speaker used to start and end her talk:

'The person I'm going to tell you about is ...'
'The reason why I think he is popular is because ...'

Now make opening and closing sentences for talks on the following topics, using the language in the box below.

1 Your favourite story.
2 Your favourite weekend activity.
3 A happy occasion.
4 A relative.
5 Your best birthday.
6 Your best holiday.

The person The thing The occasion The activity The experience The place The holiday	I'm going to tell you about	is ...
The reason why	I enjoy (doing) this I admire him/her I remember it	is because ...
	it was my best ... it was my favourite ...	was because ...

EXAM PRACTICE

5 In the exam, you will have one minute to prepare for the talk and you can make notes in that time. You could use a simple list or a mindmap to organise your thoughts.

▶ *Focus on IELTS* page 62

a Spend one minute making notes on the task in Exercise 2 above.

b Now use your notes to talk about the topic for two minutes. Time yourself and record yourself if you can.

Focus on writing *Presenting arguments*

Task 2 Discussion topic
▶ *Focus on IELTS* pages 63–65

With some question types in Task 2, you need to discuss more than one type of evidence, argument or point of view before reaching your conclusion. This is called the **evidence-led** approach.

ANALYSING THE QUESTION

TIP Read carefully to identify the main topic, which aspect or aspects of the topic you need to cover, and the actual question you are being asked.

1 Look at the Task 2 prompt below and answer these questions.

1 Is the main topic a) modern lifestyles, b) positive changes in lifestyles or c) positive and negative changes in lifestyles?
2 What information do you have to give in your conclusion?

> *Modern lifestyles are completely different from the way people lived in the past. Some people think the changes have been very positive, while others believe they have been negative.*
>
> *Discuss both these points of view and give your own opinion.*

ANALYSING A SAMPLE ANSWER

TIP Remember to organise your ideas clearly and support your arguments with examples or evidence.

▶ *Focus on IELTS* pages 23–24, 241

2 a Read the sample answer on page 43 and answer these questions.

1 What is the purpose of the first paragraph?
2 What is the purpose of the first sentence in paragraphs 2 and 3?
3 Which opinion does the writer agree with? Where does he state his opinion?

b Find examples of logical links in the sample answer and put them in the appropriate category.

Addition: ....

Contrast: ....

Introducing examples: ....

Concession: ....

Summing up: ....

Cause and effect: ....

c What evidence is used to support the main arguments in paragraphs 2 and 3 of the sample answer? Complete this paragraph plan.

> *Paragraph 2*
> *Argument: changes have been positive*
> *Evidence: improvements in healthcare,.........*
> *..*
> *..*
> *Paragraph 3*
> *Argument: changes have been negative*
> *Evidence: impact on environment*
> *..*
> *..*

It is undeniable that the average person's lifestyle has changed enormously during the last few decades owing to the huge impact of modern technology and economic development.

Some people believe that modern life is much better than in the past. As evidence of this, they point to improvements in healthcare and education and the general increase in the standard of living. Furthermore, they argue that machines have changed working conditions and reduced the need for hard physical labour, and they talk about the large leisure industries that have transformed people's free time.

On the other hand, it can also be argued that some changes have had a negative impact on our lives. For example, there has been a negative impact on both the natural and human environments. In addition, stress from all the pressure in today's schools and workplaces may have reduced the quality of life in social terms. Having access to more things and more entertainment cannot compensate for the loss of social relationships. One reason for this loss is that families spend less time together and, as a result, crime rates and divorce rates have increased and people have lost any sense of community.

In conclusion, I think there is evidence to suggest that some of the changes we have experienced in the modern world have affected our lives in a negative way, especially in terms of the family and the environment. But overall, it is clear that most of these changes have been good for the majority of people. Nevertheless, I feel we need to ensure that these positive changes can be sustained and shared more in the future.

FACT OR OPINION?

3 Underline the expressions in the answer that introduce opinions. Add them to your Vocabulary notebook. Put them in two groups:

1 Expressions that introduce subjective, personal opinions.
   Example: I think ...
2 Expressions that introduce objective opinions, based on fact.
   Example: It is undeniable that ...

EDITING FOR LANGUAGE

4 **a** Add the correct prepositions to these expressions. Then check in the sample answer above.

1 in terms .... something
2 the impact of something .... something
3 to compensate (somebody) .... something
4 to have access .... something
5 the need ....
6 .... a (positive/negative) way

b Correct the mistakes with prepositions in these student responses.

A The impact of computers to working conditions has been good. About the environment, however, the changes have been negative.

B Such changes have affected our world by a negative way. And even higher salaries cannot compensate on long working hours.

C There is no need of physical labour any more, and people have more access different activities than before.

SPEED WRITING PRACTICE

5 Plan and write your own answer to the Writing task on page 42. You should finish your answer in 35 minutes and then take five minutes to edit it. Remember to check for the most common types of grammatical and vocabulary mistakes you make.

TIP Write at least 250 words for Task 2. Under-length answers will lose marks. Don't write too much, as you won't have time to check your work.

1 Topic vocabulary overview

Module C (*Focus on IELTS* Units 5 and 6) dealt with topics relating to work, attitudes and beliefs, and social changes.

a Put the expressions in the box under the appropriate heading below.

> values patterns conditions priorities
> attitudes to delegate overworked sick pay
> notions expectations workload efficiency
> perceptions awareness salaries pressure
> multi-tasking views

Work	Belief and opinions
patterns	values
	priorities

b Complete the mindmaps below using words from the box.

> conditions sense stress technology
> facilities standard breakdown economic
> pressure healthcare schedules pace

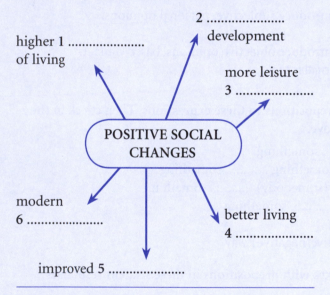

higher 1 .... of living

2 .... development

more leisure 3 ....

POSITIVE SOCIAL CHANGES

modern 6 ....

better living 4 ....

improved 5 ....

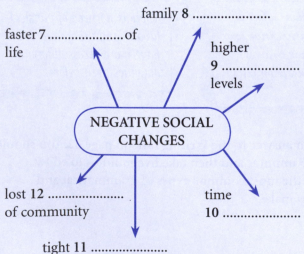

family 8 ....

faster 7 .... of life

higher 9 .... levels

NEGATIVE SOCIAL CHANGES

lost 12 .... of community

time 10 ....

tight 11 ....

c Now complete these extracts using words and expressions from Exercises 1a and 1b.

Listening Section 4: Cultural differences in 1 .... of time

> So it would be true to say that different cultures have widely different 2 .... towards punctuality. In Western countries, for instance, people have definite 3 .... that people will keep appointments and turn up on time. The kind of relationships we have with people, and also society's 4 .... as a whole, are reflected in our 5 .... of acceptable time-keeping. But other cultures have vastly different 6 .... , seeing other things as being more important.

Reading: Counting the cost of stress

> Workers today commonly consider themselves to be 7 .... and underpaid. Certainly the use of 8 .... in the workplace has speeded up transactions and increased the 9 .... on employees: they need to turn work around faster and meet 10 .... on a daily basis. People increasingly find that they have to put in longer hours and do several things at once in order to cope with the increased 11 .... Reduced staffing levels mean that people are no longer able to 12 .... tasks to colleagues, but the effect of this is that workers become increasingly isolated and there is an overall drop in working 13 ....

Speaking Part 3: Social change

> Oh, the way we live today is totally different from the way my grandparents lived. But I think we've lost a lot really. I mean, 14 .... is a common problem, what with divorce and things … and I think that young people miss out on family life today. And people don't know their neighbours anymore … I think we've definitely lost the 15 .... that our grandparents had.

d Look back through the units and add more words to the mindmaps.

2 Sentence rewriting

In academic writing it is common to use noun phrases when referring to, or discussing, research.

Rewrite the following sentences as shown without changing the meaning.

1 a) Family problems could be linked to the spread of technology.
   b) There could be .... between family problems and the spread of technology.

2 a) Professor Dillon argues that cultural awareness is the key issue.
   b) Professor .... is that cultural awareness is the key issue.

3 a) Stress and heart disease are thought to be connected.
   b) There is thought to be ....
   ....

4 a) Most people would like to combine a satisfying job with a good family life.
   b) The .... a satisfying job with a good family life appeals to most people.

5 a) Einstein discovered a new law of physics that changed the development of science.
   b) Einstein's ....
   .... changed the development of science.

6 a) The employees suspect that the management may not be telling the truth.
   b) There is .... among the employees that the management may not be telling the truth.

7 a) Professor Cartwright found that stress is widespread in the workplace.
   b) Professor .... indicated that stress is widespread in the workplace.

3 Speaking: Using colloquial language

Using colloquial language appropriately in the Speaking Module will help you to sound fluent and natural.

Use the expressions in the box connected to time, work and leisure to complete the responses to the examiner's questions.

show up late	take up (an activity)		
wind down	get to	sort out	come up with
not a big deal	strikes me	deal with	

Examiner: How often do you go out in the evenings?
Candidate: Not as much as I'd like, I'm afraid. I don't go out much during the week, because I have to 1 .... work on time every day. I hate to 2 .... 'cos it makes me feel rushed all day. And I don't find it easy to 3 .... excuses.
Examiner: How do you like to spend your free time?
Candidate: Well, after work I like to 4 .... by listening to music for a bit. And recently I decided to 5 .... the guitar, so I like to play around with that.
Examiner: How do you manage to make time for work/study and leisure?
Candidate: Oh, it's 6 .... I like my work – it's not too stressful or anything. I can easily 7 .... what I have to do every day. But of course, I need to plan ahead when I want some time off.
Examiner: What advice would you give to help someone to manage their work and free time?
Candidate: I'd just tell them to switch off as soon as they leave work. It 8 .... that people just don't do that. I find that if I write a list of problems I have to 9 .... , then I can stop worrying about them. So, yeah, write things down and then switch off.

4 Writing: Reference links

► *Focus on IELTS* pages 217–218

Look at the following extract from a Writing Task 2 on time management and choose the most appropriate link word.

Schools need to prepare 1 their/the students for adult life and a rapidly changing world. One subject 2 it/which could usefully be taught in schools today is time management. 3 It/This is one aspect of adult life 4 that/in which students are not well prepared for, and yet 5 it is/they are often the greatest pressure that 6 they/these will have to deal with. Lessons could focus on simple strategies 7 for example/like making lists and prioritising things, and using diaries to keep track of deadlines and exam dates. 8 These/Which would encourage the students, 9 they/who will be the workers and managers of the future, to take control of 10 their/our own lives. In 11 the/this way, the next generation may not suffer the same levels of stress as adults experience today.

▶ THE CULTURAL SCENE

Focus on listening 1   *Multiple choice (multiple answers); list and short answers*

Section 3
▶ *Focus on IELTS* Exam briefing page 42

In Section 3 of the Listening Module, you hear two, three or four people talking about an academic topic. They may be students or teachers. They could be talking about a particular course assignment or project, or a more general academic topic, such as study skills.

PREDICTING THE TOPIC

1 You are going to hear two students talking about a music course. First, look through questions 1–10 in the exam task opposite. Which of the following topics does each set of questions relate to?

Example: Course content   *Questions 4–6*

1   Computer equipment   ....

2   Knowledge or skills needed for the course   ....

3   Assessment   ....

4   Dates of course   ....

MULTIPLE CHOICE (MULTIPLE ANSWERS)
▶ *Focus on IELTS* page 79
▶ Module B page 23

2 In Module B, you answered multiple-choice questions with a single answer. In an alternative task type, you have to choose more than one answer.

a   Look at the instructions for questions 1–3 and 4–6 in the exam task. How many answers do you have to choose for each set of questions?

LISTENING FOR SIGNALS

> **TIP** The options (A–G) may not be in the same order in the recording as in the question.

b   As you listen, pay attention to words that signal key information. Which of the phrases below might signal information relevant to

a) things that are **necessary** for the course?   b) course **activities**?

1   you've got to be able to …
2   we often look at …
3   you really need to …
4   but that's not all, we can …
5   What are the requirements?
6   … are essential

SHORT-ANSWER QUESTIONS
▶ *Focus on IELTS* pages 42 and 79

3 Short-answer questions usually focus on factual information. You may have to answer single questions, or complete a list. You should not write complete sentences for your answers.

PREDICTING POSSIBLE ANSWERS

Look at questions 7–10 of the Listening task.

1   Which questions involve completing a list?
2   What type of factual information does each question require? (e.g. a number)

> **TIP** Keep your answers as short as possible, and never go over the word limit.

EXAM PRACTICE

4 🎧 Now listen to the recording and answer questions 1–10.

Questions 1–3
*Choose **THREE** letters A–H.*

According to Josie, which **THREE** things are necessary for Music 103?

A ability to read music

B ability to sing

C computer skills

D ability to play a musical instrument

E good maths

F independent learning skills

G membership of the music department

Questions 4–6
*Choose **THREE** letters A–H.*

Which **THREE** of the following activities does Music 103 involve?

A designing a software programme

B writing and playing back your own music

C writing music for films

D attending lectures at the university

E listening to examples from the internet

F going on study tours abroad

G comparing modern and classical music

Questions 7–8
List **TWO** more things a student's computer needs for Music 103.
*Write **NO MORE THAN TWO WORDS AND/ OR A NUMBER** for each answer.*

• **7** .... *megabytes of RAM*

• CD-ROM

• **8** ....

Questions 9–10
Answer the questions below.
*Write **NO MORE THAN TWO WORDS AND/ OR A NUMBER** for each answer.*

9 When does the next course begin?

....

10 How many assignments must be done to pass the course?

....

> **TIP** Remember that correct spelling is necessary for IELTS Listening.

USEFUL VOCABULARY

5 Section 3 is often about different types of academic course.

a Complete the sentences below, then check your answers with the recording or tapescript.

1 Josie is m............ in maths and this year she is doing four maths m............ .

2 However, she is also doing an o............ course in music.

3 This is a d............ l............ course, so students do not have to attend l............ .

4 Good maths is essential, and so are computer s............ .

5 The course includes quite a lot of t............ as well as practical work.

6 The course is worth three c............ .

7 Students have to write a............ and take one e............ .

b Choose a course you are interested in (e.g. business studies, computer studies, tourism, English language). Find out some of the types of activities on this course and list them in your Vocabulary notebook.

► Ideas for speaking and writing page 141

Focus on speaking *Answering different question types*

Part 1 Interview
▶ *Focus on IELTS* pages 68–69

1 In Part 1, you will be asked sets of questions on different topics. The questions may use a range of grammatical structures and ask for different types of information. Listen carefully to identify the type of information and the verb forms you can use in your response.

QUESTION FORMS

Match the question words below with the information they are asking for.

Example: 1 *e)*

1 How often …?	a) a preference
2 What kind of …?	b) an opinion about the value of something
3 When …?	c) a procedure or method
4 Where …?	d) a person or institution
5 Why …?	e) the frequency of (doing) something
6 Who …?	f) a place
7 Would you rather …?	g) a date or time
8 How do you ...?	h) a specific type (of something)
9 How important ...?	i) a reason

GIVING RELEVANT ANSWERS

2 You don't need to respond in complete sentences or use the same words as the question, but using similar structures will help you to give relevant answers. Don't repeat the whole question.

a Match the following questions and answers.

1 'How often do you listen to music?' 2 'When did you last go to a concert?' 3 'Would you prefer to listen to music at home or at a concert?'	a) 'Oh, I'd much rather hear live music. I find it has much more atmosphere.' b) 'Well, it all depends. I nearly always play music when I'm at home – but I'm afraid I don't often just sit and listen to it …' c) 'I'm not sure. Oh yes, I went to hear a group of Bulgarian singers at the City Hall last month and they were fantastic.'

b ∩ Now you will hear six speakers answering these questions about art. Match the questions to the speakers.

1 'What kind of artwork do you like?'
2 'When did you last visit an art exhibition?'
3 'Where do they usually hold exhibitions in your country?'
4 'Who should pay for public works of art?'
5 'Would you rather have a painting or a photograph of a person?'
6 'Would you prefer to have a painting or a photograph of a place?'

Speaker A ......
Speaker B ......
Speaker C ......
Speaker D ......
Speaker E ......
Speaker F ......

EXTENDING YOUR ANSWERS
▶ Module A page 16

3 One way the speakers in Exercise 2 extended their responses was by giving reasons. Underline the words that introduce reasons in these two answers. How are they different grammatically?

1 'I suppose I like ceramics best – mainly because of their feel and texture.'
2 'I'd prefer to have a photograph of someone I know because paintings of people can be really different …'

EXAM PRACTICE

4 Practise giving your own extended answers to the questions in Exercise 2, and record yourself if you can.

Focus on reading *Sentence completion (words from text); multiple choice (multiple answers)*

FORMING A GENERAL
PICTURE

1 a Read the title, the subtitle and the first paragraph of the text below. Then decide which answer (A or B) best describes the probable topic of the whole article.

  A Dust in the home
  B Dust in public buildings

b Read the first sentence or two of each paragraph. Decide which sets of paragraphs deal with each of these topics.

  1 Why dust is a problem   Paragraphs A to ......
  2 Where dust comes from   Paragraphs ...... to ......
  3 Solutions to the problem   Paragraphs ...... to ......

Fighting the dust

We used to think that dust blew in through the window. Now we know better, says Alison Motluk

A It's hard to defend yourself against dust. Attack it, and it scatters and escapes you, but the moment your guard is down it silently returns – on lampshades and bookshelves, in corners and under beds. And that's just in your home. Imagine having to look after a larger place, somewhere packed with delicate objects, with tens of thousands of people passing through each year. So serious is the fight against dust that those responsible for running museums, art galleries and historic buildings have realised it can only be won by making it the subject of systematic research.

B Cleaning exhibits in museums and historic buildings takes a lot of time and money. But a more serious problem is that the process of removing dust can sometimes cause damage. Morten Ryhl-Svendsen of the National Museum of Denmark's analytical lab in Copenhagen is studying dust deposition on 1000-year-old Viking ships on display at a museum in Roskilde. 'Every time the ships are cleaned, some bits break off,' he says. 'Though some fragments can be retrieved from the vacuum cleaner bag and replaced, cleaning is clearly accelerating the exhibits' decay. And no matter how small the breakage, each represents the disappearance of some information about the objects,' Ryhl-Svendsen says.

C Several studies have been launched in the past few years, attempting to put the study of dust on a scientific footing. Researchers have been investigating where it comes from, and the best way of keeping it under control. 'The conventional view is that dust comes from outside the building,' says Peter Brimblecombe, an atmospheric chemist and dust expert at the University of East Anglia in Norwich, UK. He is involved in a study at London's Tate Gallery which is beginning to overturn that idea. In the study, microscope slides were placed on top of the frames of several paintings and left there for seven days. Some were in older galleries, where ventilation was mainly through open doors and windows; others were in newer areas where the air within the room was continually recirculated by air conditioners. The amount of dust that had collected was measured and analysed, and it was found that the air-conditioned areas still had considerable amounts of dust.

D Ryhl-Svendsen and a colleague used a similar technique to study the dust on the Viking ships in Roskilde. They positioned sticky patches at various locations in and around the open ships. When they analysed the dust they had collected, they discovered a toxic plasticiser believed to come from floor tiles elsewhere in the museum, together with textile fibres, skin flakes and hair.

E Both studies indicated the same culprits: people like you and me visiting the exhibitions. Where there were large numbers, dust levels were high. And the objects that visitors got nearest to were the ones that were most densely shrouded in fluff. Skin flakes and strands of hair contribute to the problem, but the biggest menace turns out to be clothes. We are surrounded by an invisible cloud of fibres

49

shoulders and the waist. Dust kicked up by feet is heavier and usually falls back to the ground. So clear plastic barriers up to shoulder level could cut out a good deal of the dustiness, say the researchers.

H They also discovered that the more vigorously people move, the more fibres their clothes shed, which suggests there might be some benefit in changing the way visitors are directed past exhibits. People tend to be most active at the beginning of their visit – adjusting rucksacks, taking off jackets and coats – so the most precious exhibits should be displayed last. This would have the added advantage, from a conservation point of view, that visitors will be getting tired by then and may spend less time admiring the exhibits. And no twists and turns, advises Brimblecombe: 'Design routes so people don't turn corners sharply or walk back and forth.'

I Brimblecombe has also found that for each additional metre people are kept back from furniture or pictures, the quantity of dust they deposit is halved. At least two metres should separate a piece of antique furniture, for example, from a visitor's woollen jacket. It seems that the best way to protect museums and their contents for future generations to enjoy is to keep the current generation as far away as possible.

coming from the things we wear – woollen sweaters, coats, scarves and so on. In the case of the Viking ships, a noticeable proportion of the fibres were thin strands of blue denim from visitors' jeans.

F So what is the answer? The electronics and pharmaceutical industries have already developed sophisticated devices such as air showers to clean anyone who sets foot inside their premises. They're effective, but not exactly what a tourist might expect on a visit to a historical building.

G It turns out that much of the dust causing the problem is shed from our clothes between the

SENTENCE COMPLETION
(WORDS FROM THE TEXT)
▶ *Focus on IELTS* page 33
▶ Module B page 20
LOCATING THE ANSWERS

2 You have already done a sentence completion task with a **bank of answers. You may also have to complete sentences using a word or words from the text.**

a Read through sentences 1–9 in the exam task on page 51, and underline key words. (The key words in sentences 1–3 have been underlined for you.) Use them to locate which part of the text each sentence relates to. Key words may be the same in the text and sentences (e.g. proper nouns) or they may be parallel expressions.

Example:
Question 1: *The authorities ... in buildings containing historical items*
Paragraph A: *those responsible for running ... museums, art galleries and historic buildings*

b When you complete the gaps in the sentences, make sure that:

- the word or words you write are exactly the same as in the text
- you keep within the word limit specified (usually between one and three words)
- your completed sentence makes sense and is grammatically correct

Look at the completed question below, which relates to paragraph A of the text. What is wrong with this answer?

> **1** The authorities are aware that .....*researchers*...... is needed to solve the problem of dust in buildings containing historical items. ✗

TIP The sentences are in the same order as the information in the text.

c Now complete the exam task.

Questions 1–9
Complete the sentences below with words taken from the Reading Passage.
Use **NO MORE THAN TWO WORDS** *for each answer.*

1   The authorities are aware that .... is needed to solve the problem of dust in buildings containing historical items.

2   Keeping historical items clean is difficult because of the time, expense and potential .... that is involved.

3   Small pieces broken from ancient .... exhibited in Roskilde have later been rescued from vacuum cleaner bags.

4   Ryhl-Svendsen says that even small breakages are serious as they mean .... is lost.

5   Brimblecombe's research at London's Tate Gallery does not support the idea that dust enters the building from ....

6   Brimblecombe and Ryhl-Svendsen used microscope slides and .... to collect dust samples for analysis.

7   Their research findings suggest that levels of dust depend both on visitor .... and on their closeness to the exhibits.

8   The researchers found that the most serious threat came from the .... of visitors.

9   It was found that a significant component of the dust on the Viking ships consisted of .... from visitors' jeans.

MULTIPLE CHOICE (MULTIPLE ANSWERS)

► *Focus on IELTS pages 52–53*

TIP In multiple-choice questions, the options (A, B, C, etc.) may be in a different order from the related information in the text.

3 You have already done a multiple-choice task with single answers. Another type of multiple-choice question has several correct answers.

a Read the question in the exam task below. Scan the text to find which paragraphs it refers to. (*the key word is 'solutions'*)

b Read through the relevant section of the text carefully and find the items that match the options in the list. Look for synonyms and parallel expressions to help you.

Questions 10–13
Choose FOUR letters A–H.
Which **FOUR** of the solutions below are recommended by the researchers to prevent exhibits from being damaged?

A   wide space between people and exhibits

B   restrictions on visitor numbers

C   location of most valuable exhibits at end of route

D   no rucksacks in exhibition rooms

E   visitors use air showers before entry

F   transparent walls between visitors and exhibits

G   no sudden changes of direction for visitors

H   coats and jackets to be left at entrance

► Ideas for speaking and writing page 141

Focus on listening 2 *Table completion; note completion*

Section 4

▶ *Focus on IELTS page 45*

In Section 4 of the Listening Module, you listen to an academic talk or lecture. There is only one speaker. You are given time at the beginning to look through the questions, but there is no pause in the middle of the recording. Because of this, it is particularly important to follow the stages of the lecture. The exam task can help you to do this.

1 a Look at the exam task below and answer these questions.

   1 What is the general topic of the lecture?
   2 What is the focus of the first part of the lecture? What is the focus of the second part?

   b Which of these two phrases from the recording probably introduces the second part of the lecture?

   a) Many of the features that give this art its special place in the world …
   b) It's thought that the first inhabitants of Bali …

> **TIP** In the table, read across the rows as you listen (not down the columns).

2 ♩ Now complete the exam task. Remember to check the number of words you can write.

Questions 1–5
Complete the table below.
Write NO MORE THAN THREE WORDS for each answer.

Date	Event	Importance for art
3000 BC	rice farmers from **1**	built temples with wood and stone carvings settled in Bali
14th century	introduction of Hinduism	artists employed by **2** .... and focused on epic narratives
1906	Dutch East Indies Company established	art became expression of opposition to **3** ....
1920s	beginning of **4**	encouraged use of new materials, techniques and subjects
1945	independence	new art with scenes of **5** .... (e.g. harvests) reflecting national identity

Questions 6–10
Complete the notes below.
Write NO MORE THAN TWO WORDS for each answer.

Characteristics of Balinese art today:

- present everywhere in Balinese life
- production or discussion of art does not require any **6** ....
- has been able to develop because of the **7** .... of the island

- constantly practised because closely related to **8** ....
- production of art is a **9** .... process
- art is not expected to be **10** ....

▶ Ideas for speaking and writing page 141

Focus on writing *Problems and solutions*

Task 2

▶ *Focus on IELTS* page 44

For Task 2, you may be asked to discuss a problem and suggest solutions to it.

ANALYSING THE QUESTION

1 Read the Writing task below and answer these questions.

1 What is the main topic of this task?
   a) violence in films
   b) reasons for violence in films
   c) social problems caused by violence in films
   d) effects of films on young people.

2 What two aspects of the topic do you have to write about?

WRITING TASK 2

You should spend about 40 minutes on this task.

Present a written argument or case to an educated reader with no specialist knowledge of the following topic.

> *Many people believe that the high levels of violence in films today are causing serious social problems.*
>
> *What are these problems and how could they be reduced?*

You should use your own ideas, knowledge and experience and support your arguments with examples and relevant evidence.

Write at least 250 words.

GENERATING IDEAS

2 Make notes for the task using the headings below and your own ideas.

Problems   Suggested action

ORGANISING AND
SUPPORTING YOUR IDEAS

3 a To answer this task, you will need to write at least four paragraphs.
      Decide what kind of information you will write in each paragraph 1–4.

   Paragraph 1: ....

   Paragraph 2: ....

   Paragraph 3: suggested measures/action

   Paragraph 4: ....

   b Now read the sample answer on page 54. Divide it into four separate paragraphs, using your paragraph plan to help you.

c   **Answer these questions about the sample answer.**

Problems

1   How many problems are mentioned?
2   What expressions are used to introduce them? Underline them.
3   What effects are mentioned?
4   What expressions are used to introduce them? Underline them.

Suggested action

5   How many suggestions for action are given?
6   What expressions are used to introduce and link the ideas? Underline them.

Conclusion

7   What expression is used to introduce the conclusion? Underline it.

SAMPLE ANSWER

The increasing amount of violence that is shown regularly in films has been a cause of concern for some time. Such films make violence appear entertaining, exciting and even something to be copied. However, it seems to be increasingly clear that this development is causing problems in our society. First of all, those who enjoy such films eventually stop associating the violence with any real consequences. They therefore lose their sense of reality and no longer take violence seriously or have any sympathy with the victims. This is bad for both individuals and for our whole society. Another worrying trend is that in these films the heroes are shown as people to be admired, even though they are very violent characters. This leads impressionable people to believe that they can gain respect and admiration by copying this aggressive behaviour, and so the levels of violence increase, especially in major cities throughout the world. What is needed to combat these problems is definite action. The government should regulate the film industry on the one hand, and provide better education on the other. Producers must be prevented from showing meaningless violence as 'fun' in their films. Instead, films could emphasise the tragic consequences of violent acts and this would educate people, especially young people, to realise that violence is real. To conclude, I think that viewing violence as entertainment may indeed cause serious social problems and that the only way to improve this situation is by regulating the industry and educating the public about the real human suffering that such violence brings.

PRESENTING SOLUTIONS:
MODAL VERBS

4   When making suggestions for solving a problem, we often use modal and semi-modal verbs such as *should, must, have to, need to, could* and *may be able to.*

a   Underline three modal verbs used in the sample answer to suggest action to be taken. Which verb expresses a) a strong obligation, b) a possibility, c) a strong suggestion?

b Complete the language box with modals from the list in Exercise 4a in order of strength.

Governments The UN Parents	_must_ .... _may be able to_	take action find ways take measures	to reduce this problem. to improve this situation. to stop this trend.

c Complete these sentences with a suggestion from the list (a–e) below. Fill the gaps with an appropriate modal verb.

1 Smoking is increasing among schoolchildren. To reverse this trend …
2 City streets are full of litter. To reduce this problem …
3 Many people in the world do not have enough to eat. To improve this situation …
4 Farmers use too many chemicals on food crops. To reduce this problem …
5 City crime is growing. To stop this trend …

a) the authorities .... increase the police force in urban areas.

b) alternative pest controls .... be introduced.

c) local communities .... take responsibility for cleaning their areas.

d) schools .... teach children about the health consequences.

e) rich countries .... increase their international aid budgets.

JUSTIFYING SOLUTIONS: CONDITIONALS
▶ *Focus on IELTS* pages 221–222

5 In academic writing we often need to justify the measures we suggest or the action we recommend. This can be done by using conditionals.

Example:
Smoking is increasing among schoolchildren. To reverse this trend, schools must teach children about the health consequences. <u>*If* schools *do not take action* soon, the health of the next generation *will be damaged*</u>.

a Which of the justifications below predict

a) the positive results from the suggested action?
b) the negative results if action is not taken?

1 If schools do not take action soon, …
2 Unless action is taken, …
3 If this is done, …
4 Otherwise the problem will …
5 This would reduce …
6 Such measures will …

b Now write your own suggestions and justifications for each of the problems 1–5 in Exercise 4c.

SPEED WRITING PRACTICE

6 Using your ideas and paragraph plan from Exercises 2 and 3, write your own full answer to the Task 2 question. Don't look at the sample answer while you are writing. You should not take longer than 35 minutes. Spend the last five minutes editing your answer.

1 Topic vocabulary overview
The topics covered in Module D (*Focus on IELTS* Units 7 and 8) were related to different aspects of culture.

a Complete the mindmaps below. (All the words come from Module D and/or *Focus on IELTS* Units 7 and 8.)

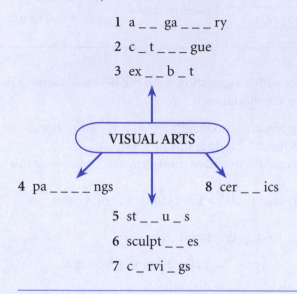

1 a _ _ ga _ _ _ ry
2 c _ t _ _ _ gue
3 ex _ _ b _ t

VISUAL ARTS

4 pa _ _ _ _ ngs
8 cer _ _ ics

5 st _ _ u _ s
6 sculpt _ _ es
7 c _ rvi _ gs

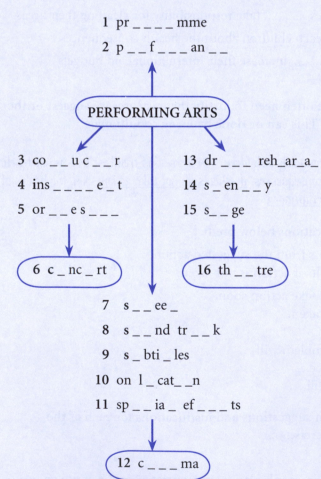

1 pr _ _ _ _ mme
2 p _ _ f _ _ _ an _ _

PERFORMING ARTS

3 co _ _ u c _ _ r
4 ins _ _ _ _ e _ t
5 or _ _ e s _ _ _

13 dr _ _ _ reh_ar_a_
14 s _ en _ _ y
15 s _ _ ge

6 c _ nc _ rt
16 th _ _ tre

7 s _ _ ee _
8 s _ _ nd tr _ _ k
9 s _ bti _ les
10 on l _ cat _ _ n
11 sp _ _ ia _ ef _ _ _ ts

12 c _ _ _ ma

b Now complete these extracts using words and expressions from the completed mindmaps. You will need to put them in the correct form.

Speaking Part 1: Talking about films

> **Examiner:** Let's talk about films. What kind of films do you enjoy watching?
>
> **Candidate:** Well, not old films – and not films in foreign languages, because I don't like having to read 1 .... What I really like are exciting films with lots of 2 .... , like the *Lord of the Rings* films. And I like those films because they were shot 3 .... – in New Zealand, I think, and it's really beautiful with the mountains and everything.

Listening Section 2: Introduction to an art gallery

> The gallery will be showing an exhibition of eighteenth-century art, including landscape and still life 4 .... , carved stone 5 .... showing mythological figures, and 6 .... , such as cups and plates, showing the important influence of Chinese art on the West during this period. An illustrated 7 .... giving full details of the exhibits is available at the desk, price $10.

Writing Task 2: The funding of cultural activities

> Many cultural activities involve a great deal of expense. In the case of concerts, as well as the expense of the concert hall, the 8 .... and members of the orchestra must be paid. A performance of a play at the 9 .... involves paying the actors, and also the cost of the 10 .... and costumes. If these and other cultural activities are to be maintained at a high standard, support in the form of government subsidies is needed.

c Look back through the units and add more words to the mindmaps.

2 Parallel expressions; avoiding repetition
▶ *Focus on IELTS* page 193
As well as using pronouns to link sentences and avoid repetition, writers also link sentences by using words with similar meanings.

Complete these extracts using words from the box. Underline the expression in the first sentence which has a parallel meaning to the word you add.

competence   emotions   exhibits   exhibition
fragments   qualities   technique   threat

1 On display in the Upper Gallery of the museum are objects which were used on expeditions to the North and South Poles. These .... include notebooks, clothing and equipment.

2 The first people to develop a method for making paper were the Chinese. They used a .... which involved washing plant fibres in water and then drying them.

3 A display of children's art opens at the Star Gallery this Saturday. This .... will consist of paintings and sculptures by children from local schools.

4 When this ceramic bowl was found in the pyramid, it had been broken into small pieces. These .... were carefully collected together and reassembled.

5 The effects of pollution are a growing menace to the Parthenon and other historic buildings in the centre of Athens. This .... has now been recognised and action is being taken to control pollution levels.

6 The ability to speak several foreign languages is necessary for the post of cultural tour guide, and a high level of .... is required in at least one of these.

7 Psychologists agree that music is very closely linked to our feelings. This connection between music and the .... has been the subject of several experiments.

8 Researchers have found that individuals who are skilled at music tend to have a number of positive features. These include .... such as creativity, energy and the ability to work well in a team.

3 Problems and solutions

a **Decide if the following expressions would be used to describe problems (P) or solutions (S).**

1 what people should do about this is ...   ..S..
2 one thing that would improve the
   situation is ...   .
3 it is a cause for concern that ...   .
4 the government should take measures to
   solve these problems, for example by ...   .
5 another worrying trend is ...   .
6 this trend could be reversed if ...   .
7 ... is needed to combat these problems.   .....
8 ... causes many problems.   .....

b **Use some of the phrases to complete this extract from a writing text.**

I *certainly think* **1** .... *some of our most beautiful and historic buildings are in danger of being destroyed. Lack of money for repairs and preservation* **2** .... *and* **3** .... *the increasing number of old buildings being pulled down to make room for car parks and office blocks.*
Rapid action **4** .... *in order to avoid the loss of our cultural heritage.*
5 .... *raising the public's awareness of the importance of these buildings to our culture. In addition, I think that*
6 .... *passing laws*

4 Linking expressions
Choose the correct linking expressions in this extract from a Part 3 Speaking task.

Well, in my country the government spends a lot of money supporting things like opera and classical music, **1** *and yet / what's more* only a minority of people actually enjoy that sort of thing. **2** *In fact / However*, there's hardly any money spent supporting the arts in schools, even though lots of children would like to have the chance to learn to paint or to play an instrument. So I think more should be spent on this – **3** *after all / what's more* these children are the artists of the future, aren't they?

5 Describing research
Complete each sentence by choosing the best ending from the list a–g below.

1 If no steps are taken to preserve them, future ...
2 The authorities at the Carlton Art Gallery say that systematic ...
3 The authorities have decided to launch ...
4 In order to put their work on a more scientific ...
5 In the past, staff received little formal ...
6 A team of staff have carried out an intriguing ...
7 The results of the study ...

a) training in conservation issues, but this is now provided for everyone.
b) a study into the best way of preventing the deterioration of the exhibits.
c) generations may not be able to enjoy some of our most important works of art.
d) indicate that sunlight is a major factor in the deterioration of exhibits.
e) footing, they have set up a major research project.
f) research is needed to identify the best way of preserving paintings and sculptures.
g) study into the effects of sunlight on a number of different items on display.

1 Vocabulary

Rewrite each sentence without changing the meaning, using the word in brackets. Write one word in each space.

1 There is a close connection between music and mathematics. (linked)
Music and mathematics ....
....

2 One of the most interesting exhibits is this stone carving. (objects)
This stone carving is one of the most interesting
....
....

3 Punctuality is regarded in different ways by different people. (attitudes)
People ....
towards punctuality.

4 There has been a complete breakdown in communication. (completely)
Communication ....
....

5 Their findings suggest that the damage is done by ordinary people. (research)
The results ....
.... indicate that the damage is done by ordinary people.

6 It's not easy to think of new ideas. (come)
It's hard ....
.... new ideas.

7 His illness may be partly stress-related. (caused)
His illness may be partly ....
....

8 A study was done on the effects of music on unborn children. (carried)
They ....
.... on the effects of music on unborn children.

2 Reading: Multiple choice

a Read the text and choose the correct letter, A, B, C or D to answer questions 1 and 2.

A museum under the sea

In early 2000, a Franco-Egyptian team discovered an entire sunken city – complete with houses, temples, toppled statues and port facilities – in the Mediterranean Sea off the coast of Egypt. The city is believed to be Herakleion, a port that guarded a branch of the River Nile before the river shifted and, for reasons unknown, the land slipped beneath the sea. The discoveries delighted archaeologists and historians alike.

Further along the coast, in Alexandria, archaeologists have already mapped a 2.5 hectare area under the water scattered with 2,500 pieces: columns, statues and obelisks inscribed with names of Pharaohs. This ancient world, a stone's throw from the city's seaside promenade, has, thus far, been reserved for a few lucky divers. But now these discoveries have sparked calls to build the world's first underwater museum, allowing visitors to cast their eyes on a history swallowed by the sea centuries ago. Projects totaling US$8 billion have been proposed, including undersea plexiglass tunnels, diving platforms, glass-bottomed boats and tourist submarines. Such ambitious plans have the endorsement of the Egyptian government, underwater archaeologists and UNESCO, which wants Alexandria's offshore area designated a World Heritage Site.

1 What event led to the destruction of the city of Herakleion?
   A The city was flooded by the River Nile.
   B The River Nile changed its position.
   C The city was attacked by enemies.
   D The sea level rose for unknown reasons.

2 The creation of an underwater museum in Alexandria
   A has been overseen by underwater archaeologists.
   B is opposed by UNESCO.
   C has attracted large numbers of tourists.
   D is supported by the government of Egypt.

b Find words or expressions in the text which mean

1 quite close to   ....
2 up to the present time   ....
3 have led to requests   ....
4 look at   ....
5 covered up   ....

3 Writing: Task 2

a Read the task, which requires an argument-led approach, and the first and last paragraphs of a sample answer below.

What is the writer's general opinion about the topic?
a) The writer supports the preservation of historic buildings in their original form.
b) The writer is against the preservation of historic buildings in their original form.

> *Some people argue that historic buildings should be preserved in their original forms. Others argue that this is both inadvisable and impossible.*
>
> *Discuss both these views and give your own opinion.*

(Paragraph 1) Nearly every country has old buildings which are significant because of their historical connections or their artistic value. Often, buildings may combine both of these qualities. In cases like this, it may seem vital that these buildings should not be pulled down or changed in any way.

(Paragraph 2) …… …… ……

(Paragraph 3) …… …… ……

(Paragraph 4) In conclusion, therefore, I feel that although we should not lose sight of the original purposes and nature of our historic buildings, there is no need for them to be frozen in time. A great building can support changes as long as these are carried out with respect for its original nature.

b The sentences below make up paragraphs 2 and 3 of the writing task above. Decide which three sentences should go in each paragraph. Then write the letters a–f in the correct order in the spaces next to the paragraph numbers above.

a) Some people even say that any furnishings or decorations which would not have been in the original building should be removed and replaced with the originals, or else with exact replicas.

b) It would be very difficult to decide what the 'original' form of such buildings was, and if we returned to this, I think we would lose much of historical and aesthetic value.

c) They say that any later additions to the building should be pulled down or removed.

d) In my country, buildings such as churches, palaces and great houses have been developed and added to over the centuries by the people who used them, reflecting the changes that have taken place in our society during that time.

e) However, it can be argued that this view does not reflect the organic nature of most significant buildings.

f) Many people believe that these buildings should not only be preserved, but should be returned to a form as close as possible to the way they first appeared.

4 Speaking: Part 2

Look at the prompt card and a candidate's response below. The answer is too short to fill two minutes. To expand it, match reasons from the list a–h below to the numbered gaps.

> **Describe something you do in your free time.**
>   **You should say**
>   **what kind of activity you do**
>   **when you do it**
>   **where you do it**
>   **and explain why you like doing it.**

Well, something I like to do, especially if I'm feeling a bit stressed, is to go out for a walk, quite a long walk but not rushing, just walking at a normal speed, er, 1 …………………… . I quite often go out for a walk in the evening if I've had a hard day at work 2 …………………… or sometimes I go out for a long walk at the weekend, er, 3 …………………… . If it's just a short walk, I go to the park, or I walk down the side streets near my home – I don't like walking on the main road 4 …………………… . But if I'm going for a longer walk at the weekend, I usually go out into the country – I get the bus or the train or something. I might even go out to the mountains, er, 5 …………………… . Anyway, I find it really relaxing; it always makes me feel better afterwards. I'm not sure why, er, 6 …………………… 7 …………………… . 8 …………………… .

a) I think one thing's the change of pace, it sort of slows me down.

b) … it's much better than just sitting in front of television in the evening or something like that,

c) And finally, if I go right out into the country, the whole environment is so different.

d) … because I find if I walk fast it doesn't relax me.

e) because of the noise – you end up even more stressed.

f) And it's good just getting out of the house and being out of doors. It helps me to kind of get things into perspective, you know?

g) if it's been a really bad week.

h) because I really love being high up, and the air is so pure.

▶ NATURAL FORCES

Focus on listening *Labelling a map; table completion*

Section 2

In Section 2 of the Listening Module, you may hear someone giving information about a place of special interest.

Above: A Maori couple
Right: Lake Rotomahana

1 You are going to hear a tour guide speaking to a group of tourists in New Zealand. How much do you know about New Zealand? Try this quiz, then check your answers in the Key.

1 The population of New Zealand is
   A 10.7 million.
   B 3.2 million.

2 Its original inhabitants are known as
   A Aborigines.
   B Maoris.

3 The capital city is
   A Wellington.
   B Auckland.

4 The country consists of
   A two main islands.
   B four main islands.

5 The main exports are
   A electrical products.
   B meat and milk products.

6 Tourists go there to
   A see castles and temples.
   B admire natural scenery.

7 The nearest continent to New Zealand is
   A Australia.
   B Asia.

LABELLING A MAP
▶ *Focus on IELTS* Exam briefing page 80

2 In Module B, page 24, you labelled a plan of a small area around a school. You may also have to label a map of a larger area.

Read the instructions for Questions 1–4 on page 61. To prepare for listening, look at the map and mark these statements true (*T*) or false (*F*).

1 Lake Rotoiti is at the top left of the map.
2 Lake Tarawera is directly north of Lake Rotomahana.
3 The Lakes Motel is on the road numbered SH 5.
4 The SH 30 and SH 5 meet just outside Rotorua Town.
5 E is about 12 kilometres from Rotorua Town.
6 One mountain is shown on the map.
7 F is between Mount Tarawera and Lake Rotomahana.
8 You have to label nine places on the map.

EXAM PRACTICE

3 🎧 **Now listen to the recording and complete the exam task.**

- Notice that for Questions 1–4, you only have to identify **four** of the places marked A–I on the map. You write the appropriate letter next to each named place on the list.

TABLE COMPLETION
▶ Module C, page 38

- Remember that there will be a short break in the middle of the recording. This will give you time to read the instructions for Questions 5–10, and identify the topic and the type of information you need to listen for.

> **TIP** Before you listen, think about the pronunciation of unusual words in the task so you will recognise them when you hear them.

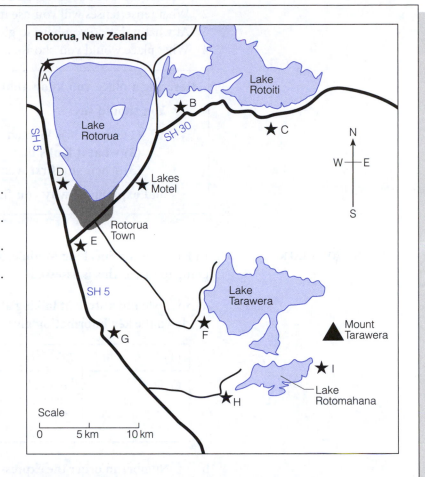

Questions 1–4
Label the map.
*Write the correct letter **A–I** next to Questions 1–4.*

1 Hell's Gate Thermal Reserve ......

2 Arts and Craft Institute ......

3 Volcanic valley ......

4 Tamaki Village ......

Questions 5–10
Complete the table below.
Use **NO MORE THAN ONE WORD AND/OR A NUMBER** *for each answer.*

Name of attraction	Special features	Cost
Hell's Gate Thermal Reserve	• very **5** .... volcanic area • boiling whirlpool • hot waterfall (temperature **6** ....°C)	adults $12 children $6
Arts and Crafts Institute	• see traditional Maori **7** .... • learn about use of geothermal waters for cooking and medicine	free
Volcanic valley	• formed by volcanic eruption in **8** .... • boat trip on lake	adults **9** .... children $5
Tamaki Village	• tour by Maori guide • 'Hangi' – traditional feast cooked over hot **10** .... in ground	no extra charge

▶ Ideas for speaking and writing page 141

Focus on speaking 1 *Describing a place*

In Part 2 of the Speaking Module, you may be asked to talk about a place you know. This could be somewhere you remember from the past or somewhere that is special to you for other reasons.

Part 2 Long turn
ANALYSING THE TASK

1 Read the candidate task card below and answer these questions.

1 Is the topic about an urban or rural place?
2 What tense/tenses will you use to talk about 1–4?
3 At what point do you have to give reasons?
4 What place would you choose to describe?

Describe a place you know that has a beautiful natural environment.

You should say:

  (1) where it is located
  (2) what it looks like
  (3) when you first went there

and explain (4) why you find this place especially beautiful.

ORGANISING YOUR TALK

2 In Part 2 of the Speaking Module, it is important to organise what you are going to say, as this is assessed.

a 🎧 Listen to a student talking about the topic in Exercise 1 and note down the key information given for prompts 1–4 on the task card.

(1)	(2)	(3)	(4)
Crete	beautiful mountains		

b 🎧 Number in order the expressions used by the speaker to signal the different parts of the talk. Then listen again and check.

  ☐ 1 Well, the place I'd like to talk about is …
  ☐ And the reason why …
  ☐ The first time I went there was when …
  ☐ What attracted me to this place was …

EXAM PRACTICE
▶ *Focus on IELTS* page 105

3 Spend one minute making notes for your own talk on the task in Exercise 1, using a list or mindmap. Use your notes to talk for two minutes on the topic. Time yourself and record yourself if you can.

DEALING WITH ROUNDING-OFF QUESTIONS

4 At the end of Part 2, the examiner may ask you one or two 'rounding-off' questions about your topic. Although long answers are not required for these, you can give fluent, idiomatic short answers.

a Look at the short answers below. Which would you choose for each question?

1 Do you often go to this place?   No, I've only been once before.
                                       No, but I wish I could.
                                       Yes, as often as I can.

2   Would you recommend this place to other people?

No, that would spoil it.
Yes, definitely!
I suppose so.

3   Do you think you'll go to this place again?

Probably not, it's too hard to get to.
I'll certainly try.
I hope so.

b   🎧 Listen to the exchanges on the recording. Underline the words in the answers which are stressed. Then practise saying these short responses as fluently as you can.

Focus on speaking 2 *Describing problems and solutions*

Part 3
▶ *Focus on IELTS* page 236

In the Speaking Module, the Part 2 topic is developed in Part 3 to a more abstract level. For example, in Part 3 you may be asked to consider problems associated with the Part 2 topic, and to suggest possible solutions to these problems.

TOPIC DEVELOPMENT

1   For the Part 2 task in the previous section, you described a place you know with a beautiful natural environment. This could be developed to discuss problems and solutions related to the environment.

a   Look at the questions below and think about how you would answer them.

1   What do you think is the main environmental problem in your country?
2   What could be done to deal with this problem?
3   Do you think this problem will get better or worse in the future?

b   🎧 Now listen to a student answering questions 1–3 above about his country, and complete the following notes.

> *Problem:* biggest problem is pressure on ....
> *Cause:* population is ...., forests being ....
> for agriculture, ...
> *Result:* loss of ....
> *Solution:* government should
> – introduce ....   – offer ....
> schools have to ....
> *Future:* If action taken, ... Otherwise ....

2   Read the notes below about another environmental problem. Use them to help you answer the questions in Exercise 1a.

> *Problem:* air pollution
> *Cause:* industrial emissions, traffic → health problems
> *Solution :* control factory emissions, reduce traffic ...
> *Future:* Unless something done ...

EXAM PRACTICE

3   Answer questions 1–3 in Exercise 1a with your own ideas and record yourself if you can.

Focus on reading *True/False/Not Given; table completion; multiple choice (multiple answers)*

FORMING A GENERAL PICTURE

1 **a** Read the heading and subheading of the text on page 65 and look at the photo. Before you continue, find out how much you already know about the *Titanic*. Decide if the following sentences are true or false. Then check your answers in the Key.

1 The *Titanic* was the biggest passenger ship that has ever existed.
2 It was considered to be unsinkable.
3 It sank in a storm on its first voyage.
4 All 2,224 of the passengers and crew were lost.
5 There were only enough lifeboats for half the passengers.
6 The real wreck was filmed by James Cameron for his film *Titanic*.

b Quickly read paragraph A and the first sentence only of the other paragraphs, and answer the following questions.

1 What do rusticles look like?
2 What do they contain?
3 How are they harming the *Titanic*?
4 Are rusticles ever useful for anything?

DEALING WITH SPECIALIST VOCABULARY

2 Texts in the Reading Module may contain academic or specialist words and expressions. Some specialist words – for example *rusticles* – may be explained in the text. Other terms can be guessed from the context.

a Scan the text to find these words and try to work out what they probably mean. Underline other words in the context which help you to guess.

1 hull (paragraph A)
2 rust (paragraph A)
3 salvage company (paragraph B)
4 brittle (paragraph B)
5 microbes (paragraph C)
6 consorms (paragraph C)
7 permeate (paragraph C)
8 susceptible (paragraph E)
9 rivets (paragraph E)
10 consume (paragraph F)

b Check your ideas by matching the words to the definitions on page 143.

SCANNING TO FIND SPECIFIC SECTIONS OF THE TEXT

3 IELTS Reading texts often have two or three different task types. It may help you to answer the questions more quickly if you start by looking through all the tasks and finding the part of the text each task refers to.

Read the instructions for each task on pages 66 and 67 and look through the questions quickly. Check back with the text as necessary.

1 In which **one** paragraph of the text will you find the answers to questions 6–10? (*use the title of the table to help you*) ....

2 In which paragraphs will you probably find the answers to questions 1–5? ....

3 In which paragraphs should you look for the answers to questions 11–14? ....

4 Now complete the three exam tasks.

Eating up the Titanic

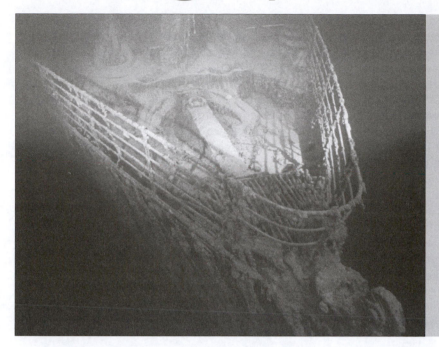

Colonies of iron-loving bacteria are eating up the most famous shipwreck in the world. But the news isn't all bad

The wreck of the *Titanic*

A In 1985, seventy-three years after it had sunk on its maiden voyage from Southampton to New York, the *Titanic* was discovered lying 3,800 metres below the surface of the sea. The first images the world saw of the wreck showed the metal hull or body of the ship, draped in what look like strange underwater icicles. These structures are called 'rusticles' from *rust* (the reddish brown substance that forms on iron when it is in contact with water) and *icicle*.

B A decade later, microbial ecologist Roy Cullimore was called on to investigate biological activity on the *Titanic* after the salvage company recovering objects from the wreck noticed it seemed to be deteriorating. By carefully guiding the robotic claws of the French submarine *Nautile*, Cullimore was able to collect some rusticles to bring back to his laboratory for analysis. Gathering them was a tricky business – rusticles are brittle and have a tendency to snap in the fast water flow created by the propellers of the submarine. A second expedition brought up more rusticles when a large section of hull was lifted from the sea bed. The largest of these, measuring 45 centimetres long, now hangs on Cullimore's office wall.

C Each rusticle is made up of communities of bacteria, fungi and other microbes that have joined forces to build a sort of rusting tower block to sustain them and protect them from the outside world. The outer walls have a layered appearance, much like the annular growth rings in trees. Inside, each rusticle seems to contain at least five distinct communities of bacteria, or 'consorms', that live in harmony, with each type of consorm performing a specific task. They are mostly clustered around water channels that run through the structure. There are also fungal growths towards the outside of the structure where the channels meet the surface. Along with the microbes, rusticles contain up to 35 per cent iron compounds in the form of ribbons that permeate the entire structure, in much the same way that nerves or blood vessels do in an animal. Chemically, these compounds are dominated by various ferric oxides, hydroxides and carbonates.

D Cullimore's work has revealed that the microbial communities work together to 'feed' on the ship, actively removing iron from it. And the effects can be dramatic. In 1996, he estimated that they were removing 100 kilograms of iron a day. As the rusticles grow, the decay rate accelerates, and Cullimore predicts that the wreck will be unrecognisable within 100 years or so.

E However, the rusticles colonise some parts of the ship but leave others alone. To find out why, Cullimore has placed various steel samples on the *Titanic*'s deck. His findings suggest that the most susceptible areas are where the steel was ripped or twisted when the ship sank, because the fractures allow microbes to get in more easily. The rusticles also seem to consume the parts of the ship made of wrought iron, such as the rivets, more easily than steel. This is bad news not just for the *Titanic*, but for other ships and undersea structures such as oil rigs, because it is the rivets which hold the whole thing together. 'When you destroy a rivet, you're weakening the whole section,' says Cullimore.

F Iron-loving bacteria such as those found in rusticles can also be useful, however. Sean Tyrrel from Cranfield University has worked on projects to design iron filters for wells in developing countries, to prevent problems caused by iron-rich water. There's been a great interest in using groundwater to provide drinking water because it is generally regarded as unpolluted and can be safely consumed without the need for treatment. But iron-bearing groundwaters are often noticeably orange in colour, causing discoloration of laundry, and have an unpleasant taste which is apparent when the water is drunk or used for food preparation. 'If there's a lot of iron in the water, people reject it,' Tyrrel says. He and his colleagues have found that under the right conditions, certain bacteria will take up the iron from the water and consume it, leaving it clear. The rusticles research should provide more clues about how to harness these bacteria for good.

G And the reach of rusticles doesn't end there. Cullimore's research has convinced him that iron-loving bacteria could be harnessed for all sorts of industrial uses. He sees rusticles as a sort of biological concrete, which has given him the idea that microbes could be added to normal concrete to improve its performance. Such bioconcrete might even be grown using microbes, instead of being mixed and allowed to harden as it is at present, before being used for buildings.

H Scientists still have much to learn about the specific types of microbes present in rusticles and how they interact with each other. But what is certain is that the various consorms must use a common language to successfully build and sustain their mutual community. Cullimore ultimately hopes to begin to understand this language. 'If we could learn how they communicate, then we could say "Hey, you shouldn't be growing here, wouldn't you rather be growing over there?"'

TRUE/FALSE/NOT GIVEN

▶ Module A page 9

- Underline key words in the statements.
- Find matching information in the text.
- Look for parallel expressions.

Questions 1–5

Do the following statements agree with the information given in the reading passage?

Write

TRUE	*if the statement agrees with the information*
FALSE	*if the statement contradicts the information*
NOT GIVEN	*if there is no information on this*

1 Underwater photographs of the *Titanic* show that the wreck is covered in rusticles.

2 Rusticles were first discovered on the wreck of the *Titanic*.

3 Roy Cullimore investigated whether rusticles were involved in the sinking of the *Titanic*.

4 Rusticles are difficult to collect because they break easily.

5 The rusticle in Cullimore's office is the largest one in existence.

TABLE COMPLETION

▶ *Focus on IELTS* page 91

▶ Modules C and D, pages 38 and 52 (Listening)

> **TIP** Note form is normally used in tables.

Table completion is a common task in both the Reading and Listening Modules.

- Read the headings at the top and on the left-hand side of the table to identify the type of information that is required.
- Use the exact words from the passage for your answer.

Questions 6–10
Complete the table below.
*Choose **NO MORE THAN TWO WORDS AND/OR A NUMBER** from the passage for each answer.*

Structure of a rusticle

Component	Description	Location
walls	appear **6**	outer surface of rusticle
consorms	• bacterial **7** .... • work together • each does a different **8**	mainly near water channels
water channels		throughout the rusticle
fungal growths		at junction of water channels and **9** .... of rusticle
10	ribbons	throughout the rusticle

MULTIPLE CHOICE
(MULTIPLE ANSWERS)
▶ Module D page 51

• Read the question.
• Find the correct section of the text.
• Check for parallel expressions in the options and text.

Questions 11–12
*Choose **TWO** letters A–G.*

The microbes found in rusticles

    A are unable to consume steel sections of boats.

    B may live for over 100 years.

    C could affect a range of underwater metal structures.

    D avoid structures made of wrought iron.

    E are destroyed if the rusticle grows too big.

    F cause fractures and rips in steel plates.

    G use iron from the ship as a source of food.

Questions 13–14
*Choose **TWO** letters A–G.*

Bacteria similar to those found in rusticles could

    A make better concrete for use in building.

    B remove harmful microbes from polluted water.

    C help locate sources of groundwater.

    D remove iron from water used for drinking and washing.

    E remove traces of iron from concrete.

    F convert harmful microbes to useful ones.

    G improve communication systems.

▶ Ideas for speaking and writing page 141

Focus on writing *Describing diagrams showing natural processes*

Task I Diagrams

▶ *Focus on IELTS* page 102–104

In the Writing Module, you may be asked to describe a diagram that shows a natural cycle or a natural process.

UNDERSTANDING THE DATA

1

a Read the instructions for the Writing task below and answer these questions.

1 What is 'El Niño' and what does it do?
2 What do the diagrams compare?

b Look at the first diagram, which shows a cross section of the Pacific Ocean, and read the labels to help you understand the process illustrated.

Under normal conditions,

1 from which direction do the strong trade winds blow?
2 what do they do to the warm water at the surface of the sea?
3 how does this affect the weather in Australia?
4 what happens to the cool water below the surface?
5 what are the two results of this in the Eastern Pacific?

c Now look at the second diagram to identify what the differences are under El Niño conditions.

TIP The diagrams in Writing Task I do not require world knowledge. Any information you will need in your description is given in the task.

WRITING TASK 1

You should spend about 20 minutes on this task.

El Niño is the name of a warm ocean current that affects weather patterns on both sides of the Pacific Ocean. The diagrams compare normal conditions in the Pacific with El Niño conditions.

Write a report for a university lecturer describing the information shown.

Write at least 150 words.

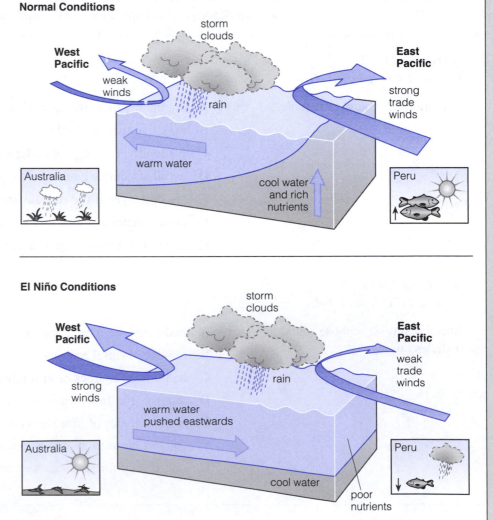

LINKING IDEAS USING -ING PARTICIPLE CLAUSES
▶ *Focus on IELTS* page 129

2 **a** Compare these sentences.

1 Strong trade winds blow warm surface water westwards. **This process causes** storm clouds to form and **brings** rain to Australia.
2 The trade winds blow warm surface water westward, **causing** storm clouds to form and **bringing** rain to Australia.

The second sentence uses an *-ing* clause to present the information in a more economical way.

b Now join these pairs of sentences in the same way.

1 The warm water builds up in the west. **This process allows** cool water to rise to the surface in the east.
2 The cool water brings rich nutrients to the surface. **This process enables** the numbers of fish to increase near Peru.
3 In El Niño conditions, warm surface water flows eastwards. **This process brings** rain to Peru.
4 Storm clouds are formed in the eastern Pacific. **This process reduces** rainfall in Australia.
5 The warm water forms a layer on top of the cool water. **This process prevents** the cool water from rising to the surface.

ORGANISING THE DESCRIPTION

3 **a** Complete this paragraph plan for the writing task.

> Paragraph 1: Introduce information
> Paragraph 2: Describe ....
> Paragraph 3: Describe ....
> Paragraph 4:...

b Complete the sample answer below using logical links from the box. Use each word or phrase once only.

> *also   the second   so   while at the same time   the first
> consequently   in these conditions   while*

SAMPLE ANSWER

> The diagrams illustrate how differences in the wind conditions over the Pacific Ocean can affect the weather in Peru and Australia.
>
> 1 .... diagram shows that in normal conditions the trade winds blowing from the east are stronger than the weak winds from the west. 2 ...., they blow the warm surface water westwards, bringing rain to Australia, 3 .... allowing cool water to rise from the deep ocean in the east. This water brings rich nutrients, enabling the numbers of fish to increase in the waters off Peru. It 4 .... brings good weather to Peru and the east Pacific.
> 5 .... diagram indicates that when the wind from the western Pacific is stronger than the trade winds, the ocean currents are changed. 6 .... warm surface waters flow eastwards, bringing rain to Peru, 7 .... the rainfall in Australia is greatly reduced. The cold water from the deep does not rise to the surface in the east, 8 .... there are fewer nutrients available and the fish decline.

WRITING THE CONCLUSION

4 Remember that your conclusion should summarise the information, not explain it.

Choose which of these three final sentences best summarises the information in the diagrams.

Overall, the diagrams suggest that

a) … both Australia and Peru benefit from El Niño conditions.

b) … it is changes in the relative wind strength that brings about El Niño conditions.

c) … El Niño conditions are caused by different weather in Australia and Peru.

GRAMMAR

5 Read the sample answer again and answer these questions.

1 What tenses are used in the description?
2 Underline all examples of passive verb forms.
3 Underline all examples of *-ing* participle clauses.

EDITING FOR LANGUAGE

6 a Find ten common mistakes in this extract from a student answer and match them to the list.

The diagram give information about the El Niño current in the Pacific Ocean.

At the beginning, in normal conditions we can see that the wind is blown the warm water to the west causes cool water to rise up to the suface in the east. This bring rich nutrients, abling the number of fish to increase. In this conditions Peru get sunshine and Australia gets rain.

In addition, in El Niño conditions the weather is different …

Common mistakes
1 Wrong spelling
2 Active/passive verbs confused
3 Agreement (subject–verb or modifier–noun)
4 Wrong word form
5 Wrong word or expression

b Now correct the mistakes.

SPEED WRITING PRACTICE

7 Without looking again at the sample answer, do the writing task. You have already spent time analysing the task so you should spend no more than 15 minutes on writing and editing. Remember:

• Don't copy your introduction from the Writing task.
• Focus on the main differences.
• End with a summary of the data.
• Write at least 150 words.

Topic vocabulary overview
Module E (*Focus on IELTS* Units 9 and 10)
introduced a range of language connected with water
resources and environmental problems.

a Complete the diagrams below using the jumbled
words.

1 litquay .....*quality*.......

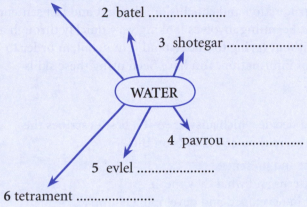

2 batel ....

3 shotegar ....

WATER

4 pavrou ....

5 evlel ....

6 tetrament ....

7 sherf ....

8 grinkdin ....

9 sweta ....

WATER

13 eas ....

10 iran ....

11 dugron ....

12 tasl ....

b Complete the diagrams below using words from
the box.

> effect   resource   pollution   supply   risks
> consumption   domestic   plant   system
> emissions   illegal

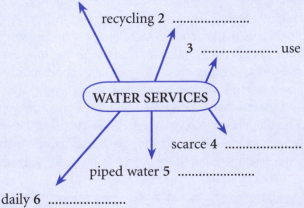

drainage 1 ....

recycling 2 ....

3 .... use

WATER SERVICES

scarce 4 ....

piped water 5 ....

daily 6 ....

vehicle 7 ....

air 8 ....

9 .... dumping

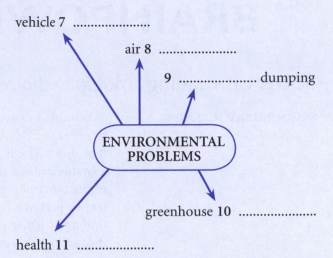

ENVIRONMENTAL
PROBLEMS

greenhouse 10 ....

health 11 ....

c Now complete these extracts using words and
expressions from the completed diagrams in the
correct form.

**Listening Section 4: Maximising water resources
in dry climates**

> Where resources are limited, one way to
> overcome the perennial problem of
> 1 .... is to build a water
> 2 .... This means that local
> communities can re-use their 3 ....
> and so conserve their scarce resources. Of
> course, today water 4 .... techniques
> are cheaper and more environmentally-friendly
> than in the past.

Reading: Regional differences in water use

> In countries with wetter climates most water
> tends to be used for 5 .... and
> industrial processes. In drier countries, however,
> water is a 6 .... and has to be used by
> the agricultural sector. The highest level of 7
> .... tends to be in areas where
> intensive irrigation systems are used.

Speaking Part 3: Environmental problems

> I think in the future the level of 8 ....
> in big cities will get worse ... and that will
> present all sorts of 9 .... , such as
> breathing problems and so on. I think it's
> inevitable because we'll have more and more
> cars. So the 10 .... will just go on
> increasing, and they're the major problem,
> aren't they?

d Look back through the units and add more words
to the diagrams.

▶ # BRAINPOWER

Focus on reading *Multiple choice (single answer); Yes/No/Not Given*

SKIMMING AND SCANNING

Skimming involves selective reading of the most important parts of a text, in order to find out how the text is organised and get a general idea of what it is about. The main information is likely to be contained in the title and any subheading; the introduction and conclusion; the first and last sentences of the other paragraphs. Scanning involves looking very quickly through a text or part of a text, without trying to understand it in detail, in order to find a particular piece of information. You have been using these skills throughout this course.

1   **Skim the text below and decide which answer (A–C) best describes the overall topic. Spend no more than 45 seconds on this.**

   A   Education in the past and present
   B   Changes in work patterns and what they mean
   C   Education and work in developed and developing countries

2   **Now find the answers to these questions.**

   1   Which two time periods does paragraph A contrast?
   2   Underline a new expression that the writer explains in paragraph A. How does the writer show this is a new expression?
   3   In paragraph B, find another new expression that is explained by the writer.
   4   Which **one** key word in the first sentences of both paragraphs C and D introduces the topic of both those paragraphs?
   5   Underline a key phrase in the first sentence of paragraph E.
   6   Match paragraphs F–H to these topics.
      1 solutions   2 advantages   3 problems

The knowledge society

A   A CENTURY ago, the overwhelming majority of people in developed countries worked with their hands: on farms, in domestic service, in small craft shops and in factories. There was not even a word for people who made their living other than by manual work. These days, the fastest-growing group in the developed world are 'knowledge workers' – people whose jobs require formal and advanced schooling.

B   At present, this term is widely used to describe people with considerable theoretical knowledge and learning: doctors, lawyers, teachers, accountants, chemical engineers. But the most striking growth in the coming years will be in 'knowledge technologists': computer technicians, software designers, analysts in clinical labs, manufacturing technologists, and so on. These people are as much manual workers as they are knowledge workers; in fact, they usually spend far more time working with their hands than with their brains. But their manual work is based on a substantial amount of theoretical knowledge which can be acquired only through formal education. They are not, as a rule, much better paid than traditional skilled workers, but they see

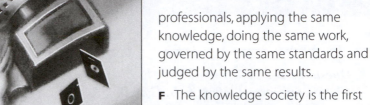

themselves as professionals. Just as unskilled manual workers in manufacturing were the dominant social and political force in the twentieth century, knowledge technologists are likely to become the dominant social – and perhaps also political – force over the next decades.

C Such workers have two main needs: formal education that enables them to enter knowledge work in the first place, and continuing education throughout their working lives to keep their knowledge up to date. For the old high-knowledge professionals such as doctors, clerics and lawyers, formal education has been available for many centuries. But for knowledge technologists, only a few countries so far provide systematic and organised preparation. Over the next few decades, educational institutions to prepare knowledge technologists will grow rapidly in all developed and emerging countries, just as new institutions to meet new requirements have always appeared in the past.

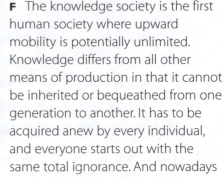

D What is different this time is the need for the continuing education of already well-trained and highly knowledgeable adults. Schooling traditionally stopped when work began. In the knowledge society it never stops. Continuing education of already highly educated adults will therefore become a big growth area in the next society. But most of it will be delivered in non-traditional ways, ranging from weekend seminars to online training programmes, and in any number of places, from a traditional university to the student's home. The information revolution, which is expected to have an enormous impact on education and on traditional schools and universities, will probably have an even greater effect on the continuing education of knowledge workers, allowing knowledge to spread near-instantly, and making it accessible to everyone.

E All this has implications for the role of women in the labour force. Although women have always worked, since time immemorial the jobs they have done have been different from men's. Knowledge work, on the other hand, is 'unisex', not because of feminist pressure, but because it can be done equally well by both sexes. Knowledge workers, whatever their sex, are professionals, applying the same knowledge, doing the same work, governed by the same standards and judged by the same results.

F The knowledge society is the first human society where upward mobility is potentially unlimited. Knowledge differs from all other means of production in that it cannot be inherited or bequeathed from one generation to another. It has to be acquired anew by every individual, and everyone starts out with the same total ignorance. And nowadays it is assumed that everybody will be a 'success' – an idea that would have seemed ludicrous to earlier generations. Naturally, only a tiny number of people can reach outstanding levels of achievement, but a very large number of people assume they will reach adequate levels.

G The upward mobility of the knowledge society, however, comes at a high price: the psychological pressures and emotional traumas of the rat race. Schoolchildren in some countries may suffer sleep deprivation because they spend their evenings at a crammer to help them pass their exams. Otherwise they will not get into the prestige university of their choice, and thus into a good job. In many different parts of the world, schools are becoming viciously competitive. That this has happened over such a short time – no more than 30 or 40 years – indicates how much the fear of failure has already permeated the knowledge society.

H Given this competitive struggle, a growing number of highly successful knowledge workers of both sexes – business managers, university teachers, museum directors, doctors – 'plateau' in their 40s. They know they have achieved all they will achieve. If their work is all they have, they are in trouble. Knowledge workers therefore need to develop, preferably while they are still young, a non-competitive life and community of their own, and some serious outside interest – be it working as a volunteer in the community, playing in a local orchestra or taking an active part in a small town's local government. This outside interest will give them the opportunity for personal contribution and achievement.

MULTIPLE CHOICE (SINGLE ANSWER)

▶ Module C page 36

3 **Now do the exam task on page 74.**

- Read the stem of the multiple-choice question.
- Scan to locate the information in the text.
- Look for parallel expressions in the text and options.

Questions 1–5
Choose the correct letter, **A, B, C** *or* **D.**

1 According to the writer, a hundred years ago in the developed world, manual workers

   A were mainly located in rural areas.

   B were not provided with sufficient education.

   C were the largest single group of workers.

   D were the fastest growing group in society.

2 The writer suggests that the most significant difference between knowledge technologists and manual workers is

   A their educational background.

   B the pay they can expect.

   C their skill with their hands.

   D their attitudes to society.

3 He predicts that in the coming years, knowledge technologists

   A will have access to the same educational facilities as professional people.

   B will have more employment opportunities in educational institutions.

   C will require increasing mobility in order to find suitable education.

   D will be provided with appropriate education for their needs.

4 According to the writer, the most important change in education this century will be

   A the way in which people learn.

   B the sorts of things people learn about.

   C the use people make of their education.

   D the type of people who provide education.

5 The writer says that changes in women's roles

   A mean women are now judged by higher standards.

   B have led to greater equality with men in the workplace.

   C are allowing women to use their traditional skills in new ways.

   D may allow women to out-perform men for the first time.

YES/NO/NOT GIVEN

▶ *Focus on IELTS* Exam briefing page 14

▶ Module A page 9

4 In Modules A and E, you looked at a task where you had to decide if statements were True, False or Not Given. This focused on factual information. In another, similar task you have to answer questions about the writer's opinions. In this case, you are told to answer *Yes/No* instead of *True/False.* The third option is still *Not Given.*

LOCATING THE ANSWERS

> **TIP** Remember that different sets of questions may be based on different parts of the text.

a Read question 6 in the exam task on page 75. Use the underlined key words to help you to locate the part of the text where you will find the answer for this question. The rest of the questions will follow on in order from that part of the text.

NO OR NOT GIVEN?

b It can be difficult to distinguish between *No* (or *False*) and *Not Given.* You can often make a *No/False* true according to the passage by adding a negative. You can't do this for *Not Given.*

Read the information in the text that relates to question 6. What does this information tell you?

a) Parents can pass knowledge down to their children.
b) Parents cannot pass knowledge down to their children.
c) Neither a) nor b). (= Not Given)

c Now complete the exam task.

Questions 6–13

Do the following statements agree with the views of the writer in the reading passage?
Write:

YES   *if the statement agrees with the views of the writer*
NO   *if the statement contradicts the views of the writer*
NOT GIVEN   *if it is impossible to say what the writer thinks about this*

6 In the knowledge society, knowledge can be passed down from parents to children.

7 Everyone is expected to be successful in the knowledge society.

8 The knowledge society means that some people may become successful by accident.

9 The knowledge society has both good and bad points.

10 Schoolchildren should not study so hard that they risk becoming ill.

11 It is right for schools to encourage a high degree of competition between their students.

12 When choosing outside interests, knowledge workers should avoid the need to try to do better than other people.

13 Outside interests are more fulfilling if they involve helping other people.

USEFUL
VOCABULARY

5 Complete the notes below with information from the reading text. Then use them to help you summarise, orally or in writing, the main points given in the text about the knowledge society.

> *Past:*   *most people* 1 .... *workers*
>
> *Present:* *being replaced by* 2 ...., *e.g. doctors,*
>   *lawyers, etc.*
>
> *Future:*   3 ...., *e.g. computer technicians, software*
>   *designers, etc. (need formal education +* 4 .... *education)*
> *Knowledge society:*
> • *benefits: change in* 5 .... *+ upward mobility*
> • *drawbacks:* 6 .... *+ emotional trauma*

▶ Ideas for speaking and writing page 142

Focus on listening *Multiple-choice questions (single answer); matching*

Section 3
► *Focus on IELTS* Exam
briefing page 42

In Section 3, you may hear a conversation between students and/or tutors about a research project, a report, a case study or some other type of assignment.

PREDICTING INFORMATION

1 Look at questions 1–5 below.

1 Who will you hear in the conversation? What are their roles (e.g. student/ teacher)?
2 What have Sami and Irene done for their research project?

UNDERSTANDING QUESTIONS BASED ON DIAGRAMS

2 In the Listening Module, you may need to answer questions based on graphs or pie charts.

Look at question 5. This shows three pie charts. Answer these questions.

1 What does the dark shaded area of each pie chart represent?
2 Pie chart A suggests that about 25% of students recommended a booking system. What percentage is suggested by pie chart B? How about C?

MULTIPLE CHOICE (SINGLE ANSWER)
► Module B page 23

3 ∩ Listen to the first part of the recording and answer questions 1–5.

• Underline key words in the questions.
• Listen for related words.
• Choose the closest option.

Questions 1–5
Choose the correct answer, A, B or C.

1 Sami and Irene decided to do a survey about access to computer facilities because

A no one had investigated this before.

B their tutor suggested this topic.

C this was a problem for many students.

2 Sami and Irene had problems with the reading for their project because

A the language was too technical.

B not much had been written about the topic.

C they could not locate the books in the library.

3 How did Sami and Irene get the main data in their survey?

A from face-to-face interviews

B from observation of students

C from online questionnaires

4 The tutor suggests that one problem with the survey was limitations in

A the range of students questioned.

B the number of students involved.

C the places where the questions were asked.

5 What proportion of students surveyed thought that a booking system would be the best solution?

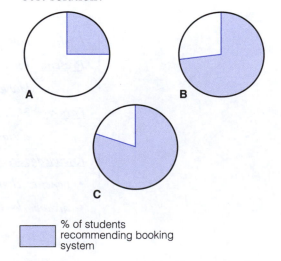

% of students recommending booking system

MATCHING

4 In the Listening Module, you may have to match two sets of information such as people and places, or suggestions and advantages/disadvantages.

a Read the instructions for the task below and look at the list of information in the box. What **type** of information do you have to listen for?

b Read the list of suggestions 6–10. They are in the same order as the information you will hear. What is the first topic you have to listen for?

c ⌒ Now listen to the recording and complete the task. As you are listening for each item, look quickly though the list of options in the box. When you hear the answer, write the letter only (**not** the complete phrase) next to that item. Then listen for the next item.

TIP Remember to listen for parallel expressions, as you will probably not hear the exact words.

Questions 6–10

What disadvantage was mentioned in relation to each suggestion?

Choose your answers from the box and write the letters A–H next to questions 6–10.

6 different rooms for educational
   and recreational use   ......

7 restrictions on use by classes   ......

8 new computers   ......

9 24-hour access to computers   ......

10 booking system   ....

Disadvantages
A against university regulations
B inconvenient for users
C involves long waits
D lack of alternative resources
E need for security arrangements
F not a long-term solution
G more work for staff at centres
H too expensive

IDENTIFYING PARALLEL
EXPRESSIONS

5 a ⌒ Listen to the second half of the recording again and complete the following sentences. Write one word in each gap.

1 It would be a .... if you had to get up and go to another room.

2 There's .... else they can ....

3 It wouldn't really .... the problem ....

4 There would have to be .... around all the time to make sure the equipment didn't get ....

5 It means the .... at the open access centres have to .... it.

b Match each of the completed sentences 1–5 to one disadvantage from the box in the exam task above.

▶ Ideas for speaking and writing page 142

Focus on speaking 1 *Describing a past event*

Part 2 Long turn
ANALYSING THE TASK

1 Read the candidate task card below and number the prompts you need to talk about.

> **Describe a special school or college event that you remember well.**
>
> **You should say:**
>
>   **what the event was**
>   **what happened during it**
>   **who was there**
>
> **and explain why you remember this event so well.**

CHOOSING WHAT
TO TALK ABOUT

2 In the exam, you can't choose your speaking task, but you do choose which event/memory/person, etc. to talk about. You need to choose quickly as you only have one minute to prepare.

> **TIP** If you can't think of an appropriate topic quickly, make one up.

Look at the types of event you could talk about in the box below. Which ones are   a) social events?   b) academic events?   c) sporting events?

> *a debate   a championship final   a party   a special dinner   a guest lecture*
> *a graduation   a prize-giving ceremony   a tournament   a sports match*

ANALYSING SAMPLE
ANSWERS

3 🎧 Listen to three extracts. What event is each speaker describing? Choose from the box in Exercise 2. Note down the vocabulary that helped you identify each event.

Speaker A is describing a ....

....

Speaker B is describing a ....

....

Speaker C is describing a ....

....

EXPLAINING

4 The last part of the Part 2 task always asks you to explain something. In this task, you need to give reasons why you remembered this event.

a Read the extract below. Is this the final part of extract A, B or C in Exercise 3?

   1 '*Why I remember it all so well was because of* the strong feelings I had, … you know, one part of my life was ending and a new part about to begin. I felt sad … and happy at the same time. I don't think I'll ever forget it.'

b Now complete the explanations below for the other two topics. This time, try to use your own ideas.

   2 '*The reason I remember it was* because we all … Yeah, everybody helped to make it a really good event.'

   3 '*I remember it so well because* it was so … It was our biggest win ever!'

EXAM PRACTICE

5 Now spend one minute making notes on the task in Exercise 1. Talk about your event for two minutes. Record yourself if you can.

Focus on speaking 2 *Giving opinions*

Part 3
TOPIC DEVELOPMENT

1 The Part 2 task on page 78 used the setting of a school or college for an academic, social or sporting event. Look at the list of possible Part 3 topics arising from this task and write two questions each for topics 2–4.

Topic 1 The importance of social events for schools/colleges
What benefits can social events bring to a college?
Are there any dangers in encouraging social events?

Topic 2 The value of sport in education
Topic 3 The aims of primary education (now and in the future)
Topic 4 Academic success today

INTRODUCING OPINIONS
▶ *Focus on IELTS* page 223

2 We often use adverbial expressions like the ones below to indicate what we think about a topic. We usually say these when we start to speak.

a Underline the best word to complete each sentence.

1 *Inevitably/Personally*, I don't think organised social events are very important.
2 *Clearly/Frankly*, there should be some role for sport in schools.
3 *Surprisingly/Obviously*, the first aim of primary education is to teach students basic literacy skills.
4 *Generally/Inevitably*, it's hard to get a job these days with no qualifications, though it's always possible.
5 *Surprisingly/Inevitably*, ability is usually judged by exam results.
6 *Frankly/Clearly*, I don't believe exams are necessarily the best way to assess a person.
7 *Typically/Surprisingly*, weak students sometimes get pretty good exam results.
8 *Predictably/Surprisingly*, most people find exams are stressful.

b Which adverbs above are used to indicate that:

a) you are only giving your own opinion about something ....

b) you are saying something direct and honest ....

c) this situation is usually true or this is what usually happens
............, ...

d) a fact can be easily noticed or understood ...., ...

e) this situation was expected or certain to happen............, ...

f) this situation was unexpected ....

JUSTIFYING OPINIONS

3 **a** Extend each of the statements 1–8 in Exercise 2a by giving reasons.
Example:
1 *Personally, I don't think organised social events are very important because students often prefer to have a separate social life, outside college.*

b ∩ Listen and compare your ideas with the native speakers on the recording.

EXAM PRACTICE

4 Look back at Exercise 1. Answer the questions you wrote on these topics, using language and ideas from Exercises 2 and 3. Record yourself if you can.

Focus on writing *Presenting an opinion (1)*

Task 2
THESIS-LED APPROACH
▶ *Focus on IELTS* page 122

In Task 2, you may be asked to agree or disagree with a statement or opinion, rather than being required to discuss opposing views. In this case you may choose simply to give your own opinions on the topic and justify these. This is called the thesis-led approach.

ANALYSING THE QUESTION

1 Look at the Writing task below and answer these questions.

1 What is the main topic?
2 What aspect(s) of the topic do you have to write about?
3 What question do you have to answer in your conclusion?

WRITING TASK 2

You should spend about 40 minutes on this task.

Present a written argument or case to an educated reader with no specialist knowledge of the following topic.

University education should be restricted to the very best academic students, rather than being available to a large proportion of young people.

To what extent do you agree or disagree?

You should use your own ideas, knowledge and experience and support your arguments with examples and relevant evidence.

Write at least 250 words.

GENERATING IDEAS

2 Look at the Writing task again.

1 What is your opinion on this topic? Do you agree or disagree?
2 Note down some reasons you could use to justify your opinion.

> *Access to university should/ should not be restricted because:*
> *a)* ....
> *b)* ....
> *c)* ....

ORGANISING AND SUPPORTING YOUR IDEAS
▶ *Focus on IELTS* page 123

3 **a** Put the following paragraph plan in the correct order: (1) opening, (2) middle and (3) closing paragraphs.

Justify your opinion.
Introduce the topic.
Summarise your thesis/point of view.
State your thesis/point of view.

b How many of the reasons you noted in Exercise 2 could you include in the middle section?

ANALYSING A SAMPLE ANSWER

4 **a** Read the sample answer on page 81 and answer these questions.

1 Does the writer agree or disagree with the statement?
2 How many reasons are given? Number them.
3 What words are used to introduce these reasons?

b The sample answer would score a low band. Identify and tick **five** problems from the list A–H.

University education should be restricted to the most academic students, rather than being available to a large proportion of young people. I disagree with this opinion for several reasons. Firstly, individuals today need much higher-level skills and technical knowledge. Furthermore, societies cannot continue to develop unless more citizens are educated. Finally, it is only fair that anyone who could benefit from a university education should have access to one. In conclusion, it is important to encourage students to get a higher level education today. (84 words)

A Inaccurate use of language
B Underlength answer
C Language copied from the task
D Poor punctuation
E The conclusion does not answer the question
F Ideas are not developed
G No paragraphing
H No signposting link words

WRITING THE INTRODUCTION

TIP Remember not to copy language from the task in your introduction.

5 Choose the best alternatives to expand and reword the introduction in Exercise 4.

In the past, **1** tertiary/university education was **2** limited/restricted to a small proportion of people who were **3** the most academic/the very best academic students. Today, however, **4** a large proportion of /many more young people have the possibility of going to university, and I think that this is a much better situation for several reasons.

DEVELOPING AND SUPPORTING YOUR IDEAS

6 a Look back at the sample answer in Exercise 4. Can you think of ways to develop the reasons given for the writer's opinion?

b Match the ideas and examples below with reasons 1–3 in the sample answer.

A

In order to progress and compete in the modern world, each country needs people who can develop modern technologies further and apply them in new fields.

B

Therefore, there should be equal opportunities for everyone to realise their full potential. Going to university is part of this.

C

For example, many professions require advanced computer skills and an ability to adapt to a rapidly changing workplace. Schools do not have the resources to equip students with these skills, so universities have to fulfil this role.

DRAWING CONCLUSIONS

7 Remember to refer back to the original task when writing your conclusion. If the task asks you an explicit question, answer it directly.

Complete the conclusion below, using your own opinions and summarising your reasons.

In conclusion, I partly agree/totally agree/disagree with the statement because I believe ...

SPEED WRITING PRACTICE

8 Write your own response to the task, using your ideas from Exercises 2 and 3. Spend no more than 35 minutes on this and write at least 250 words. Use the last five minutes to edit your work.

▶ Answer Key page 160

1 Topic vocabulary overview

Module F (*Focus on IELTS* Units 11 and 12) was about education and learning both in and out of the workplace.

Complete these extracts with words or phrases from the boxes. Use each word or phrase once only. There are some extra words in each box that you don't need to use.

Listening Section 3: Foundation English Course

| class | curriculum | Department | lectures self-access centre | seminars | thesis | tutorials undergraduate |

Student: Can you tell me a bit about what the Foundation course involves?

Tutor: Well, the course is run by the 1 .... of English as a Foreign Language in the university. It's to help you develop the language skills you'll need to cope with your undergraduate course later on – for example, listening and note-taking practice to prepare you for the 2 .... , and speaking activities to help you take an active part in 3 .... – taking part in a group discussion – as well as in one-to-one 4 ....

Student: And how is the course organised?

Tutor: Well, in the morning you have an English 5 .... Then in the afternoon you work on your own in the 6 .... We have all sorts of materials there so you can choose what's best for you.

Speaking Part 3: Changes in education

| campus | Faculty | full-time | lecturers | part-time professors | semester | subjects | undergraduates |

Examiner: In what ways is education changing in your country?

Candidate: Well, one big change is that the curriculum is changing for secondary schools – it includes a much wider range of 7 .... now – things like information technology, for example. And then the universities are becoming more flexible. For example, they take both 8 .... and .... students, so it means you can study and work at the same time.

And in my university the 9 .... haven't all come straight from school – lots of them have had some sort of job after leaving school, like me, before coming to university. And in the 10 .... of Engineering, where I study, quite a lot of the university staff – the 11 .... and even the top 12 .... – have had experience in industry, they haven't just worked in universities all their lives.

Reading: The effect of environment on learning

| brain cells | learning capacity | mental nerve fibres | stimulation |

Learning appears to be very much influenced by environment. For example, when rats are kept in conditions where they have high levels of 13 .... , their 14 .... appears to increase. Tests carried out to assess their 15 .... activity (e.g. through setting them a series of increasingly difficult puzzles to solve) show that this is also greater. In addition, scientists claim that the 16 .... of the cells in these rats' brains are longer.

2 Word formation: adjective endings

a Complete the adjectives in the list below by adding the correct suffix.

1 act _ _ _
2 benefic _ _ _
3 domin _ _ _
4 ludicr _ _ _
5 substant _ _ _
6 adequ _ _ _
7 domest _ _
8 effici _ _ _
9 overwhelm _ _ _
10 systemat _ _

b Now complete these sentences using a suitable adjective from Exercise 2a. They are on the topic of the knowledge society.

1 To past generations, it would have <u>seemed a</u> <u>...................... idea</u> that everyone could achieve success in life.

2 In days gone by, the .... majority of people were manual workers.

3 In the past, an uneducated woman who needed to earn money usually went into .... service.

4 The .... effects of the spread of education have been particularly felt by women.

5 In modern society, women make a .... contribution to the labour force, holding key positions in many companies.

6 To ensure that there will be a sufficient number of knowledge technologists in the future, some kind of .... preparation is needed now.

7 An .... level of education is needed by those intending to become software designers or computer technicians, but a university education is not essential.

8 In the future, knowledge technologists are likely to become a .... force in society.

9 Work-related stress can be avoided or reduced by playing an .... part in voluntary work, sports or local government.

10 In spite of technological progress, in many areas even the most .... machine cannot replace a worker.

c Underline the phrases containing adjective/noun collocations that you have completed in the sentences above. The first one has been done for you.

3 Language of research

In the Reading and Listening Modules of the exam, you often have accounts of the stages of research projects and the way researchers gather information.

Complete the following sentences by adding one word made from the jumbled letters. Then underline the phrase in each sentence which describes general research methods.

Example: We chose the area of student motivation as the starting ......<u>point</u>...... for our research. (otpni)

1 We had to do a lot of background .... before we began. (nagerid)

2 We decided we wanted to observe the .... of students in language classes. (ebavhoriu)

3 We carried out a .... to discover student attitudes to language learning. (usyrev)

4 We designed a .... and asked all the students to complete it. (aeireusqntnoi)

5 We also selected a random .... of students to interview. (aselmp)

6 We then conducted face-to-face .... with these students. (tneiewrivs)

7 We compared the .... of the students in the final exam with their .... of motivation. (reponfacrme, elvle)

8 We found that the .... of the successful students were highly motivated. (amojtryi)

4 Linking ideas: concession and contrast
► *Focus on IELTS page 219*

a Number the sentences below to make a connected paragraph.

☐ On the other hand, they might find that it was difficult to readapt to life as a student when the time came for them to return to their studies.

☐ Even though they would have relatively few qualifications, they would gain valuable work experience.

☐ However, for some of them it might be better to take a break from education for a year or two, and get a job instead.

☐ They might even decide not to do a university course at all, despite the problem that lack of qualifications might cause them later on.

☐ Most people go to study at university immediately after leaving school.

b Underline the linking expressions in the sentences.

1 Vocabulary

Read the pairs of sentences below and put a tick (✓) if they mean the same thing and a cross (✗) if they are different. Underline any phrases which make the meanings different.

1 a) Several students got poor results in the most recent examinations.
   b) Some students did badly in the latest exams.
2 a) Access to library computer facilities is open to postgraduate students.
   b) The use of the computers in the library is restricted to postgraduate students.
3 a) He was given an honorary degree in celebration of his personal achievements.
   b) The university awarded him an honorary degree in recognition of his personal contributions.
4 a) There was a marked improvement in pupil performance.
   b) Pupil performance improved considerably.
5 a) There is a growing body of evidence that links academic progress to physical exercise.
   b) All the evidence so far suggests that academic progress and physical exercise are connected.
6 a) Changing wind patterns play a part in altering our weather systems.
   b) Changes in our weather systems can be attributed in part to changes in wind patterns.
7 a) Global climate is vulnerable to any small increase in temperature.
   b) The slightest rise in temperature can affect the world's climatic system.
8 a) The Department Head had an important influence on his graduate students.
   b) The Head of Department exerted unnecessary pressure on the postgraduates working with him.

2 Reading: Table completion

> **Bamboo, the phenomenon of the vegetable kingdom**
>
> With more than 1,500 species colonising a multitude of habitats from sea level to 12,000 feet, bamboo is one of the most successful plants on earth. It can also add significant solutions to environmental problems to its list of successes.
>
> It is one of the most adaptable plants, with many valuable uses. For instance, it can grow in such degraded soils that it can be used to 'repair' soil damaged by overgrazing and poor agricultural techniques. In addition, its complex root network is ideal for preventing soil erosion and flooding. Unlike most tree species, harvesting does not kill the bamboo, so topsoil erosion and other adverse effects of tree-felling are kept to a minimum.
>
> Perhaps even more importantly, given that carbon dioxide emissions are thought to be responsible for global warming, bamboo produces more than 35% more oxygen than trees. Research has demonstrated that bamboo can absorb as much as 12 tonnes of carbon dioxide per hectare per year, giving the plant a potentially crucial role in stabilising our planet's atmosphere.
>
> People have also used bamboo for an astonishing variety of functions over the last 4,000 years. Today, the durability and resistance to shrink or swell that characterises bamboo means that it can be used as an eco-friendly alternative to slow-growing hardwoods for a range of products for the construction industry, such as wooden flooring.

a Read the text and complete the table below. Use NO MORE THAN THREE WORDS AND/OR A NUMBER for each answer.

HELP
Work across the table from left to right.

Special features of bamboo	Can be used to
• large number of species • large range of 1	• help solve 2 ....
• can grow on overgrazed land	• 3 ....
• 4 .... • can survive 5	• stop erosion & water run-off • reduce effects of tree-felling
• 6 .... than other plants • absorbs large amounts of CO_2	• regulates the Earth's 7 ....
• 8 .... • does not shrink or swell	• make products for building industry

b Find words and expressions in the text which mean:

1 can change to fit different conditions

....

2 harmful consequences

....

3 possibly very important

....

4 a huge range

....

5 not harmful to the environment

....

3 Speaking: Part 2

a Read the task instruction and number the sentences from the candidate's response in the correct order according to the sequence markers. Underline the sequence marker in each sentence.

Examiner: I'd like you to describe how you learnt English.

Candidate:

☐ Now it's one of my main ambitions – to speak English really well.

☐ At that stage being back at school in my home town seemed a bit boring, so I kind of lost interest.

☐ So during that time I learnt a lot – and had a really good accent of course.

☐ Well, first I started classes in kindergarten.

☐ But later I started to get into pop music and English bands …

☐ But eventually we came back home and I started to forget everything.

☐ and from then on I started to work hard again.

☐ And after that, when I was still a little kid, my family moved to the US for a while.

b Write what you would say to describe the different stages you went through to learn English.

....

....

....

....

....

....

....

....

4 Writing: Task 1

Complete the answer to the Writing task below by choosing the correct linking words from the box and adding the relevant figures from the table.

The table below gives information about the daily cost of water per person in five different countries. (Figures are based on the minimum daily requirement per person of 11.5 litres.)

Write a report for a university lecturer describing the information below.

Cost of minimum daily water requirement by country

Country	Daily cost per person (US$)	Cost as percentage of average daily wage
Tanzania	6.4 cents	5.7%
Uganda	4.1 cents	3.2%
Pakistan	1.76 cents	1.1%
UK	1.3 cents	0.013%
US	0.85 cents	0.006%

while   for instance   both   respectively   however   overall   whereas   also   first of all   despite

The table compares the amount people have to pay for their minimum daily water in five countries. It 1 .... shows the percentage of the average daily wage this represents in each place.

2 .... , we can see that Tanzania and Uganda have the highest daily water costs 3 .... the UK and US have the lowest. This means, 4 .... , that Tanzanians pay 5 .... , 6 .... Americans pay a mere 7 .... for the same amount of water.

These differences are even greater when we consider the percentage of the average daily wage this cost represents. In 8 .... Tanzania and Uganda, the cost is significant, representing 9 .... and 10 .... 11 .... In the UK and US, 12 .... , the cost is only a tiny fraction of the daily wage at 13 .... and 14 .... And, 15 .... the daily cost of water in Pakistan being similar to that in the UK, it represents as much as 16 .... of the daily wage.

17 .... , the table shows that there are huge differences between the cost of water in the developing countries and the industrialised west.

► INSIDE INFORMATION

Focus on speaking 1 *Expressing preferences*

Part 1 Interview
**UNDERSTANDING THE
QUESTIONS**

1 **a** **Read these questions. What is the general topic?**

1 Do you prefer talking to people on the phone or face-to-face?
2 Do you prefer making calls on a land line or a mobile phone?
3 How popular is text-messaging compared to talking on the phone?
4 Do people in your country prefer to write letters or e-mails?
5 How popular is faxing compared to e-mail?
6 Would you rather get a letter or an e-mail?

b **Which of the questions above are asking about**

a) your own personal preferences?
b) preferences among the general public?

c 🎧 **Listen to part of an IELTS interview. How many questions does the examiner ask? Tick them in the list above.**

**USEFUL LANGUAGE:
EXPRESSING PREFERENCES,
GIVING REASONS**

2 **a** 🎧 **Listen to the recording again and complete these extracts using up to three words.**

1 … a mobile can be used anywhere … But .... , I'd rather use a land line.
2 Young people are definitely texting more, ... making calls.
3 I think maybe older people .... to make calls.
4 I think nowadays .... is for e-mails.
5 … perhaps some people .... to write letters in some situations.
6 .... get a letter if it's about something important.

b **What reasons does the candidate give for each of the preferences expressed in 1–6?**

EXAM PRACTICE

3 Practise giving your own answers to questions 1–6 in Exercise 1. Use the expressions from Exercise 2 and give reasons for your answers. Record yourself if you can.

Focus on listening 1 *Note completion; short answers; multiple choice*

Section 1
WRITING ADDRESSES

1 In Sections 1 and 2 of the Listening Module, you often have to write addresses.

a Use the jumbled letters to make six words that can be used in a similar way to *Road* or *Street* in addresses.

1 IDEVR   ....   4 LILH   ....
2 EVEUAN   ....   5 NAEL   ....
3 YAW   ....   6 QSARUE   ....

b 🎧 Now listen and check your answers.

EXAM PRACTICE

2 🎧 Read questions 1–7, then listen to the whole recording and do the exam task. There will be a short break in the middle to give you time to look at questions 8–10.

NOTE COMPLETION
▶ Module A page 14

SHORT-ANSWER QUESTIONS
▶ Module D page 46

- Look through the questions and predict what sort of information is needed.
- Use the exact words from the recording in your answer.
- Remember that only one or two words are usually needed for each answer.

Questions 1–3
Complete the notes below.
Write **NO MORE THAN THREE WORDS AND/OR A NUMBER** for each answer.

<table>
<tr><td colspan="3" align="center">**Sinclair Electrical Services**</td></tr>
<tr><td>*Example*
Customer called about</td><td>*Answer*
<u>television</u>.............. repairs</td></tr>
<tr><td>Customer's name:</td><td>Mrs **1** ....</td></tr>
<tr><td>Address:</td><td>**2** ....
Sommerton</td></tr>
<tr><td>Phone:</td><td>**3** ....</td></tr>
</table>

Questions 4–7
Answer the questions below.
Write **NO MORE THAN THREE WORDS AND/OR A NUMBER** for each answer.

4 What is the problem with the TV?

....

5 What may have caused the problem?

....

6 What is the TV make and model number?

....

7 How old is the TV?

....

MULTIPLE CHOICE (SINGLE ANSWER)
▶ Module B page 23, Module F page 76

Questions 8–10
Choose the correct letter, A, B or C.

8 Where is the customer's house?

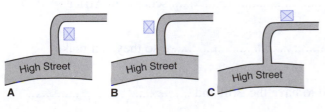

9 When will the electrician call at the house?

A Friday afternoon

B Saturday morning

C Monday morning

10 How did the customer first hear about the repair service?

A from a neighbour

B from the phone book

C from the Internet

CHECKING YOUR ANSWERS

3 In the Listening Module, you have time to check your answers at the end of each section, and also when you transfer your answers at the end of the test.

a Look at these incorrect answers for questions 4–7. Why is each one wrong?

> 4 *no volum*
> 5 *power is cut*
> 6 *is a Schneider model SVV5002*
> 7 *seven years ago*

b Now check that you have not made any similar mistakes in your own answers.

Focus on reading *Sentence completion; classification; multiple choice (single answer)*

SKIMMING

► Module F page 72

1 a Read the title and subheading of the text opposite and answer these questions.

1 Does the writer, Mike Chege, think that access to information technology is important for the world's poor?
2 What two examples of digital technology are given in the subheading?

b Skim the text, looking at the first sentence in each paragraph, and answer these questions. Spend no more than one minute on this.

1 Find and underline the two key questions that the writer asks.
2 What four main topics are discussed in relation to the first question?
3 What two examples are given in relation to the second question?

SENTENCE COMPLETION
(WORDS FROM THE TEXT)

► Module D page 50

TIP Each sentence in the task may summarise information from several sentences in the text.

2 Now do the exam task below.

- Underline key words in the sentences.
- Use them to find which part of the text the first sentence relates to.
- Think about what type of information you need and look for it in the text.
- Write the exact word(s) from the text in the gap.
- Continue in the same way for the remaining sentences.

Questions 1–5
Complete the sentences below with words taken from the Reading Passage.
*Use **NO MORE THAN THREE WORDS** for each answer.*

1 The example of the Tanzanian company's telecommunications bill demonstrates how information and communication technology can cut ....

2 In Africa, use of the Internet enables .... of diseases such as meningitis to be controlled.

3 An international organisation has subsidised a .... scheme in Africa which depends on ICTs.

4 E-government provides people with a source of .... so they can make their own choices in life.

5 In order to allow global use of ICTs, people need to have the skill and .... to use this technology.

BRIDGING THE DIGITAL DIVIDE

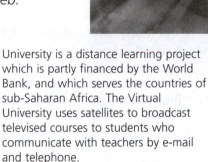

When addressing the issue of global access to information technology, some people claim that the world's poor are more concerned about having enough to eat than about using e-mail or surfing the World Wide Web. **Mike Chege** *disagrees.*

A In what concrete ways can information and communication technologies (ICTs) benefit the two-thirds of humanity who are more concerned about their next meal than about e-mail or eBay?

B First, there are the economic advantages of these technologies. Besides providing business with the opportunity to access real-time market information and complete business transactions electronically, ICTs can reduce costs and provide a channel to market goods and services. One small company from Tanzania replaced $20 faxes with 10 cent e-mails and saw its telecommunications bill go from over $500 per month to $45 per month. In the business-to-consumer segment you will find examples like EthioGift.com which sells gifts, including sheep and goats, over the Internet. And in India, which is fast becoming a global centre for telemarketing, customer support and other call centre services, ICTs are transforming the economy. With the legalisation of Internet telephony, India has captured an even bigger chunk of the global outsourcing market, with calls from the US accounting for 80 per cent of call centre business. Schools are even training young men and women to speak in an American accent in order to handle the calls.

C Health services also benefit from ICTs. Using the Internet, doctors in poor countries can keep up to speed with the latest developments in their field as well as seek help from their peers. This technology can also facilitate the control of diseases. Throughout Africa, for instance, individual cases of meningitis are tracked over the Internet so that epidemics can be stopped early. In addition, ICTs can assist in allowing healthcare professionals to extend their reach through telemedicine into the remotest and most underserved areas.

D ICTs can make it easier to reach a broad segment of the population in education too. The African Virtual University is a distance learning project which is partly financed by the World Bank, and which serves the countries of sub-Saharan Africa. The Virtual University uses satellites to broadcast televised courses to students who communicate with teachers by e-mail and telephone.

E Finally, we come to what has been dubbed 'e-government'. E-government initiatives focus on making government transparent and accountable by providing citizens with direct access to information. Critics might argue that when you're being stalked by war, hunger and disease, this may not be a priority. But e-government is about more than just the ability to pay your taxes online or apply for a driving licence over the Internet. It is about giving citizens access to information which allows them to make informed decisions on subjects that affect their lives.

F But how can those people who need ICT capabilities most, be best helped to bridge the Digital Divide? Throwing computers and modems at people (as someone colourfully put it) will not in itself help much. Other important issues that need to be addressed include improving computer and keyboarding skills and increasing people's confidence in their ability to use the new technology.

G A good example of how this can be done is the Information Village Project, a computer intranet linking ten villages near Pondicherry, India. The project, started with a $120,000 grant from the International Development Research Centre, Canada, provides locally relevant information on product prices, healthcare, weather and fishing conditions. A team of volunteers from each village gathers up the information and feeds it into the computer in the local language (Tamil). It is then available to all users of the intranet. There is also a multimedia component to make the information accessible to illiterate users. Most of the operators and volunteers providing the primary information are women, and their role in the project raises their status in the community. Since most of the villages experience erratic power supply, the project can run on solar power as well as mains electricity.

H Another Indian creation, the Simputer (short for Simple, Inexpensive, Multilingual computer) was conceived by a team of computer scientists at the Indian Institute of Science in Bangalore. It is a small, hand-held, battery-powered computer about 12 cm by 7 cm that has a touch-sensitive screen. You use a stylus to tap on icons and to input information. Because each display page shows only a few possible commands, even illiterate users should be able to learn by trial and error the purpose of the icons and buttons on each page. The Simputer also has software that can turn text into speech. This works for various Indian languages and allows the Simputer to read the text aloud on its tiny built-in speakers. It also has a slot for 'smart' cards, a feature that its makers see as crucial. Because the device lacks a hard drive, smart cards act as the device's portable storage units. In this way, many people can use one Simputer without having to share their private information with one another. The Simputer costs $200 – a sizable chunk of the yearly per capita income for many of its users. But one Simputer can enable an entire village to access the Internet, perform transactions, keep track of agricultural prices and educate its children.

I So bridging the Digital Divide is not something that happens after addressing the 'core' development challenges; it is a key component of addressing those challenges in the 21st century. Failure to address the Digital Divide will only exacerbate the existing social and economic inequalities between countries and communities.

CLASSIFICATION

3 In this type of task, you have to match numbered features to a set of general categories. It is therefore similar to a matching task (see Module B page 22). The task may involve relating information from different sections, so the questions may not be in the same order as the information in the text.

a Look at the exam task below (questions 6–11). Underline the two key names in the list A–D. Then scan the text and find the two paragraphs which refer to these.

b Read question 6 and look through both paragraphs to see if this feature relates to either (or both) of the key names, then choose the correct answer A, B, C or D.

c Continue in the same way with questions 7–11.

Questions 6–11
Classify the following features according to whether they apply to

> **A** *the Information Village Project only*
> **B** *the Simputer only*
> **C** *both the Information Village Project and the Simputer*
> **D** *neither the Information Village Project nor the Simputer*

  6 use of the technology is not limited to individuals

  7 information can be kept secure and private by individual users

  8 must have a mains electricity supply

  9 initially supported by an overseas agency

10 can only be used by people who can read and write

11 knowledge of English not required

MULTIPLE CHOICE
(SINGLE ANSWER)
► Module C page 36

4 In the exam, in some cases each set of questions may relate to a separate part of the text.
At other times you may need to look back through the whole text for each new set of questions. This is one reason why it is useful to get a general picture of the text before you read.

a Look at question 12 in the exam task on page 91 and underline two key phrases in the stem. Then scan the text quickly to find the related information. The information for question 13 will follow after this in the text.

b Now look at question 14. This is a different type of multiple-choice question, as it is testing the main idea of the text. Which two paragraphs of the text often summarise the main idea?

c Now complete the exam task.

Questions 12–14
Choose the best answer, A, B, C or D.

12 What reason is given for the increasing importance of call centres to the Indian economy?

   A the availability of workers with the right accent

   B a change in the legal system

   C local familiarity with outsourcing techniques

   D the country's geographical position

13 The writer says that in both health and education

   A more training is needed in the use of ICTs.

   B international organisations need to provide more support with ICTs.

   C ordinary people are gaining more skill in the use of ICTs.

   D ICTs can help to provide services to more people than before.

14 Overall the writer's main argument in this passage is that

   A ICT access is a basic need for a fairer world.

   B the digital divide is the cause of our present inequalities.

   C the developed world should do more to provide ICT training.

   D the digital divide may never be successfully bridged.

▶ Ideas for speaking and writing page 142

Focus on writing *Advantages and disadvantages*

Task 2

ANALYSING THE QUESTION
▶ *Focus on IELTS* pages 63 and 122
▶ Module C page 42

1 **Read this Writing task and decide what you have to write about.**

> You should spend about 40 minutes on this task.
>
> Present a written argument or case to an educated reader with no specialist knowledge of the following topic.
>
> > ***E-mail has had a huge impact on professional and social communication, but this impact has been negative as well as positive.***
> >
> > ***Do the disadvantages of using e-mail outweigh the advantages?***
>
> You should use your own ideas, knowledge and experience and support your arguments with examples and relevant evidence.
>
> Write at least 250 words.

GENERATING IDEAS

Advantages of using e-mail
fast and easy way of communicating socially

Disadvantages of using e-mail
volume of e-mails increases workload

2 a **Match the ideas 1–6 to the appropriate headings on the left.**

   1 fast and easy way of communicating socially

   2 volume of e-mails increases workload

   3 allows viruses into IT system

   4 allows people to send attachments with different sorts of information

   5 fast responses expected – this increases pressure

   6 makes communication between companies cheaper and easier

b   Which of the ideas in Exercise 2a are related specifically to the workplace?

c   Can you add any more ideas of your own?

ORGANISING YOUR IDEAS
▶ Module C page 42
▶ Module F page 80

3   Which of the paragraph plans below follows

a) an argument-led approach (in which you discuss more than one point of view before reaching your conclusion)?

b) a thesis-led approach (in which you give your own opinions and justify them)?

1
> *Introduce topic.*
> *Give opinion – more advantages – and examples.*
> *Briefly discuss disadvantages.*
> *Conclusion: repeat opinion.*

2
> *Introduce topic.*
> *Discuss disadvantages of using e-mail.*
> *Discuss advantages.*
> *Conclusion: opinion — more advantages.*

ANALYSING A SAMPLE ANSWER

4   a   Read the sample answer below. Does it follow a thesis- or argument-led approach?

> *E-mail has had a huge impact on professional and social communication but this impact has been negative as well as positive.*
>
> *One disadvantage of using e-mail in the workplace is that it causes extra work. It also increases pressure on workers. Another disadvantage is that people spend too long online. Using e-mail can also allow viruses to get into your computer system.*
>
> *One advantage of using e-mail is that it is a fast and easy way to communicate. It is easy to stay in contact with family and friends.*

b   This answer would score a low band. Identify the problems with:

1   the overall length
2   the introduction
3   the development of the argument

4   the use of link words
5   the conclusion
6   the range of language used

PARAPHRASING THE INTRODUCTION

5   Complete this paraphrase of the introduction in the Writing task.

> *It is certainly true that the use .... greatly changed the way .... at work as well as socially. But it is also true that not all the effects of this innovation ....*

DEVELOPING AND SUPPORTING YOUR IDEAS

6   Think of some ways to develop the ideas in Paragraphs 2 and 3, for example, by giving an explanation or an example, or describing a result. Make notes.

Example:

> *Paragraph 2*
>
> *Disadvantages of using e-mail in the workplace:*
> *– causes extra work – people get more e-mails than they can reply to every day, feel stressed.*
> *– increases pressure – ....*

USING A RANGE OF LANGUAGE

7 You can avoid repetition by using parallel expressions in your writing. Which words in the box below are alternative ways of referring to:

a) advantages? ....

b) disadvantages? ....

> *a drawback   an obvious benefit   a negative effect   a good point*
> *the downside   a frequent/common criticism   an objection*
> *an argument in favour of   a positive aspect*

LINKING IDEAS

8 a Put the linking expressions from the box in the correct category below.

> *This is because   In other words,   so*
> *A common example of this is when   Another objection to … is that*

Addition: ....

Introducing examples: ....

Cause and effect: ....

Clarification: ....

b Which of the following sentences would be suitable to introduce paragraph 3 of the sample answer in Exercise 4?

1 Moreover, the main benefit of using e-mail is that it is a fast and easy way to communicate.

2 On the other hand, an argument in favour of e-mail is that it is a fast and easy way to communicate.

3 In spite of these negative effects, e-mail has brought important benefits.

DRAWING CONCLUSIONS

9 Which of the two conclusions below is more appropriate for the sample answer in Exercise 3 and why?

1

> To sum up, while there are some obvious drawbacks to using e-mail, this fast and user-friendly technology has greatly improved our ability to communicate both professionally and socially. Therefore, I think e-mail has brought us many more benefits than disadvantages.

2

> In conclusion, there are obvious advantages and disadvantages to using e-mail, and we need to try to overcome the problems.

SPEED WRITING PRACTICE

10 Write your own full answer to the task in Exercise 1. Spend no more than 35 minutes on this. Use the last five minutes to edit your work.

▶ Answer Key page 163

Focus on listening 2 *Table completion; summary completion*

Section 2

TABLE COMPLETION

▶ Module C page 38

1 🎧 Read the title and headings of the table in the exam task below. Think about what type of information is needed for each item. Then listen and answer questions 1–5.

Questions 1–5
Complete the table below.
*Write **NO MORE THAN THREE WORDS AND/OR A NUMBER** for each answer.*

Thursday October 15th **Radio 6**	
Time	**Programme**
7.00	'Animal Talk'
1	Charity broadcast: Rare Species Protection Group
8.00	2 '................................'
8.30	'What's your view?' The effects of the 3 ....
9.00	4 ....
9.20	Book of the week: *Just-so Stories* 'How the 5 .... was written.'

SUMMARY COMPLETION

2 For this task, you complete a summary with words from the recording.

a Read through the summary below to find out what the topic is.

b The following extract from the recording relates to question 6 of the exam task. Read question 6. You need to find something that is 'strong'. Does the answer come before or after this word in the recording?

> They're both mammals, they both live in groups and the social bonds they form are extremely strong. For example, when a new elephant is born …

TIP You may need to keep key words in your memory for a short time as you listen.

c 🎧 Now listen and complete the exam task.

Questions 6–10
Complete the summary below.
Write NO MORE THAN THREE WORDS AND/OR A NUMBER for each answer.

'Animal Talk'

This programme is about communication systems of killer whales and elephants. Both of these are mammals which have strong 6 ...., live for a long time and have large 7 ....

Killer whales communicate mainly through 8 .... in the water but little is known about the purpose of this communication. Elephants send messages through the air in a process which is called 9 '................................' because the messages cannot be heard by humans, and they can also receive messages through their 10 ....

▶ Ideas for speaking and writing page 142

Focus on speaking 2 *Describing a newspaper article*

Part 2

In Part 2, you may be asked to talk about information you have read, heard or seen in the media.

1   Read the candidate task card below and number the prompts you need to talk about.

Describe a newspaper or magazine article that you found interesting.

You should say:

what it was about
where you read it
how it made you feel

and explain why you found this article interesting.

SAMPLE ANSWER

2   a   🎧 Listen to a student talking on this topic. What does the speaker say about points 1–4?

1   Well, I read a very interesting article last week. Basically it was about …
2   I read this article in a …
3   Anyway, the article actually made me feel …
4   And the reason I found this article interesting was because …

b   Listen again and number these phrases in the order you hear them.

☐ the article explained   ☐ it suggested that   ☐ it was based on

☐ it also gave some advice about   ☐ it really described

EXAM PRACTICE

3   a   Read the short newspaper article below and underline the key points. Then spend one minute making notes on points 1–4 of the task above.

Several countries, including the UK, have recently implemented measures to ban the use of hand-held cell phones by drivers. Researchers claim that the risk of accident during or just after a cell-phone conversation is four times higher than would be expected in normal driving conditions. Studies have shown that calls are much more distracting for the driver than listening to the radio or talking to passengers. The problem is that drivers are not aware of this and as a result are not aware of the real dangers that this activity poses.

---

b   Now talk for two minutes about the article above. Time yourself and record yourself if you can.

c   Now think of another article you have read and try the task again.

1 Topic vocabulary overview

Module G (*Focus on IELTS* Units 13 and 14) covered a range of topics connected with communications, the business world and the media.

a Complete the diagrams below using words from the box. Use each word once only.

> *services headlines make (n) broadcast*
> *transactions system card series access*
> *technology coverage decisions costs*
> *means edition income centre episode*
> *developments affairs*

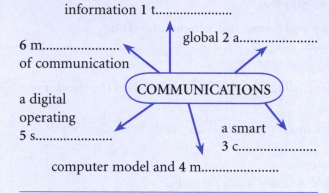

information 1 t.....................

global 2 a.....................

6 m..................... of communication

COMMUNICATIONS

a digital operating 5 s.....................

a smart 3 c.....................

computer model and 4 m.....................

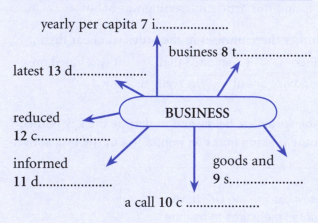

yearly per capita 7 i.....................

business 8 t.....................

latest 13 d.....................

BUSINESS

reduced 12 c.....................

informed 11 d.....................

goods and 9 s.....................

a call 10 c ....

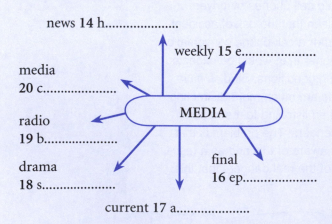

news 14 h.....................

weekly 15 e.....................

media 20 c.....................

MEDIA

radio 19 b.....................

drama 18 s.....................

final 16 ep.....................

current 17 a...................

b Now complete these extracts using words and expressions from the completed diagrams.

Writing Task 2: Changes in communication

> There is no doubt that there have been huge advances in 1 .... in recent years. The arrival of the Internet has given us 2 .... to information, regardless of where we live. But also e-mailing has changed our regular 3 .... , greatly reducing our use of fax and land line telephones, for instance.

Listening Section 3: Impact of technology

> **Student:** We wanted to see how local businesses had been affected by the 4 .... in technology, and we were amazed to see how much people exploited the Internet. Most of their 5 .... are now carried out via e-mail, and this has, of course, 6 .... by cutting fax and phone bills and so on. In turn, this has meant that yearly 7 .... has increased and families seem quite a bit better off than they did in our last study. What was particularly impressive was the fact that nearly all the small companies had websites that are obviously effective for marketing because now all kinds of 8 .... are exported from the region.

Speaking Part 1: Watching TV

> **Examiner:** What kind of TV programmes are most popular where you live?
>
> **Candidate:** Well, I'd say that people generally watch TV for entertainment, and that's why 9 .... are so popular. Apparently, there's almost no traffic on the roads when it's the 10 .... of a good programme …
>
> **Examiner:** Do a lot of people watch more factual programmes as well?
>
> **Candidate:** Oh yeah, especially the news – and 11 .... programmes, you know, like documentaries and so on. But in my house we just catch the 12 .... and then go back to watching something more cheerful.

2 Hyphenated adjectives

a Match 1–10 with the endings a–j.

1	user-	a)	held
2	labour-	b)	in
3	built-	c)	friendly
4	long-	d)	operated
5	hand-	e)	saving
6	high-	f)	sensitive
7	battery-	g)	in
8	touch-	h)	term
9	phone-	i)	tech
10	short-	j)	lasting

b Complete these sentences with the correct adjective from Exercise 2a.

1 Schools and hospitals need more modern, ... equipment these days.

2 A lot of studies concentrate on the .... implications of a new technology, rather than seeing what happens over longer periods.

3 I think computer menus are more .... when they use icons.

4 It is now illegal in some countries to use a .... cell phone while driving.

5 There is no need to buy extra equipment as this model has .... loud speakers.

6 Old houses were built of .... , materials, which is why they are still standing.

7 Interactive computers often have .... screens so you don't need to use the keyboard or mouse.

8 People have used radio .... programmes to complain about high taxes.

9 There is less manual work now that so many . ... devices are available.

10 You can use .... lap-top computers almost anywhere.

3 General words

Rewrite each sentence, using the words given in brackets, to produce a parallel sentence with a similar meaning. Make any necessary changes to the form of the word given and to the rest of the sentence (e.g. adding or removing prepositions).

1 There are exciting new developments taking place now in the area of communication technology. (innovation/occur/field)
Currently, exciting ....

2 Perhaps one of the most important aspects of modern life is the availability of information. (significant/feature/contemporary)
Some people think that one of the ....

3 Scientists first had the concept of connecting separate computers to form a network many years ago, but they had no idea of the long-term implications. (notion/link/produce)
Although ....

4 But governments need to address several major issues relating to electronic media. (consider/question/concern)
However, it is essential ....

5 For example, people are expressing growing concern over the way that technology can be used to invade their privacy. (show/anxiety/violate)
People ....

6 In addition, the possible effect of technology on businesses such as the entertainment industry could be very serious. (potential/impact/catastrophic)
The ....

4 Speaking: Using colloquial language

Complete the candidate responses using the colloquial expressions from the box.

quite far down   cheap and cheerful   loads of
why bother   the odd one out   a lot in common
high on the list   in depth   left out   keep in touch

Examiner: We've been talking about ways of communicating. So let's consider text-messaging. Do you think that's a good way to communicate with friends?

Candidate: No, I'm afraid I'm 1 .... 'cos I hate using text-messaging even though all my mates use it all the time. I have to admit, it makes me feel a bit 2 .... when they get 3 .... messages, but I really think it's only popular because it's 4 .... You end up sending mindless messages most of the time.

Examiner: So what do you think is a better way to communicate with friends?

Candidate: Well, I'd much rather *talk* to someone than write to them … so for me, calling comes pretty 5 .... , but writing e-mails and texting come 6 ....

Examiner: So what do you think are the limitations of text-messaging?

Candidate: It all depends on the person, I suppose, and the relationship, of course. If two people have got 7 .... , maybe they don't really need to talk 8 .... about anything, so text-messages are just to 9 .... But I think if you haven't got anything to say, 10 .... to send a message?

► FUTURE PROSPECTS

Focus on speaking 1 *Making predictions*

Part 3
► *Focus on IELTS* page 159

In Part 3 of the Speaking Module, you may be asked to talk about possible future developments or changes.

SAMPLE ANSWER

1 🎧 **Read the following discussion between an examiner and a candidate. Then listen and fill the gaps with up to three words.**

Examiner: Now let's consider space exploration in the future. Do you think there will be more space exploration or less in the next few decades?

Candidate: Well, I suppose it's still a bit of a race at the moment, so in the short term I think there will ....*definitely*.............. be more research and investment. And I think this is **1** .... to continue in the long term.

Examiner: Why do you say that?

Candidate: Because I think there's **2** .... that the Earth won't be able to support the growing population, so we'll **3** .... need to look for somewhere else to go.

Examiner: I see. So what future developments might take place in space exploration, do you think?

Candidate: Mmmm, it's hard to say. I think it's **4** .... that people will land on Mars in the not too distant future. And I think we'll **5** .... discover new planets and maybe even new galaxies. But I think it's **6** .... that we'll find any aliens.

Examiner: So how do you think the technology from the space industry will affect our lives?

Candidate: I think we **7** .... see big developments in transport, but there's **8** .... of us all having our own spaceship or anything like that.

EXPRESSING PROBABILITY
► *Focus on IELTS* page 232–233

2 **a** How does the speaker in Exercise 1 feel about each of the predictions he makes? Match the expressions you wrote in Exercise 1 to a heading in the box.

99% sure	75% sure	Not very sure
	(positive) *likely, ...*	
	(negative) *unlikely, ...*	

b Which of the expressions above were used with:

1 impersonal subjects (*there/it*)?
2 personal subjects (*we*)?

CONDITIONALS
▶ *Focus on IELTS* pages 221–222

3 Conditional clauses are often used to introduce or develop arguments and opinions. When we think the situation is possible or likely in the future, we use *If/Provided/Unless* + present, + future.

a Complete the following sentences with ideas of your own. Remember to indicate how sure you feel about your predictions.

1 If there are rapid changes in technology, then older people ....

2 If more and more people work from home, then workplaces ....

3 Provided we have sufficient food and healthcare, people ....

4 Unless we find alternative energy sources, fossil fuels ....

5 If more and more people do all of their shopping online, shopping malls ....

6 Unless we make some efforts to save minority languages, ...

b ⌂ Listen and compare your answers with the recording.

EXAM PRACTICE

4 Now answer the Part 3 questions below, using the language you have practised in Exercises 1–3. Record yourself if you can.

1 How do you think your lifestyle will change in the near future?
2 What kind of education do you think your grandchildren will have?
3 Do you think the world will be a better place in the future?
4 Do you think we will have more or fewer species of wildlife in the future? Why?
5 Do you think zoos will still exist in the future?
6 How will people's attitudes towards animals change in the future?

Focus on listening *Multiple choice (multiple answers); note completion; classification*

Section 3
▶ *Focus on IELTS* page 42
▶ Module D page 46

Section 3 is always an academic discussion of some kind. This could be a tutorial in which a student is discussing a project, getting feedback on some work or asking for advice.

PREDICTING THE TOPIC

1 Read through questions 1–5 in the exam task on page 100 and answer these questions.

1 Why is Eliot having this tutorial?
2 What is the specific topic that Eliot has been studying?
3 What do the notes in questions 2–5 tell you about this topic and what do you know yourself? (e.g. Why is it necessary? Where might it take place?)

EXAM PRACTICE
MULTIPLE CHOICE
(MULTIPLE ANSWERS)
▶ Module D page 46

2 ⌂ Listen to the first part of the recording and answer questions 1–5.
● Check how many answers you have to choose.
● Listen for words that signal key information.
● Remember that the order of the options (e.g. A–F) may be different from what you hear.

Question 1
*Choose **TWO** letters A–F.*

What were the **TWO** main problems with the first part of Eliot's essay?

A   insufficient research

B   lack of organisation

C   lack of concrete examples

D   narrow focus

E   inclusion of irrelevant material

F   insufficient supporting evidence

TIP Where there are two answers for a single question, remember to write **both** answers next to that question number when you transfer your answers.

Questions 2–5
Complete the notes below.
*Write **NO MORE THAN THREE WORDS** for each answer.*

Captive breeding

Introduction

- a **2** .... of captive breeding

Advantages of captive breeding programmes

- allow preservation of species from extinction
- could give new function for **3** .... in future
- allow reintroduction of species into wild

Disadvantages of captive breeding programmes

- captive breeding is **4** ....
- psychological effects of captivity
- danger of **5** .... for captive animals
- poor success in reintroduction to wild

CLASSIFICATION
QUESTIONS

3 In classification questions, you have to match points from the listening to a short set of general groups or classes, usually three or four. The points will be numbered in the same order as you hear them.

a   Look at the instructions for questions 6–10. Do you have to listen for:

a) Eliot's feelings about the subject?
b) research findings about the subject?

b   The phrases below come from this part of the listening. Which option (A, B or C) from the classification task might each phrase relate to?

1   I couldn't actually find any statistics about …
2   … the research suggests this is less crucial.
3   All the data shows that's absolutely essential.

c   🎧 Now listen to the rest of the recording and complete the task.

Questions 6–10

What does Eliot say about the following factors related to the release of captive animals into the wild?

A   the data shows that this factor is very important

B   the data shows that this factor is less important

C   no data is available for this factor

*Write the correct letter, **A**, **B** or **C** next to questions 6–10.*

6   training in survival skills before release   ......

7   provision of food and shelter after release   ......

8   employment and education of the local community   ......

9   medical screening of animals   ......

10   acclimatisation   ......

▶ Ideas for speaking and writing page 142

Focus on writing 1 *Describing how something works*

Task 1 How something works
► *Focus on IELTS* pages 162–3

Task 1 may require you to describe how something works. To tackle this type of task, you first need to understand what the structure or device is used for. In your description, you should:

1 say what it consists of and describe the most important parts
2 describe the process involved.

UNDERSTANDING
THE DIAGRAM

1 Read the instructions for the Writing task below, and look at the diagrams. Answer these questions to help you understand the process illustrated.

1 What is this structure used for?
2 Where is it built?
3 What three main parts does the structure consist of?
4 What happens to the air when a wave enters the chamber? What is the effect of this?
5 What happens when the wave flows back out of the chamber?

WRITING TASK 1

You should spend about 20 minutes on this task.

The diagrams show a structure that is used to generate electricity from wave power.

Write a report for a university lecturer describing the information.

Write at least 150 words.

Generating electricity from waves

ORGANISING
THE DESCRIPTION

2 a How many paragraphs will you need for your answer? Complete the paragraph outline below.

> Paragraph 1: Introduction – say what the diagrams show
> Paragraph 2: Describe the structure
>
> ....
>
> ....
>
> ....

b What expressions will you use to introduce each paragraph?

c Compare your ideas with the underlined expressions in the sample answer in Exercise 3 below.

ACTIVE AND
PASSIVE VERBS

3 When describing processes and how things work, we often use passive verbs. But be careful, it is very unusual for all the verbs to be in the passive voice. Choose the correct verb form to complete the sample answer below.

> The two diagrams show how electricity can 1 produce / be produced from the power of sea waves.
>
> The process involves a structure which 2 builds / is built onto the side of a cliff or sea wall. This structure 3 consists / is consisted of a large chamber. One end is open to the sea, and the other leads into a closed vertical column. A turbine 4 is positioned / positions inside this column and this 5 uses / is used to generate the electricity in two phases.
>
> The first diagram indicates that when a wave 6 is entered / enters the mouth of the chamber, air 7 forces / is forced up the column. This movement of air 8 is turned / turns the turbine, thereby producing electricity.
>
> The second diagram shows that when the wave retreats, air 9 sucks / is sucked out of the column and chamber. This movement similarly turns the turbine in the same direction, and this 10 is generated / generates electricity.
>
> In conclusion, ...

WRITING THE
CONCLUSION

4 Which of the following conclusions best summarises the information in the diagrams?

In conclusion,
a) … we can see that sea waves can generate electricity.
b) … we can see that this process produces electricity from waves as they both advance and retreat.
c) … we can see that this structure is useful for generating electricity.

SPEED WRITING
PRACTICE

5 Use the underlined paragraph beginnings to write your own answer to this task. Do not look at the rest of the sample answer. Spend no more than 15 minutes on writing. Then edit your work.

> **TIP** When you have more than one diagram, make sure your conclusion relates to the information in both or all the diagrams.

Focus on reading *Locating information; note completion; multiple choice (single answer)*

SKIMMING
▶ Module F page 72

1 a Read the title of the text on page 104. Do you think it is 'inevitable' that everyone will eat genetically modified food in the future? Do you know if any of the food you eat now has been genetically modified? If not, would you like to know?

b Skim the text and choose the best summary of its organisation, A or B. Spend no more than two minutes on this.

A Specific example + important event ➔ Disadvantages ➔ Advantages ➔ Return to first example

B Specific example + important event ➔ Advantages ➔ Disadvantages ➔ Writer's opinion

c Why do you think the text starts with the specific example of one small town, rather than a general statement?

LOCATING INFORMATION

2 In this task, you have to locate information in paragraphs or sections of the text. You need to be able to identify specific types of information (e.g. examples, explanations, contrasts).

a Read paragraph A of the text, then look through items 1–8 to find ideas that match the information in the paragraph. To help you, some key expressions in the paragraph have been underlined.

TIP The numbered items (questions 1–8) are **not** in the same order as the information in the text.

TIP Some paragraphs may have more than one matching item.

b When you have found a possible item, check that it matches the text exactly (e.g. if the item refers to a contrast between two things, check that the two things are actually contrasted in the paragraph).

c Read the rest of the text paragraph by paragraph and complete the task, following the same procedure.

Questions 1–8
The reading passage has eight paragraphs labelled **A–H**.
Which paragraph contains the following information?
NB You may use any letter more than once.

1 an example of a part of the world which valued Brazil's GM-free status

2 an important decision that has been made by Brazilian authorities

3 an account of one organisation's efforts to reassure the people of Brazil about   GMOs

4 the effect on public attitudes to science of the continued ban on some GM techniques

5 the reason why other countries felt threatened by Brazil's ban on GM products

6 an example of a small community which has, up to now, been free of GMOs

7 a warning about the possible effects of GM technology on the food chain

8 a method of raising awareness of both positive and negative aspects of GMOs

Genetically modified crops: accepting the inevitable?

A Cabaceiras is a town of around 5,000 people situated in Brazil's northern state of Para. The people are mostly small-scale vegetable farmers, with specialist, traditional knowledge handed down over hundreds of years. But now the natural purity of their produce is under threat from one of the 21st century's most controversial technological issues: genetically modified organisms (GMOs). Previously one of the world's last major agricultural exporters to remain GMO free, the Brazilian government has now decided to allow the biotechnology industry to sell GM seed to the country's farmers.

B Many people in Brazil feel the acceptance of transgenic crops is a dangerous move. Before this decision, Brazil was the world's largest exporter of GM-free soya. In 2001, sales of this product alone earned the country US$ 4.1billion – just under one-third of the country's total income from agricultural exports. Its main market was Europe, where consumers are still suspicious as to whether food species that have been genetically engineered in a laboratory may affect their health. Several UK supermarket chains, for example, insist on GM-free soya and refuse to buy from the USA, where 69 per cent of all soya crops are GM.

C European law requires all produce containing more than one per cent of GM ingredients to be labelled as such. At the time when Brazil was totally GM-free, Adriano Campolini, policy director of the development agency ActionAid, pointed out, 'Brazil faces pressure from countries like the USA and from the biotech industry to come into line. They are afraid that Brazil will have a competitive advantage because of its GM-free status.' Fearful that health and safety worries were being ignored, ActionAid joined with other non-governmental organisations to stall attempts in Brazil's congress to legalise GMOs, insisting there must be further research. They gained support among rural peasants such as those who live in Cabaceiras through a public education campaign, staging mock jury trials at which scientists, large-scale farmers, peasants and civic leaders alike were invited to debate the case for and against.

D Even now, small family farmers like Lilian Marques, 33, who lives in Cabaceiras with her family, fear GM technology could harm them and their businesses. Lilian is well aware of the possible effects on health of eating GM food, but she also has other concerns. 'I am afraid that the rich farmers will plant GM seed now it is legalised,' she explains. 'The wind could bring the pollen to our plantation, then it will be as if we have planted GM seed too. We produce only natural vegetables, yet we could not be sure what we were eating.'

E There are other potential consequences that trouble many in this fragile Amazon region, whose biodiversity is the richest on the planet. Some fear there may be a risk of chemical pollution from the products that must be used on the crops. One type of GM maize has even been engineered to be insect-resistant – if a caterpillar eats the leaf, the caterpillar dies. 'Maybe GM crops could be harmful to the forest and the animals that we eat,' Lilian suggests. 'What if an insect eats from the crop, then an animal eats the insect, then we eat the animal?'

F The biotech industry says such fears about GM technology are misguided. Monsanto, the international food biotechnology company, has launched a campaign in Brazil, costing US$ 2 million, to provide information to the public about genetically modified crops. The company insists the process that kills the insects is harmless to humans and that 'Round-up' – the herbicide used on GM crops – is 'no more toxic than table-salt'. 'We are as close to 100 per cent as science can ever be that GM products are safe for human health and the environment,' says spokesman Gary Barton. Monsanto hails the USA and Argentina – the other two largest exporters of soya – as examples of agricultural exporters that thrive on GM crops, whose merits it says include increased resistance to disease, improved nutritional value and increased levels of production. 'Three and a half million farmers around the world wouldn't have adopted biotechnology in their fields if they weren't seeing any benefits,' says Barton.

G It is not just the biotechnology companies that have an interest in Brazil lifting its GM ban, though they will undoubtedly reap the biggest profits. Francisco Campos, a professor of plant molecular biology in the northeastern city of Fortaleza, has made his own scientific breakthrough but cannot implement it because the embargo has only been lifted on GM soya, not other crops. 'We need plants to feed animals in order to have milk and meat. In this region, most of the plants we use for animal food, like cassava and prickly pear, are nutritionally deficient. But we can now insert a gene to add nutritional quality. In my laboratory, we have created our first transgenic cassava like this, but we are not allowed to put it to use. This GM ban undermines the confidence people have in science and its ability to help feed our nation.'

H But the villagers in Cabaceiras are not convinced. 'In my view, people still don't know if GM seed is good or bad,' says Lilian. 'Therefore, I don't want to take the risk.'

NOTE COMPLETION

TIP Remember, when writing notes, you can leave out words such as articles and some verbs if they are not necessary for the meaning.

3 This task tests your understanding of the main ideas of part or all of the text, as well as the way the text is organised. Notes use headings, subheadings, letters and numbers to show how pieces of information relate to one another. They may also use special layout features, e.g. indentation.

a Look carefully at the way the notes are laid out in questions 9–13 below.

1 What are the two main subheadings?

2 How many main points are given under the first subheading? How many are given under the second subheading?

3 What do you notice about the position of the three examples of benefits given for GM crops on the page?

b Look at the headings again. Use the key phrase *GM technology* to find the parts of the text which deal with this topic. What information is given first in the text, arguments for or arguments against?

c Now complete the exam task.

Questions 9–13
Complete the notes below.
*Choose **NO MORE THAN THREE WORDS** from the passage for each answer.*

Arguments against GM technology

a) health could be affected by eating GM foods

b) danger of **9** .... from GM crops being carried to plantations of non-GM produce.

c) danger of **10** .... from products such as insecticides

Arguments for GM technology

a) insecticide and **11** .... products used on GMOs are safe

b) GM crops bring many benefits
   e.g. less danger of **12** ....
   more nutritious
   more productive

c) already used by 3.5 m farmers world-wide

d) new type of **13** .... plant developed through the insertion of an extra gene could improve yields of meat and milk if used as animal food.

MULTIPLE CHOICE
(MAIN IDEA)
▶ Module G page 90

4 Read the last paragraph of the text again. How far do you think Lilian's comment reflects the writer's message? Now read question 14. Which option, A–D, comes closest to this idea?

Question 14
*Choose the correct letter, **A**, **B**, **C** or **D**.*

Which of these statements best summarises the reading passage?

A The concerns of ordinary people about GMOs should not be dismissed.

B The environmental and economic disadvantages of GM use outweigh the advantages.

C Multinational companies should not be allowed to restrict the use of GM technologies.

D Uneducated people should be reassured about the value of GMOs.

▶ Ideas for speaking and writing page 142

Focus on writing 2 *Discussing different views*

Task 2

▶ *Focus on IELTS* pages 63–65

ANALYSING THE QUESTION

▶ Module C page 42
▶ Module F page 80

1 Read the Writing task below and answer these questions.

1 How many opinions should be discussed?
2 Is the thesis-led or the argument-led approach more appropriate for this question?

WRITING TASK 2

Some people think that genetically modified (GM) crops are a positive development. Others, however, argue that they are potentially dangerous.

Discuss both these views and give your own opinion.

Write at least 250 words.

ANALYSING A SAMPLE ANSWER

2 a Divide the sample answer below into paragraphs.

1 Which paragraph gives the arguments a) against GM crops? b) in favour of GM crops?
2 What is the writer's opinion? Where is it given?
3 What recommendation does the writer make?

▶ *Focus on IELTS* pages 217–218
▶ Module C page 42

b Now complete the sample answer with suitable link expressions.

GM food products have been at the centre of a global debate for several years. Some people claim that the genetic engineering of food products brings many advantages. 1 ...., they argue that food production can be massively increased by making crops more resistant to pests. 2 ...., they believe that food can actually be improved by adding vitamins or removing problem genes that lead to allergies, 3 .... in peanuts. Fruit and vegetables can 4 .... last much longer if the gene that ripens them is modified. 5 .... they can be stored for much longer periods and so there will be less waste. 6 ...., people who oppose the widespread use of GM techniques worry that there could be long-term negative effects. They are concerned that so far the GM industry has not been able to prove that they are safe. The issue is 7 .... how safe such foods are for humans, 8 .... what long-term effects they may have on the environment and wildlife populations. 9 ...., there is some evidence to suggest that GM crops may contaminate nearby plants. 10 ...., I personally tend to agree with these concerns. I think that 11 .... there may be obvious benefits to GM crops, 12 .... they present more potential dangers. Their impact could be so large and so irreversible that more long-term studies should be carried out before their use spreads any further.

---

c Find words and expressions that indicate:

1 positive attitudes to the topic: *many advantages, ...*
2 negative attitudes to the topic: *oppose, worry that ...*

SPEED WRITING PRACTICE

3 Now write your own answer to the task in Exercise 1. Don't look at the sample answer while you are writing. Spend no more than 40 minutes on this task.

Focus on speaking 2 *Talking about hypothetical situations*

Part 2 Long turn

In Part 2 of the Speaking Module, you may be asked to describe a hypothetical situation: something you would like to do/own/learn if you could.

EXAMPLE TASK
TOPICS

1 a Look at the possible topics (1–3) and match them to the responses a–c below.

1 Describe someone you would like to meet.
2 Describe your ideal house.
3 Describe something you would like to collect.

a) … and it would have lots of big windows, because I've always loved light rooms …
b) … I've always liked different styles of painting, so I would choose pictures by different artists and I could hang them in different rooms.
c) … I've always admired him … and I'd love to ask him about how he kept his humanity during all those years … And perhaps he could explain to me how …

b Which of the underlined structures are used when the speakers are

a) talking hypothetically?   b) justifying their choices?

SAMPLE ANSWER

2 ⌒ Listen to a complete Part 2 long turn and complete the candidate task card.

> **Describe** ....
>   **You should say:**
>   ....
>   ....
>   ....
>   **and explain** ....

ORGANISING
YOUR TALK
▶ Module E page 62

3 ⌒ Number in order the expressions used by the speaker at different stages of the talk in Exercise 2. Then listen again and check.

[1] Well, the … I'd really like to be good at is …
[ ] The places I'd like to do it in are …
[ ] It's something I've always wanted to do …
[ ] That would mean I'd have to develop …
[ ] But also because …
[ ] And why would I choose this activity?
[ ] And I'd also have to develop … because that's something you obviously need …

EXAM PRACTICE

4 Now choose a topic from the list (1–3) in Exercise 1. Spend one minute making notes, then talk for two minutes. Time yourself and record yourself if you can.

1 Topic vocabulary overview
Module H (*Focus on IELTS* Units 15 and 16)
included the topics of space, developments that will
affect our future and research papers. This
vocabulary is relevant for all of the IELTS Modules.

a Complete the diagram below, using the jumbled
words to produce expressions about space.

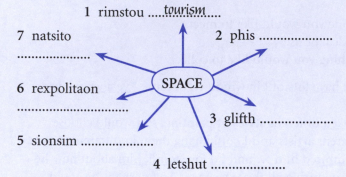

1 rimstou .....*tourism*.....

7 natsito ....

2 phis ....

6 rexpolitaon ....

SPACE

3 glifth ....

5 sionsim ....

4 letshut ....

b Complete each phrase below by choosing the best
word from the boxes. Use each word once only.

Space

> astronaut atmosphere alien launch orbit
> radiation satellite

  1 artificial ....
  2 Earth's ....
  3 rocket ....
  4 .... civilisation
  5 cosmonaut or ....
  6 solar ....
  7 in ....

Developments that will affect the future

> crops advances technology bio-tech
> engineering alternative

  8 nuclear ....
  9 .... energy
10 genetic ....
11 .... industry
12 GM ....
13 scientific ....

Research papers

> definition relevant statistical evidence rate
> points draft

14 supporting ....
15 .... material
16 .... data
17 accepted ....
18 poor success ....
19 first ....
20 key ....

c Now complete these extracts using words and
expressions from Exercises 1a and 1b.

**Speaking Part 2: Something that interested you as
a child**

> Well, when I was a kid I was really fascinated by
> everything I heard about 1 .... , so
> that's what I'm going to talk about. My big hero
> was Neil Armstrong, who is probably the most
> famous 2 .... ever because of his
> 3 .... to the moon. But I don't think
> I'd like to go into space myself. Just the thought
> of leaving the 4 .... behind
> and being up there, 5 .... , really
> terrifies me.

Reading: Developments for the future

> In a recent survey, the public were asked which
> 6 .... would have a big impact
> on their future lives. Surprisingly, it was found
> that people still worried about
> 7 .... and its potential dangers.
> One of the most frequently expressed hopes was
> for 8 .... sources for the future.
>
> Inevitably, 9 .... came high on
> the list, mainly because people thought this
> would affect several areas of their lives – like
> food production with 10 ....
> and so on. They also expected to see a big role
> for the 11 .... , especially in
> medicine.

Listening Section 3: Writing a research paper

> **Tutor:** Well I've had a look at how you've
> written up your research project, and the first
> thing you need to do is to work out what
> your main argument will be and then
> organise your 12 .... to get
> this across. Of course you'll need to provide
> 13 .... for each of these,
> just to show that your ideas are based on
> current research.
> **Student:** Right. I've certainly tried to get
> 14 .... to back up my claims,
> but it's not easy to find, so I've included
> everything that was available.
> **Tutor:** I can tell. You have to be careful to
> include only 15 .... and not
> go off at a tangent just because you've found
> something vaguely related.

d Look back through the units and add more words to the diagram and lists.

2 Probability
▶ *Focus on IELTS* pages 232–233

a Read the pairs of sentences below and put a tick (✓) if they mean the same thing and a cross (✗) if they are different. Underline any words that make them different.

1. a) It is quite probable that we will see a female President in the US before too long.
   b) There is every chance that we will see a woman in the White House before too long.
2. a) It is highly unlikely that Belgium will win the next football World Championship.
   b) It's quite possible that the Belgians will be the next football World Champions.
3. a) Brazil is bound to have a strong team.
   b) The Brazilian team is almost certain to be a strong one.
4. a) I doubt whether we will see more women's sports on TV in the future.
   b) It's quite likely that women's sports will be televised more in the future.
5. a) According to scientists, the climate will definitely get warmer in the long term.
   b) The scientific evidence suggests that temperatures are likely to rise in the long term.

b Complete the predictions below with the expression which you think is most appropriate (both are grammatically correct).

1. It is *highly unlikely / highly probable* that the whole world will achieve peace this century.
2. Global warming *will possibly / is bound to* affect every country.
3. It's *quite possible / unlikely* that the number of university graduates out of work will increase in the next decade.
4. I *am sure / doubt* that the cost of living will go down in the future.
5. The demand for housing in big cities *could possibly / will definitely* shoot up.
6. There is *every chance / no doubt* that environmental issues will be given a higher priority in the next decade.

3 Linking information
In academic English, sentences are rarely short and simple. Instead, information is linked within complex sentences.

Link the information in sentences 1–8 to make single complex sentences that avoid repetition. Use the prompts in brackets at the end of the sentences to help you.

Example: Europe's largest and most advanced satellite is called Envisat. Envisat will be launched this month. (, … ,)
Envisat, Europe's largest and most advanced satellite, will be launched this month.

1. The satellite is designed to monitor environmental change. The satellite is also designed to monitor pollution. (not only/but also)
   The satellite is designed to ....
2. Envisat has taken 14 years to develop. Envisat will transmit environmental data. Envisat will also transmit specific data on greenhouse gases and ozone levels. (which/ as well as)
   Envisat, which ....
3. The satellite cost £1.4 billion. The satellite is equipped with ten different instruments. The satellite will have a ten-year lifespan. (which/and)
   The satellite, which ....
4. It will register minute surface movements. The purpose is to give advance warning of natural disasters. Examples of natural disasters are mud-slides, floods and hurricanes. (in order to/such as)
   It will register minute surface movements ....
5. The satellite is the size of a large lorry. It will be launched on an Ariane rocket. (which)
   The satellite, which ....
6. Envisat will orbit the earth 14 times a day. The orbit will be at a height of 800 kilometres. (at a …)
   Envisat will ....
7. It will be guided by a team of 50. The team will be based in the European Space Operations Centre in Germany. (…, …)
   It will be guided by ....
8. The satellite will move in a 35-day cycle. The satellite will take just three days to draw a complete map of the world. (moving)
   The satellite, ...

1 Vocabulary

Rewrite each sentence without changing the meaning, using the word in brackets. Write one word in each space.

1 More species are at risk today than ever before. (endangered)
We now have ....
.... than ever before.

2 There is an urgent need for us to take action on a global level. (crucial)
.... for us to take action on a global level.

3 There is a growing concern about pollution. (worried)
More and more ....
....

4 People generally have very different opinions about this topic. (controversial)
This is generally ....
....

5 The evaluation made him feel less confident. (undermined)
The evaluation ....
....

6 Lots of people read this magazine. (circulation)
This magazine ....
....

7 Last week the government lifted the ban on GM research. (go-ahead)
Last week the government ....
.... for GM research.

8 The government still forbids full-scale production of GM crops in this country. (prohibited)
Full-scale production of GM crops ....
.... in this country.

2 Reading: Locating information

a The reading passage has four paragraphs labelled A–D. Which paragraph contains the following information?

NB You may use any letter more than once.

1 a description of a change in whale communications

2 an explanation of the purpose of fin whale communication

3 examples of sources of human noise

4 a reason why songs are necessary for some species of whale

5 a warning about the possible dangers of human noise

6 a description of whale communication

Human noise may disturb whales' 'Love Songs'

A Whales belt out the loudest songs on Earth – the slow, low ballads of blue and fin whales can be heard for several thousand miles. Researchers tracked down bellowing fin whales in the Sea of Cortez, and concluded that the songs were breeding displays to 'serenade' females because all the singers were male.

B The discovery makes a lot of sense because fin whales, like blue whales, do not have breeding grounds. But they don't need them because they can locate each other with these long-distance calls.

C The finding raises concerns that rising levels of ocean noise caused by commercial vessels and military sonar could interfere with these communications. Since the human contribution to ocean noise is dominated by sounds in a similar low-frequency range but produced by shipping vessels, oil and gas exploration and military activities, researchers fear the cacophony may disrupt or drown out the ocean banter of marine animals and could possibly damage their hearing.

D One study published in *Nature* in 2000 showed that low-frequency active sonar altered the singing behavior of humpback whales. Humpback songs were associated with reproduction but it is not clear whether the alterations would affect reproduction rates or were needed to compensate for the noise.

---

b Find words or expressions in the text associated with:

1 loud songs: .belt out. , ... , ...

2 a type of song: .... , ...

3 communication: .... , ...

3 Writing: Task 2

a Read the Writing task and the sample answer. Match the opening sentences 1–4 to the correct paragraphs A–D. (Ignore the numbered gaps within the paragraphs.)

> *We are becoming more and more dependent on machines to function in the modern world. Some people think this is a very negative development.*
>
> *To what extent do you agree or disagree?*

A

....
But this does not necessarily mean that the effects of our dependence are negative.

B

....
In our homes, 1 ...., washing machines and kettles and all the appliances we take for granted actually save us hours of labour.
2 .... in the workplace, computers and telephones and all the communication equipment we use form the whole basis of business and commerce.
3 .... of the positive effect of machines in our lives are endless, whether we consider transport or trade or any other sector of society.

C

....
Perhaps the health problems associated with a less physical life style, or the passive nature of much of our entertainment can be counted as disadvantages. 4 ...., these are features of modern life that individuals can change themselves.

D

....
In conclusion, ...
But without machines, our standard of living, and the economic growth and development of our society would all collapse. 5 .... who would want to go back to subsistence farming with hand-made tools? 6 .... trying to turn back history, we should appreciate the many benefits that machines bring.

1 I certainly agree about our overall dependence.

2 In contrast it is hard to find reasons why our dependence on technology is negative.

3 It would be difficult to imagine how modern life could carry on without all the machinery that we have come to rely on.

4 In fact, machines have brought benefits to every aspect of our daily lives.

b Complete gaps 1–6 with the correct linking word from the box. Remember to add punctuation or capital letters where necessary.

> similarly   however   examples   instead of
> yet   for instance

c Answer these questions.

1 Which part of the question does the writer agree with? Underline the phrases used to express this agreement directly.

2 Which part of the question does the writer disagree with? Underline the phrases used to express this disagreement directly.

4 Speaking: Part 1

Read the conversation between an examiner and a candidate. Complete the candidate's responses using sentences a–f.

Examiner: Now let's talk about your future. Where do you think you will be living in five years' time?

Candidate: Well, I'm not sure. 1 .... Who knows? That's something I hope to do in the next few years. But I suppose 2 ....

Examiner: And what sort of job do you think you'll have in the future?

Candidate: Oh, ideally an extremely-well paid one, with very few working hours! 3 .... I think I'll definitely have some sort of job, for sure. 4 ....

Examiner: What field do you expect to work in?

Candidate: Oh, 5 .... I've always been interested in it, and I love it. But I haven't got much experience yet, so I'll have to start at the bottom. 6 .... We'll see.

a) I'll probably still be at home, living with my family.

b) But that seems highly unlikely, really.

c) Of course, it's possible that I'll get promotion after a while.

d) It's quite possible that I'll be in the US.

e) There's little chance of it being such a good one, though.

f) I'll almost certainly be in IT.

111

► TRANSPORT

Focus on reading *True/False/Not Given; locating information; diagram labelling*

SKIMMING AND SCANNING
► Module F page 72

1 **a** **Read the title and subheading of the text below.**

1 What are you going to read about in the text?
2 What do you already know about this issue?

b **Skim the text to answer these questions.**

1 In which part of the world is the experiment taking place?
2 How many cities are involved?
3 What three general factors are being investigated in the experiment?

DEALING WITH
SPECIALIST VOCABULARY

2 **Find explanations in paragraphs B and C for the following expressions. You will need to understand these for the tasks.**

1 fuel cell (line 33)   2 zero emission (line 54)

CUTE buses: a new direction for public transport

It seems like a normal bus, except that it moves almost silently, and it does not give off any exhaust fumes. Instead, a small cloud of white steam emerges from the roof. But this is no ordinary vehicle. It is part of an experiment that could revolutionise public transport in our cities, providing sustainable, non-polluting transport from renewable energy resources

A Urban transport is a major problem in the countries of the European Union, where over 75% of the population lives in towns and cities. It is becoming increasingly difficult to reconcile individual needs and expectations of personal mobility with the preservation of the fabric of our cities and with the quality of life of their inhabitants. Transport is already one of the chief contributors to health and environmental problems in urban regions, and increasing levels of congestion mean that in some cities the average speed of traffic at peak times is slower than <u>it</u> was in the days of the horse and cart. In addition, exhaust fumes are a major contributor to rising levels of CO_2 emissions in the atmosphere, as well as being a source of carbon monoxide and particulate matter. With experts forecasting an increase of 30% in the total number of kilometres travelled by 2030, urban transport systems have to face the challenge of meeting citizens' needs for mobility through the development of innovative and sustainable methods of transport.

B To address this problem, the European Commission has allocated €18.5m to a project entitled CUTE (Clean Urban Transport for Europe), one of the most ambitious experiments in energy and transport taking place today. The aim of the project is to investigate the role that hydrogen and fuel cells could play in providing a safe, clean and efficient means of public transport. In order

to do this, the nine participating cities have each been supplied with three buses which are powered by hydrogen rather than by diesel fuel. The buses, produced by Mercedes Benz Citaro, contain tanks of compressed hydrogen in the roof, which supply **fuel cells**. <u>Here</u>, the hydrogen molecules are split `line 33` and electricity is produced to power the bus, together with pure water which escapes into the atmosphere as steam. The buses only need refuelling once a day and can travel at speeds of up to 100kph.

C The nine participating cities vary widely in their local conditions and the type of operating systems <u>they</u> use, allowing data to be collected and comparisons to be made between the different systems. One decision the transport authorities in each city have to make is the source of the hydrogen they use for fuel. <u>This</u> may be produced either from renewable resources, or from fossil fuels. At present only around 40% of the energy required for the production of hydrogen on the project comes from renewable resources such as wind power. Amsterdam and Hamburg both use energy from <u>this source</u> to produce the hydrogen for their buses. Stockholm also uses a renewable resource, in this case hydro power, while Barcelona profits from its high number of hours of sunshine to make use of solar power. In cases such as <u>these</u> it may be possible to have a **zero emission** system, with no harmful `line 54` by-products given off at any stage of the project. However, other cities such as Porto and London use natural gas or other non-renewable resources to produce the hydrogen.

D In addition to deciding on the means of production, the cities also have to decide on the location where the production of hydrogen is to take place. The on-site production of hydrogen removes the need for <u>its</u> transportation by truck in liquid or gas form, which is again an advantage in ecological and financial terms; <u>this solution</u> is used by several cities including Madrid. In London, however, in order to make the hydrogen available to other users, the authorities decided against on-site production, so the hydrogen production plant is some way from the bus depot.

E The varying geographical and climatic conditions of each city also allow information to be collected on a range of operating conditions for the buses. In some cities, such as London, buses have to be able to perform in congested traffic, while in Madrid and Porto in summer they have to be able to contend with the hot climate in addition to <u>this</u>. Bus transport in Porto also has to cope with extreme geographical conditions since the city is built on a steep hillside, and <u>the same</u> is true of Luxembourg and Barcelona. In Stuttgart, on the other hand, which has a widespread population, the buses' ability to travel long distances is tested.

F The overall remit of the project therefore involves comparison of performance and costs involved in three main areas: the production of hydrogen, the organisation of infrastructure (for example, the location of hydrogen refilling stations), and the use of the buses in varying operational conditions. There is still some way to go before hydrogen buses will be replacing ordinary public transport on a large scale – at present running costs are ten times higher, which does not make them a commercial proposition – but it is beginning to look as if the days of the diesel driven bus are numbered. ■

TRUE/FALSE/NOT GIVEN
▶ Module E page 66

3 Look through questions 1–9 below and complete the tasks.

Questions 1–5

Do the following statements agree with the information given in the reading passage?

Write

TRUE	*if the statement agrees with the information*
FALSE	*if the statement contradicts the information*
NOT GIVEN	*if there is no information on this*

1 Traffic may cause problems both to city buildings and to residents.

2 The most efficient way to solve urban transport problems is to increase the use of public transport.

3 The chemical reaction which produces power for the hydrogen bus takes place in the fuel cell.

4 The authorities in each city are responsible for the initial collection and analysis of the data.

5 The nine cities in the CUTE project have zero emission systems for their hydrogen buses.

LOCATING INFORMATION
▶ Module H page 103

- Read the text paragraph by paragraph.
- Look through the list of items to find matching information.
- Remember that you are looking for a specific **type** of information (e.g. a contrast, reason, etc.).

Questions 6–9

The reading passage has six paragraphs labelled A–F.
Which paragraph contains the following information?

NB You may use any letter more than once.

6 a contrast between the two main methods of hydrogen production

7 a reason why hydrogen powered buses may not be widely used for some time

8 a comparison of traffic conditions in the past and present

9 a justification for the transportation of hydrogen by road to refuel London buses

---

DIAGRAM LABELLING
▶ *Focus on IELTS* page 172

4 **In this task, you have to label a diagram using words from the text.**

a Look at the notes on the diagram below. Use the place names to help you locate the information you need in the text. (The names may occur more than once.)

b Read the sections you have marked carefully and complete the task.

Questions 10–14
Complete the labels on the diagram.
*Choose **NO MORE THAN THREE WORDS FROM THE PASSAGE** for each answer.*

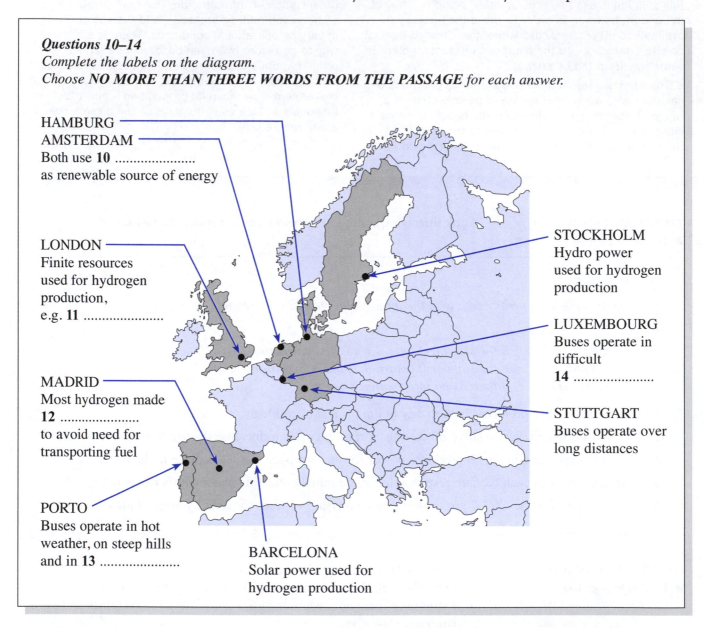

HAMBURG
AMSTERDAM
Both use **10** .... as renewable source of energy

LONDON
Finite resources used for hydrogen production, e.g. **11** ....

MADRID
Most hydrogen made **12** .... to avoid need for transporting fuel

PORTO
Buses operate in hot weather, on steep hills and in **13** ....

BARCELONA
Solar power used for hydrogen production

STOCKHOLM
Hydro power used for hydrogen production

LUXEMBOURG
Buses operate in difficult **14** ....

STUTTGART
Buses operate over long distances

GRAMMATICAL LINKS
▶ *Focus on IELTS* pages 25 and 210

5 **To answer some of the questions in the exam task above, you needed to understand grammatical links such as adverbs and personal pronouns. This is an important reading skill for IELTS.**

Look back through the text and highlight what the underlined words refer to.

1 it (paragraph A)
2 Here (paragraph B)
3 they (paragraph C)
4 This (paragraph C)
5 this source (paragraph C)

6 these (paragraph C)
7 its (paragraph D)
8 this solution (paragraph D)
9 this (paragraph E)
10 the same (paragraph E)

▶ Ideas for speaking and writing page 142

Focus on speaking 1 *Talking about problems*

Part 2 Long turn

In Module E page 63, you did a Part 3 Speaking task involving discussion of problems and solutions. You could also be asked to talk about a problem in Part 2.

ANALYSING THE TASK

1 Read the candidate task card below and number the prompts you need to talk about.

> **Describe a transport problem in your town/city.**
>
> **You should say:**
>
> > **what the problem is**
> > **what the causes are**
> > **how it affects you**
>
> **and explain how you think it might be solved.**

ORGANISING YOUR TALK

2 a 🎧 Listen to a student talking about this topic. Note down the key information given for prompts 1–4 on the task card.

(1)	(2)	(3)	(4)

b 🎧 Listen again and fill the gaps in the sentences the student used to introduce each section.

1 Well, in my city, I think .... is the poor bus service.

2 I think the reason why .... is because …

3 I .... , so it means I have to leave early …

4 In terms .... , well, I know it's not easy.

EXAM PRACTICE

TIP When discussing problems of this kind, the prefixes *over-* and *under-* are very useful, e.g. *overcrowded*.

3 a Use the candidate notes below to help you talk about another transport problem. Remember to talk for two minutes.

> 1 *Problem: using local trains, long ticket queues, dirty trains, overcrowded*
> 2 *Causes: ticket offices understaffed, train service underfunded*
> 3 *Affects me: never get a seat, uncomfortable, makes me stressed*
> 4 *Solutions: Govt. should invest more, newer trains, more staff, better ticketing systems, etc., more trains in rush hour*

b Now spend one minute making your own notes on the task in Exercise 1. Use them to talk for two minutes on the topic. Record yourself if you can.

Focus on speaking 2 *Developing a discussion topic*

Part 3 Discussion
TOPIC DEVELOPMENT

1 a For the Part 2 task in the previous section, you described a transport problem in your town or city. This could be developed in Part 3 to discuss further transport-related issues.

Look at the typical Part 3 questions below and think about how you would answer them.

1 Do you think everyone has the right to have their own private transport?

2 What do you think the effects would be if everybody had their own car?

3 What measures, if any, should the government take to restrict the use of private cars?

4 What kind of transport systems do you think might be developed in the future?

b Can you think of two more general questions to ask about transport or transport problems?

SAMPLE ANSWER

2 🎧 Listen to two native speakers answering question 1 in Exercise 1a, and compare their answers with your own ideas.

GIVING YOURSELF
TIME TO THINK

3 When answering questions on more abstract or general issues, native speakers often use opening expressions that give them time to think, as well as indicating that they are aware of the complexity of the issue.

🎧 Look at the expressions in the box and listen to the recording again. Tick the expressions which the speakers use.

It's hard to say …	*Well, conditions vary …*
It all depends (on the situation)	*Obviously I'm no expert, but …*
Every case is different …	*I'm not sure there's an easy answer (to that).*

LOGICAL LINKS:
CONTRAST

4 Use the expressions in the box below to complete the following responses to question 1 in Exercise 1a.

In the short term … but in the long term …
In the case of … but in the case of …
On the one hand … but on the other hand …

1 It's a confusing situation: .... advertisers persuade everybody to buy their own car, ... we're told that private transport is bad.

2 I think everybody does have the right to private vehicles ....
.... bicycles, ... cars there are a lot more problems.

3 .... I think everybody should be able to have their own transport, ... that situation can't be sustained.

EXAM PRACTICE

5 Now answer questions 1–4 in Exercise 1 with your own ideas, using the language you have practised in Exercises 2 and 3. Record yourself if you can.

Focus on listening *Flow chart completion; summary*

Section 4
PREDICTING THE TOPIC

Remember in Section 4 there is no break in the recording, so look through all the questions in the time you are given before the recording starts.

1   Look at questions 1–10 in the exam task below and on page 118. What is the lecturer likely to be discussing?

a) different types of tourism
b) good and bad effects of tourism
c) the history and development of tourism

FLOW CHART COMPLETION
► *Focus on IELTS* page 180

2   Flow charts are a way of summarising the different stages of a process in the form of a diagram. You need to listen carefully for words that signal the different stages.

IDENTIFYING THE
STAGES OF A TALK

You will hear the following signalling phrases during the first part of the lecture. Number them in the order in which you expect to hear them.

☐ As tourist development begins to increase …
☐ Doxey identifies four stages.
☐ If development continues to increase, …
☐ He calls the first stage …
☐ … in the final stage of the model …

EXAM PRACTICE

3   🎧 Now listen to the recording and complete both tasks.

Questions 1–5
Complete the flow chart below.
Write **NO MORE THAN TWO WORDS** *for each answer.*

Doxey's 'Irridex' model of tourism

> **TIP** The headings in inverted commas in the flow chart will be defined by the speaker, so don't worry if you don't understand them all.

> **TIP** You may hear some information about a new stage before the speaker mentions the actual name of the stage.

'Euphoria'

• tourists seen as a **1** ...., and welcomed
• tourism could bring chance of **2** ....

⬇

'Apathy'

• interest becomes 'sectionalised'
• contacts tend to be **3** ....

⬇

'Annoyance'

• problems caused by overdevelopment and **4** ....
• policy makers attempt solutions by increasing infrastructure

⬇

'Antagonism'

• open hostility to tourists
• tourists blamed for changes to **5** ....

SUMMARY COMPLETION
▶ Module G page 94

- Read through the summary and think about what sort of information is required.
- Listen for key words and parallel phrases.
- Check that the words you choose are grammatically correct.

Questions 6–10
Complete the summary below.
Write **NO MORE THAN THREE WORDS** *for each answer.*

<u>Criticisms of Doxey's model</u>

The model has been criticised as giving a **6** .... view of the effects of tourism, because it is unidirectional. It is also rather oversimplified – in fact **7** .... are more complex and varied.

<u>Positive effects of tourism</u>

Tourism may give tourists increased understanding of other societies and cultures, and in the host community it may lead to the revitalisation of **8** .... Tourism may also help groups and individuals by creating new jobs for **9** .... and by encouraging people who work in tourism to learn **10** ....

USEFUL VOCABULARY:
ACADEMIC LANGUAGE

4 This recording and task use quite formal academic language. Find academic expressions in the summary task above which mean:

1 just going one way ....
2 complicated ....
3 more ....
4 those living in tourist centres ....
5 redevelopment ....
6 making ....

▶ Ideas for speaking and writing page 142

Focus on writing *Describing information from tables*

Task I Tables
▶ *Focus on IELTS* pages 81–2

Tables compare data and may also show changes over time as well. They are often used when there is quite a lot of information, so it is important to select the key features to describe.

UNDERSTANDING
THE DATA

> **TIP** The way information is ordered in the table (i.e. left to right and top to bottom) will help you to understand it.

▶ Module A page 12
▶ Module B page 25

1 Read the Writing task below and look at the table. Answer these questions to help you understand the information given.

1 What two main areas does the table give figures for?
2 How is each main area subdivided?
3 What main difference do the figures show within each area?
4 How many years does the table deal with?
5 What are the main trends over time?
6 What kind of language can you use when describing the data?

WRITING TASK 1

You should spend about 20 minutes on this task.

The table below gives figures for student applications and acceptances for UK university courses in the field of tourism, transport and travel.

Write a report for a university lecturer describing the information below.

Write at least 150 words.

Student statistics for university courses in tourism, transport and travel, 2000–2002

	Applications		Acceptances		
year	men	women	men	women	% of total
2000	3,400	900	550	150	15.5 %
2001	3,200	800	600	200	20 %
2002	2,750	750	580	170	21.4 %

ORGANISING
THE DESCRIPTION

2 You should try to group the information rather than describing every piece of data.

Complete this paragraph outline for the Writing task in Exercise 1.

> *Paragraph 1: Introduce information*
> *Paragraph 2: Describe figures and trends related to ....*
> *Paragraph 3: ....*
> *Paragraph 4: ....*

REWORDING THE INTRODUCTION

> **TIP** Remember not to copy your introduction from the task: paraphrase instead.

3 Underline the most appropriate word(s) to complete this introduction to a sample answer.

> The table concerns university courses **1** in the field of/related to tourism, transport and travel in the UK. It shows **2** decreases/changes/increases in the **3** numbers/proportion/percentage of **4** applicants/male and female students applying for and being accepted on such courses **5** between/from 2000 and 2002.

DESCRIBING THE DATA

4 **a** Use the information in the table in Exercise 1 to complete these sentences with a word or number.

1 In all three years, more .... applied for *such* courses than .... , although *their numbers* .... considerably, from 3,400 in 2000 to .... in 2002.

2 Female .... reached little more than a quarter of the figures for .... in 2000 and 2001, and *they* .... to 750 in 2002.

3 Total applications .... during *the period*.

4 Many more .... and .... applied for *these courses* than were accepted throughout *the three years*.

5 However, the .... of applications *which* were accepted .... from about 15% in 2000 to over .... in 2002, even though the total number .... only slightly.

6 Many more .... were accepted than .... in *all three years*.

7 While total applications .... , the .... of *those* accepted .... considerably.

b Now look back at your paragraph outline in Exercise 2, and group the sentences into paragraphs 2, 3 and 4.

c Decide which of the sequencers in the box below you could use to start each paragraph.

Example: The table shows = start of introduction

> Overall,   Firstly, we can see that with regard to applications,
> The table shows   In terms of acceptances,

REFERENCE LINKS

▶ *Focus on IELTS* pages 217–218

5 To link ideas in a text and avoid unnecessary repetition, writers use a variety of reference links.

Find the words in italics in sentences 1–7 in Exercise 4 and write down what each refers to.

1 such (courses) ....
2 their numbers ....
3 they ....
4 the period ....
5 these courses ....

6 the three years ....
7 which ....
8 all three years ....
9 those ....

SPEED WRITING PRACTICE

6 Now do the Writing task below. Remember to include editing time in the 20 minutes given. Remember:

- Don't copy your introduction from the Writing task.
- Briefly describe the main features or trends and use figures to support these. Don't describe every change.
- End with a summary of the data.
- Write at least 150 words.

WRITING TASK 1

You should spend about 20 minutes on this task.

The table below gives information about the use of different modes of transport in Shanghai in 1996, and one possible projection (high motorisation scenario) for their use in 2020.

Write a report for a university lecturer describing the information below.

Write at least 150 words.

Percentage of passenger kilometres by different modes of transport in Shanghai

Mode of Transport	1996	2020 (projection)
walking	7%	3%
bicycle	27%	3%
scooter	12%	7%
bus	39%	22%
train	–	13%
car	15%	52%

▶ Answer Key page 170

1 Topic vocabulary overview
Module I (*Focus on IELTS* Units 17 and 18) dealt with topics relating to transport and tourism.

a Complete each phrase below by choosing the best word from the boxes. (All the phrases are found in *Focus on IELTS* Units 17 and 18 and/or Module I.)

Transport

congestion	construction	efficient	exhaust
helicopter	bicycle	lanes	overstretched
pedestrians	speeding	steamship	traffic
truck	vehicles	zero	

Types of transport

1 .... ⎫
2 .... ⎬ wheeled 5 ....
3 ....
4 ....

Traffic problems

6 .... fumes
7 increasing levels of ....
8 .... jams
9 dangerous driving, e.g. ....
10 .... public transport systems
11 danger to ....

Possible solutions

12 bus ....
13 .... of more roads
14 .... emission fuels
15 .... public transport

Tourism

community	impact	long-distance	season
souvenir	tourists	traditional	

16 the .... of tourism
17 the host ....
18 an influx of ....
19 .... crafts
20 the .... trade
21 .... travel
22 the tourist ....

b Look back through the units and add more words to the lists.

c Now complete these extracts with appropriate phrases from Exercise 1a.

Listening Section 4: Facing transport problems in the 21st century

> Notes:
> main source of atmospheric pollution in cities:
> 1 .... fumes from motor
> 2 ....
> São Paolo: long delays on roads because of traffic 3 .... and 4 .... , so rich people travel by 5 ....
> Solution to transport problems is not 6 .... of new roads
> Bogota: new and 7 .... public transport system has revitalised city centre

Speaking Part 2: Something I bought on holiday

> **Candidate:** One thing I've bought which I like very much is the rug which I have on the floor in my bedroom. I got it when I was in Turkey last year. I went there in winter so it wasn't the tourist 8 .... and a lot of the shops were closed, but one was open, so I went in. It was just a little shop but it was full of carpets and rugs – carpet making is a 9 .... craft in Turkey. I hadn't really meant to buy anything, but I'm glad I did because it's a nice 10 .... of my holiday. I like it because …

Writing Task 2: Effects of tourism

> The way that people spend their leisure time has been transformed by the increasing popularity of 11 .... travel. The drop in the price of air fares has meant that people can travel to faraway places for their holidays. This has both good and bad effects. Tourism may provide employment for people in the host 12 .... , but at the same time it can have a negative 13 .... on the environment and local way of life.

2 Word pairs with related meanings
In academic English, some pairs of words with the same form, e.g. both nouns or both adjectives, are regularly used together.

Find the correct ending for each sentence from the list (a–j) and then underline or highlight the pair of related words.

Example: Our city is an excellent place for research into new types of transport because of its varying <u>geographical</u> and .*b*.

1 In order to solve our city's traffic problems, we need to develop innovative and …
2 We need to convince those in government and …
3 To make the right decision, very careful comparison of performance and …
4 Any proposals must take people's individual needs and …
5 It will first be necessary to agree on the formal terms and …
6 It may take several months for the planning and …
7 Designers have to consider not just the practical aspects of the transport system, but the views and …
8 As well as this, the environmental and …
9 Better systems of transport will benefit both groups and …

a) behaviour of its potential users.
b) <u>climatic</u> conditions.
c) conditions of the project.
d) costs is necessary.
e) design stages of the project to be completed.
f) expectations into account.
g) individuals.
h) industry that changes need to be made.
i) social costs of the scheme have to be evaluated.
j) sustainable methods of transport.

3 Adjective–noun collocations

a **In the sentences below, all three nouns in italics can collocate with the preceding adjective, but only one makes sense in the sentence as a whole. Underline the correct noun in each case.**

1 Unfortunately, the local *authorities/people/ trains* are very unreliable, so most people travel by car.
2 If congestion problems affect bus services, the most practical *effect/use/solution* is usually to introduce special bus lanes.
3 The flowchart is a theoretical *claim /model/ problem* of traffic patterns which can be applied to a number of real-life situations.
4 The hydrogen bus is not yet suitable for use on a commercial *scale/centre/sector* as its running costs are still high.
5 Electricity to power the bus is produced by means of a chemical *reaction/industry/test* in which hydrogen molecules are split.

6 For the sustainable development of transport policies, it is necessary to consider environmental *disasters/causes/issues* such as prevention of pollution.
7 The initial *collection/contact/period* of the data on the European transport project is carried out by the local authorities.

b **Read each sentence again and underline the adjective that precedes the nouns in italics.**

1 What ending do all the adjectives have?
2 What is the noun form of each of these adjectives? (Note: some adjectives may have more than one related noun form.)

4 Spoken language: Giving yourself thinking time

a **Complete the gaps in these extracts from a Part 3 Speaking task. The first letter of each word has been given.**

1 **Examiner:** So do you think tourism has benefited the area where you live?
   Candidate: It's h...................... to say. In some ways it has, I suppose.
2 **Examiner:** Do you think there's a danger that tourism will destroy the traditional way of life of some cultures?
   Candidate: Well, it all d...................... o........... the situation.
3 **Examiner:** How do you think tourism is likely to develop in the coming years?
   Candidate: Obviously I'm no e...................... , but I think there will be big changes.
4 **Examiner:** What do you think can be done about the problems caused by the escalation of tourism?
   Candidate: I'm not sure there's an e........... a......................

b **Now choose one sentence from the list a–d below to continue each of the candidate's responses.**

a) For example, people may want more leisure facilities – clubs and shops and things like that.
b) In some cases there's certainly a risk that this will happen, but I don't think it has to.
c) It would be very hard to reduce the numbers of tourists, but it's also hard to see how to solve the problems they cause.
d) It's meant there are extra jobs for people, in hotels and restaurants, for example.

▶ APPEARANCES

Focus on listening *Sentence completion; multiple choice (single answer)*

Section 4
PREDICTING THE TOPIC

1 a Look at the illustrations below. They show the portraits of a man and a woman who lived the Fayum area of Egypt between 80–100 AD, together with modern reconstructions of their faces.

    1 What similarities and differences can you see between the portraits and the reconstructions?

    2 How do you think the reconstructions were made?

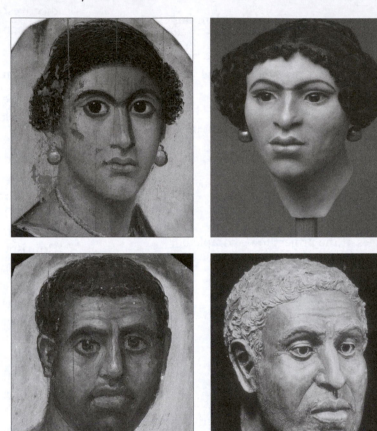

b Look through questions 1–10 in the exam task on page 125. How does the topic link to the pictures above?

SENTENCE COMPLETION

2 In this task, you have to complete a set of sentences based on all or part of the listening text. The sentences are related to the main ideas in the listening text.

PREDICTING POSSIBLE
ANSWERS

▶ *Focus on IELTS* page 23

a Read through questions 1–6 again and underline key phrases. This will give you an idea what to listen for.

b Think about what is needed in the gaps.

    1 Which gap could be filled with the name of a place?

    2 Which gap probably needs an adjective?

    3 Which gap(s) may need a short phrase? (Remember that this must be three words or fewer.)

> **TIP** Listen carefully to check whether a singular or plural word is required.

EXAM PRACTICE

3 🎧 Now listen to the recording and complete both tasks.

Questions 1–6
Complete the sentences below.
*Write **NO MORE THAN THREE WORDS** for each answer.*

1 After 322 BC, many people came from .... to settle in the Fayum.

2 The new inhabitants of the Fayum introduced the custom of placing a picture ....
of the mummy.

3 The pictures were made of coloured .... spread onto a wooden board.

4 William Petrie believed the pictures were painted .... of the person.

5 He said the pictures were unusual because of their .... style.

6 The pictures may have originally been displayed .... of the people they showed.

MULTIPLE CHOICE (SINGLE ANSWER)
▶ Module F page 76

Questions 7–10
*Choose the correct answer, **A**, **B** or **C**.*

7 The reconstructions of the faces were
mainly based on

A the original portraits of the mummies.

B models of the skulls of the mummies.

C the X-rays of the mummies.

8 In the man's portrait, the dark shadow
around his chin

A would make him identifiable as an
individual.

B suggests the artist was not trying to
flatter him.

C shows this is a different person from
the reconstruction.

9 The portrait of the woman

A has unusual features for a woman.

B suggests a particularly strong
personality.

C is very similar to the model.

10 The speaker concludes that both portraits

A are individual adaptations of a
standard.

B were probably painted by the same
person.

C are rather untypical of their genre.

**TRANSFERRING
YOUR ANSWERS**

TIP As you copy your
answers, check that you
are writing next to the
correct number.

4 When you have finished the IELTS Listening Module, you have ten minutes
to transfer your answers to the answer sheet. As you transfer your answers,
check that you have not made mistakes with spelling or grammar and that
you have not written any unnecessary words.

Look at your completed answers above. Answer these questions.

1 What is the maximum number of words you are allowed for each of
questions 1–6?

2 For questions 7–10, what should you copy onto your answer sheet?

▶ Ideas for speaking and writing page 143

Focus on reading *Multiple choice (single answer); flow chart completion; short answers*

SKIMMING AND SCANNING

1

a Read the title, subheading and the first two paragraphs of the text to find out what it is about. Answer these questions.

1 Which words in the text mean:
   a) a substance that carries genetic information specific to each individual?
   b) scientific techniques used for solving crimes?
2 How can DNA be used at present to help the police in criminal investigations?
3 What information might a DNA sample be able to provide in the future?

b Skim the rest of the text to find out which paragraphs deal with these topics.

1 Hair colour   Paragraph(s) ....
2 Facial features   Paragraph(s) ....
3 Eye colour   Paragraph(s) ....

c Underline or highlight the organisations named in this text.

Getting the picture from DNA

Working out what someone looks like from only a DNA sample is no longer science fiction. You'd be surprised what forensics experts can already do, says Clare Wilson.

A At present, if police find DNA which could be that of the criminal at the scene of a crime (for example in blood or hair), standard forensic techniques can help in two ways. If there's a suspect in custody, the police can see if their DNA matches the 'crime stain', as it is called. Or in the absence of a suspect, they can see if it matches the DNA of any known criminal held in their archives.

B Both techniques have proved their worth in criminal investigations. But what if there's no suspect and no match in the archive? Ever since DNA testing was introduced, forensic scientists have wondered how much a DNA sample on its own could tell them about what a criminal might look like.

C Scientists have already had some success with predicting hair colour from DNA samples. For example, researchers at Britain's Forensic Science Service (FSS) have developed a DNA test which will tell with 98% accuracy whether or not someone has red hair. However, the red-hair test is of limited use in Britain, where only 6% of the population are red-headed. What about blonde, brown and black-haired criminals? Hair colour is usually determined by the cumulative effect of several genes, so unfortunately there's

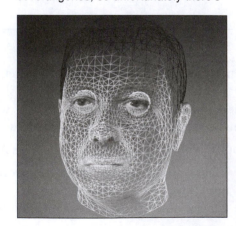

no such thing as a single gene for blonde hair that could be turned into a simple test, for example. It's the same with eye colour.

D But biotechnology firm DNAPrint Genomics of Florida, USA, is having a crack at both problems. As a starting point, research was carried out using mice to discover the genes that controlled eye colour. Similar sequences in human DNA were then investigated, and ten possible genes were found. Next, the DNAPrint researchers took DNA samples from 500 volunteers and recorded their eye colours. They then applied a technique called SNP mapping to see if they could discover any correlations between the two. (SNP stands for 'single nucleotide polymorphism' – a single 'letter' change in the genetic code. These variations account for most of the genetic differences between individuals.) The researchers sequenced the ten possible genes from each volunteer, then sifted through the sequences looking for SNPs. They found 50 in total. Then they set computers to work out how the SNPs correlated with eye colour. Of the ten genes, they found that only four really matter. By looking at these, they can classify someone as having dark eyes (black and brown), light coloured eyes (blue and grey), or hazel eyes (greenish-brown) – with 97% certainty.

E DNAPrint is now applying exactly the same technique to hair colour, identifying possible genes and looking for SNPs. Representatives say they have made some headway and can classify people into one of three groups – blonde, brown or black-haired – with some accuracy, from their DNA alone.

F Back in Britain, the Forensic Science Service has also been pursuing the genetic basis of facial features. A few years ago it helped fund a major project carried out by scientists at University College London (UCL). Over several months, an exhibit at a London museum invited visitors to leave DNA samples and have their faces scanned using 3D surface mapping. About 600 people volunteered. The UCL researchers tried to break down this data on overall facial shape into distinct features such as nose curvature or chin clefts, and correlate them to DNA sequences. But they made little progress. Just as with eye colour, there is no one gene for a big nose, so the enormous complexity of the task defeated the researchers. When the lead scientist retired, the project was wound down without drawing any firm conclusions.

G But the idea of finding genes for facial features isn't dead. Many of the genes involved are common to most mammals. So a gene for a large jaw in mice, for example, might very well be found in humans, too. One promising project has found that mice show significant variation in jaw shape and size, and has begun to unravel the genetics behind the variation. Project leader Chris Klingenberg of the University of Konstanz in Germany cautions that, as with humans, the genetics controlling jaw shape in mice is horribly complicated, but the project is making some progress. In one study of 535 mice, it has identified genes for jaw shape, jaw size and jaw symmetry and found two basic patterns resulting from the combination of these genes.

H The UK-based human rights group known as 'Liberty' has concerns, saying that the existing tests are not yet sufficiently conclusive to be used as a basis for arresting suspects. Certainly, genes never tell the whole story with physical characteristics – environment plays a key role too. Kevin Sullivan, from the Forensic Science Service, points out that when it comes to someone's facial characteristics, 'playing rugby might have more of an effect on your ear and nose shape than your genes.' But he is optimistic about the future of the research. 'Law-abiding citizens don't have anything to worry about,' he says. 'But criminals do.'

**MULTIPLE CHOICE
(SINGLE ANSWER)**
▶ Module F page 73

2 Now answer questions 1–3.

Questions 1–3
Choose the correct letter, A, B, C or D.

1 What is meant by a 'crime stain'?

 A traces of blood left at the scene of a crime

 B DNA belonging to known criminals

 C samples of blood or hair in criminal archives

 D DNA samples left at the scene of a crime

2 Forensic scientists are interested in finding out

 A if the genes responsible for criminal tendencies can be identified.

 B how far personal appearance can be predicted from DNA.

 C if hair colour could be linked to criminal behaviour.

 D whether or not DNA can be used to identify a suspected criminal.

3 What problem do scientists face in developing DNA tests for hair and eye colour?

 A the fact that these characteristics are not generally determined by one gene

 B the variation in test procedures required for these characteristics

 C the fact that these characteristics are not necessarily related

 D the variation in distribution of these characteristics from one country to another

COMPLETING A
FLOW CHART

▶ *Focus on IELTS* page 91

3 If a text includes a description of a process, you may have to complete a summary in the form of a flow chart. A flow chart is a summary of the main stages in a process and has arrows indicating the order of the stages.

a Look at the flow chart in the exam task below and answer these questions.

1 What tells you the general topic of the flow chart?
2 How many stages are there in the process?
3 Scan the text to find which section the flow chart relates to.

> **HELP**
> In this case the flow chart relates to just one paragraph.

b Now read through the flow chart stage by stage. Use parallel phrases to locate the relevant information in the reading passage, and complete the task.

Questions 4–7
Complete the flow chart below.
*Choose **NO MORE THAN THREE WORDS AND/OR A NUMBER** from the text for each answer.*

Research into the genetic basis of eye colour

Identification of genes determining eye colour in **4** ....

↓

Identification of ten possible genes in humans

↓

SNP mapping of these ten genes to find **5** .... between eye colour and DNA

↓

Identification of **6** .... SNPs

↓

Analysis of relationship between SNPs and eye colour

↓

Identification of the **7** .... genes that determine eye colour.

> **TIP** Don't worry if some of the vocabulary in the text is technical; you just need to understand the main ideas.

SHORT-ANSWER
QUESTIONS

▶ *Focus on IELTS* page 174

4 This task usually focuses on identifying factual information in a text. The questions are in the same order as the information in the text.

a Look at the exam task on page 129 to decide what type of information is required. Which question(s) are asking for:

a) a number?   b) an organisation?   c) a country?

LOCATING THE ANSWERS

> **TIP** In the Reading Module, sets of questions may focus on one section of the text, or the whole text.

b Now use key words to help you find the sections of the text where the answers are located, and complete the exam task. Use words from the text for your answer, and do not change these in any way.

Questions 8–13
*Answer the questions below using **NO MORE THAN THREE WORDS AND/OR A NUMBER** for each answer.*

8   Which American company is doing research on the genetic basis of hair and eye colour?

9   How many groups of eye colour can now be identified through SNP mapping?

10   Which British institution unsuccessfully researched data from humans on the genetic basis of facial features?

11   In which country is research being done on mice to find out about genes for facial features?

12   Which association is concerned about the possible applications of the research described in this text?

13   Which environmental factor could be important in determining your facial characteristics, according to Kevin Sullivan?

▶ Ideas for speaking and writing page 143

Focus on writing 1 *Describing a process*

Task 1 Flow chart
▶ *Focus on IELTS* pages 102–104

Diagrams describing a process are often in the form of a flow chart, which shows what happens at different stages of the process.

UNDERSTANDING
THE DIAGRAM

1   Look at the process diagram below and answer these questions.

1   What process does the diagram illustrate?
2   What special workplace is needed?
3   How many pieces of equipment are used in the process?

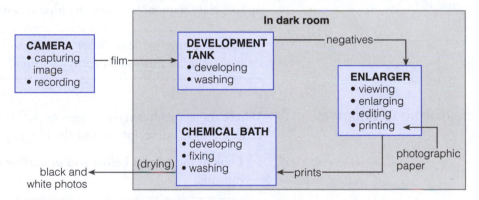

INTRODUCING
THE DESCRIPTION

2   If the process you have to describe involves pieces of equipment, it is important to mention these.

The following sentences show three alternative ways of introducing a description of the diagram above, and describing the equipment needed. Complete each sentence.

1   The diagram shows that in order to produce black and white photographs, a dark room and .... are needed, namely ....

2   The flow chart shows that the process of producing black and white photos is carried out in a dark room and involves the use of
....

3   The flow chart indicates that .... are used in the process of producing black and white photographs:
....

USING PASSIVE FORMS
▶ Module H page 102

3 If the flow chart uses words rather than pictures to explain what happens in the process, you will probably have to change the form of these words in your description. When you write your description, you may need to use passive verb forms.

Complete the following sentences using an appropriate verb from the box in the passive form. Look back at the diagram to help you.

develop (x2)	*produce*	*wash*	*view*	*fix*	*remove*
(x2) *enlarge*	*print*	*record*	*dry*	*capture*	*edit*

1 Images .... by the camera and .... onto a film in a camera.

2 The film .... from the camera.

3 It .... in a development tank in the dark room.

4 Negatives ....

5 The negatives .... in an enlarger, where the images can .... and ....

6 These .... onto sheets of photographic paper.

7 The prints ...., ..., ... and ....

8 The finished black and white photos can .... from the dark room.

LOGICAL LINKS:
SEQUENCERS
▶ *Focus on IELTS* pages 24 and 103

4 You need to use appropriate sequencing links to show the different stages of a process and the order of those stages.

Rewrite the sentences in Exercise 3 in the form of a paragraph, choosing appropriate sequencers from the box. You will not need to use all of them.

in the first stage	*once/when*	*after/before …ing*
then/next/after this/subsequently		*finally/in the last stage*

DESCRIBING ALTERNATIVES

5 Where there are alternative stages or pathways in a process, this must be reflected in the description and the language used.

a Look at the extract below and underline the language used to indicate options.

> At the editing stage, the image can be changed either by cropping
> or by focusing on one enlarged section. Alternatively, the image may be printed without editing.

b Write two similar sentences using the information below.

Black and white photographs – develop   – at a pharmacy
– by a professional photographer
– at home

SPEED WRITING PRACTICE   **6**   Now do the writing task below (including editing) in 20 minutes.

WRITING TASK 1

Production of photographs using digital equipment

You should spend about 20 minutes on this task.

The diagram shows how photographs can be produced using digital photographic equipment.

Write a report for a university lecturer describing the information.

Write at least 150 words.

DIGITAL CAMERA + smart card
• capturing image
• recording

(downloading) image →

COMPUTER
• editing (cutting/ improving/formatting)

→ sending (e-mail)
→ storing (CD)

colour photos ←

black and white photos ←

PRINTER
• printing

photo paper

▶ Answer Key page 172

Focus on writing 2 *Presenting an opinion (2)*

Task 2

SPEED WRITING PRACTICE

▶ Module C page 42
▶ Module F page 80

Write your answer to the following exam task. Follow this strategy.

• Analyse the question carefully.
• Decide what approach to follow in your answer (thesis-led or argument-led).
• Organise your ideas into a paragraph plan or outline.
• Write your answer. Remember to develop your main ideas and give reasons for your opinions.
• Write no fewer than 250 words.
• End with an appropriate conclusion.
• Edit your work.

WRITING TASK 2

You should spend about 40 minutes on this task.

Present a written argument or case to an educated reader with no specialist knowledge of the following topic.

In the modern world, the image (photograph or film) is becoming a more powerful way of communicating than the written word.

To what extent do you agree or disagree?

You should use your own ideas, knowledge and experience and support your arguments with examples and relevant evidence.

Write at least 250 words.

▶ Answer Key page 140
▶ Assessing your writing page 139

Focus on speaking *Practice interview*

GENERAL ASSESSMENT CRITERIA

In the Speaking Module, you are assessed on how effectively you can communicate. This means how clearly and fluently you can express ideas and information, the range of vocabulary and structures you use and how clear and appropriate your pronunciation is.

Part 1 Interview (4–5 minutes)
▶ Module A page 16
▶ Module D page 48

1 For Part 1, remember:

- Listen to the questions carefully and give relevant answers.
- Don't repeat the questions.
- Extend your answers by giving reasons, examples, etc.
- Use fluency markers to sound natural.
- Use linking expressions to organise your answers.

EVALUATING SAMPLE ANSWERS

a Read questions 1 and 2 below and think about how you would answer them.

> 1 How do you feel about shopping for clothes?
> 2 Would you prefer to have a lot of clothes or only a few, better-quality ones? Why?

b 🎧 Listen to three different speakers, A, B and C, answering questions 1 and 2. Thinking about the general assessment criteria above and the strategy points, decide which speaker gives the best performance and why.

c Now answer questions 1 and 2 yourself. Record yourself if you can. Listen to your recording and identify ways in which you could improve.

EXAM PRACTICE

d 🎧 Listen to another set of questions and pause the recording to answer each one.

Part 2 Long turn (2 minutes)
▶ Module C page 39

2 For Part 2, you will be given a task card, a pencil and some paper and you will have one minute to prepare.

- Use this minute to make notes that will help you to keep talking for two minutes.
- Read the task card carefully and identify the different prompts you should talk about.
- Use clear signals when you move on from one prompt to the next.
- Talk for two minutes.

EVALUATING NOTES

a Read the task card below and the notes for the task written by three different candidates. Which notes do you think are the most useful? Why?

> **Describe an advertising photo or TV image you have seen and you think was effective.**
>
> > You should say:
> > where you saw it
> > what it was advertising
> > what it showed
> > and explain why you think this photo/TV image was effective.

A *I saw an advert for petrol and it used a picture of a tiger. I don't remember what petrol company it was for. The image of a powerful, wild animal was used to give the impression that*

B

le tigre – un produit de 'Esso' –   la t l – L'image d'un animal puissant – une compagnie puissante – une avertissement qui fait de l'effet – on pensera que la soci t a les m mes traits …

C

TV advert for petrol
frequently on TV in 90s
image of a tiger, outdoors, running – powerful, strong, beautiful animal
people admired – paid attention
effective because became image of company

EVALUATING SAMPLE ANSWERS

b 🎧 Listen to three different speakers starting to answer the Part 2 task above. Thinking about the general assessment criteria and the strategy points above, decide which speaker gives the best performance and why.

EXAM PRACTICE

c Now take one minute to make notes on the task in Exercise 3. Then speak on this topic for two minutes. Record yourself, then listen to check if your talk is easy to follow.

ROUNDING OFF QUESTIONS AND SHORT ANSWERS

▶ Module E page 62

3 At the end of your long turn, you may be asked one or two rounding off questions.

- Listen for the tense in the question(s).
- Give short answers rather than long ones.
- Use idiomatic language where possible.
- Don't worry if the examiner doesn't ask you any rounding off questions.

🎧 Now listen to three possible rounding off questions. For each one, tick the best answers from a–c.

1 a) No, I never tried it.   b) No.   c) Can't remember.
2 a) Yes.   b) I doubt it.   c) Dunno.
3 a) Not sure.   b) No.   c) Occasionally, but not often.

Part 3 Discussion (4–5 minutes)

▶ Module E page 63
▶ Module F page 79
▶ Module H page 98
▶ Module I page 116

4 In Part 3, the examiner will develop the topic of Part 2 to a more abstract level. The aim is to help you to explore the topic. To do this the examiner will ask you a series of questions. Listen carefully to the questions. (Ask for clarification if you don't understand.)

- Notice what time period you are being asked about.
- Use expressions that give you time to think.
- Give reasons for your opinions.
- Try to explore the topic, rather than simply answering questions.
- Give extended answers.

EVALUATING SAMPLE ANSWERS

a Read questions 1–3 below and think about how you would answer them.

> 1 Some people think advertising can be dangerous. Would you agree or disagree with that?
> 2 Do you think that governments should use laws to protect people from advertising?
> 3 How will people be able to resist advertising in the future?

b 🎧 Now listen to a candidate answering the questions. Decide how well the speaker responds to the questions.

EXAM PRACTICE

c Now answer questions 1–3 yourself. Record yourself if you can. Listen to your recording and think about how you could improve.

d 🎧 Listen to three further questions. Pause the recording to give yourself time to answer each one.

1 Topic vocabulary overview
Module J (*Focus on IELTS* Units 19 and 20) was about the way things and people look, how our appearance is controlled by our genes, and how the things we see can be recorded on film.

a Complete the diagrams below. (All the words are found in *Focus on IELTS* Units 19 and 20 and/or Module J.)

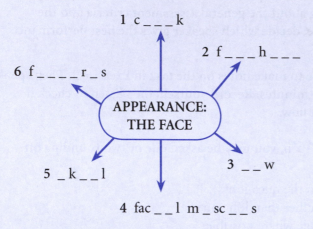

1 c _ _ _ k
2 f _ _ _ h _ _ _
6 f _ _ _ _ r _ s
APPEARANCE: THE FACE
5 _ k _ _ l
3 _ _ w
4 fac _ _ l m _ sc _ _ s

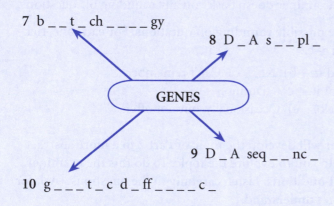

7 b _ _ t _ ch _ _ _ _ gy
8 D _ A s _ _ pl _
GENES
9 D _ A seq _ _ nc _
10 g _ _ _ t _ c d _ ff _ _ _ _ c _

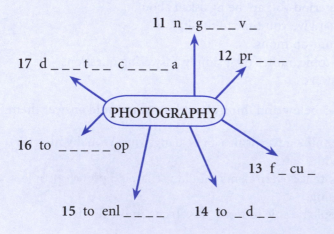

11 n _ g _ _ _ v _
12 pr _ _ _
17 d _ _ _ t _ _ c _ _ _ _ a
PHOTOGRAPHY
16 to _ _ _ _ _ op
13 f _ cu _
15 to enl _ _ _ _
14 to _ d _ _

b Now complete these extracts using words and expressions from the completed diagrams. You will need to put them in the correct form.

Speaking Part 3: Changes in photography

> **Examiner:** So how is photography different now from in the past?
> **Candidate:** Well, it's hard to be sure, but, well, I think the **1** .... is making a big difference, because you don't have to send your film away to be **2** .... , you can do it at home on your computer … so you can **3** .... the pictures yourself – to improve the colour or the composition for example, or **4** .... them if you want bigger pictures, then either make **5** .... , or just e-mail them to your friends. And so you've got much more control over how the picture turns out.

Listening Part 4: New directions in science

> **6** .... relates the study of biological processes to technology. It has important applications in many fields. One of them is forensic science. Scientists are now trying to match particular **7** .... , such as eye and hair colour, to specific **8** .... If this could be done, it would allow forensic scientists to predict someone's appearance from one **9** .... – collected from a trace of blood left by a criminal, for example.

Reading: Neanderthal man

> Neanderthals are thought to have died out around 28,000 years ago. Unlike modern man, Neanderthals had a low sloping **10** .... with a prominent ridge above the eyes. The size of the **11** .... indicates that their brain was of an equivalent size to that of humans, but analysis of DNA extracted from fossil remains shows important **12** .... between Neanderthals and modern man, and suggests that we do not descend directly from them.

c Look back through the units and add more words to the diagrams.

2 Describing a picture

In Task 1 of the Writing module, you may have to describe a picture of an object or objects. This may involve describing and comparing shapes and sizes.

Diagram A: Cross-section of a picture frame

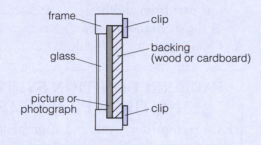

Diagrams B and C: Front view of two picture frames

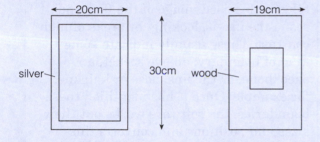

a Each of these sentences has one mistake in grammar. Find the mistakes and correct them. Use the diagrams to help you.

☐ The frame shown in diagram C is also rectangular, and it is approximate the same size, but it is made of wood instead of silver.

☐ The frame shown in diagram B is rectangle in shape.

☐ The frame itself has quite narrow, leaving a large space for the picture inside, and it is made of silver.

☐ A picture frame is consists of three main parts: the frame itself, the glass and the backing.

☐ However, this frame is much more wider than the first one, so the space left inside for the picture is only a fraction of the size of that in diagram A.

☐ The backing, which may be made of wood or cardboard, held in place by two clips, one at the top and one at the bottom.

☐ It is therefore clear that the first frame would be use for a large picture, while the second would be suitable for a small picture.

☐ Its overall high is 30 cm, and its overall width is 20 cm.

☐ The glass fits inside the frame and covering the picture or photograph.

b Now number the sentences in order to make a description of the diagrams, and decide how they should be divided up into paragraphs.

c Finally, cover up the sentences and write your own description of the diagrams. Then compare with the version in the answer key.

3 Language of research

Passive verb forms may be used in sentences describing research methods and research findings.

a Complete these sentences using the correct past tense form (active or passive) of the verb in brackets.

1 The results .... little insight into the causes of the problem. (give)

2 Later on, the same techniques .... to a new set of data. (apply)

3 The research .... in the identification of several key factors. (result)

4 The correlation between these two sets of figures .... (investigate)

5 Over 1,000 results .... , although not all of them were used in the analysis. (record)

6 When the figures were analysed, the results .... that the scientists' previous conclusions were mistaken. (suggest)

7 The findings .... conclusive evidence that the original theory was correct. (provide)

8 For several weeks, the researchers .... through the data looking for any significant patterns. (sift)

9 The importance of the discoveries .... by the amount of media attention that they received. (reflect)

b Read your completed sentences and decide whether each sentence relates to a) or b) below.

a) how the research was carried out

b) what was found out from the research

135

1 Vocabulary

Read the pairs of sentences below and put a tick (✓) if they mean the same thing and a cross (✗) if they are different. Underline any phrases which make the meanings different.

1 a) The research project was wound down in 2003.
   b) The research project was completed in 2003.

2 a) The cost of fuel is rapidly diminishing.
   b) There has been a rapid escalation in the cost of fuel.

3 a) The book does not discuss the role of environmental factors.
   b) The book does not discuss the part played by environmental factors.

4 a) The shopkeepers' income from the souvenir trade is dwindling.
   b) The shopkeepers' income from the souvenir trade is shrinking.

5 a) The results of the experiment were not conclusive.
   b) The experiment was not completed.

6 a) Researchers have not made much progress in finding a cure for the common cold.
   b) Researchers have made little headway in finding a cure for the common cold.

7 a) The rise in tourist revenue is partly accounted for by the improved tourist facilities in the area.
   b) The improved tourist facilities in the area partly explain the rise in tourist revenue.

8 a) Recent anecdotal evidence suggests that younger people are travelling more than ever before.
   b) Evidence from recent research suggests that younger people are travelling more than ever before.

9 a) As far as your appearance goes, your genes don't tell the whole story.
   b) Your appearance is not completely controlled by your genes.

10 a) The figure shows a cube with sides of 5 cm.
   b) The diagram shows a square whose sides are 5 cm in length.

2 Reading: Flow chart completion

a Read the text below and find words or phrases which mean:

1 the idea on which something is based   ....

2 a line which divides one part from another   ....

3 of the surrounding area   ....

4 find (something) difficult   ....

FACE RECOGNITION SYSTEMS AND THEIR PROBLEMS

Face-recognition systems, often based on closed circuit television systems, have slightly different methods, but the principle is broadly similar. The software takes a digitised image of the face and scans the pixels, looking for areas of high contrast. These usually indicate some kind of boundary: an eye socket, a cheekbone, or the lips, nose or hairline, for example. Once it has identified these boundaries, the software works out their sizes and positions and converts this geometry into what is called a 'faceprint'. Photographs of known criminals are fed into the software and their faceprints are calculated too. Then the software can monitor live CCTV images for the faces of these people. When it discovers a match, it raises an alarm.

That's the theory, but in the real world it's not quite so simple. The ambient light level and the quality of image from the camera can affect the accuracy of the match. The angle at which the face is presented to the camera also matters: if the software can't find two eyes it will struggle to capture a faceprint at all. The number of images in the database also has an effect. Large numbers slow down the search for matches, or produce too many possible matches.

b Complete the flow chart on page 137. Choose NO MORE THAN THREE WORDS from the passage for your answer.

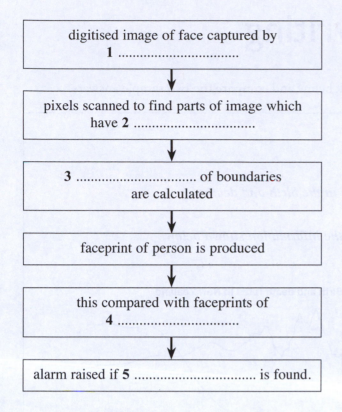

digitised image of face captured by **1** ....

↓

pixels scanned to find parts of image which have **2** ....

↓

3 .... of boundaries are calculated

↓

faceprint of person is produced

↓

this compared with faceprints of **4** ....

↓

alarm raised if **5** .... is found.

3 Speaking: Part 3

Complete the gaps in the candidate's response. The first letter of each word has been given.

Examiner: What changes do you think we might see in tourism in the coming years?

Candidate: Well, it's **1** h...................... to say. I mean, I think there are all sorts of different directions that tourism is moving in. For **2** e...................... , there's the whole **3** i...................... of space tourism, tourists going up into space, and **4** o...................... that's all very expensive and very high-tech. But on the other **5** h...................... , there's the idea of tourists **6** t...................... greater responsibility for the people and the **7** e...................... of the places they visit, and I think a lot of people are more **8** a...................... of things like eco-tourism and **9** s...................... tourism – you know, tourism which doesn't **10** u...................... up resources that can't be replaced.

4 Writing: Task 2

Read the task, which requires a thesis-led approach, and the sample answer below. Six sentences (a–f) have been removed from the answer. Decide on the best place for each of the missing sentences.

> *Some people believe that advances in technology designed to reduce crime, such as closed circuit television systems, invade the personal privacy of innocent people.*
>
> *To what extent do you agree or disagree?*

In recent years great strides have been made in the application of technology to the prevention of crime and the capture of criminals. (**1** ....) DNA testing means that a single flake of skin left at the scene of a crime can be matched against records held of suspects. (**2** ....)

As always with any type of scientific progress, concerns have been raised about the use of this technology. Some people would like to see much stricter controls put on the use of such developments, or even to see them banned completely. (**3** ....)

Firstly, these developments mean that genuine criminals can be apprehended more quickly and reliably. (**4** ....) In addition, the increased reliability of such techniques as DNA testing reduces the likelihood of innocent people being convicted and punished for crimes they did not commit. (**5** ....)

I appreciate that these techniques do to some extent affect the personal privacy of every member of society. (**6** ....)

a) A further point is that the existence of such techniques acts as a deterrent to potential criminals.

b) For example, CCTV systems and face–recognition software allow computer-based records to be kept of the faces of millions of people.

c) However, I feel that the positive uses to which they can be put, as outlined above, outweigh these dangers.

d) For example, instead of having to search manually through thousands of photographs, with all the possibility of human error that this involves, a computer-based search can be carried out in seconds.

e) I understand the reason for their concern, but feel that they are misguided for several reasons.

f) Soon it may be even possible to tell a criminal's appearance from a DNA sample.

137

Assessing your writing

Look at the Writing task below and compare the two sample answers.

WRITING TASK 1

You should spend about 20 minutes on this task.

The graph below gives information about changes in the birth and death rates in New Zealand between 1901 and 2101.

Write a report for a university lecturer describing the information shown below.

Write at least 150 words.

Birth and death rates in New Zealand

SAMPLE ANSWER A

The graph gives information about changes in the birth and death rates in New Zealand between 1901 and 2101.

In 1901 the birth rate was 20,000 and the death rate was 9,000. In 1961 the birth rate reached a peak of 66,000 while the death rate was 23,000. In 2001 there were 55,000 births and 38,000 deaths, and in 2061 there were 60,000 deaths and 48,000 births.

At the end of the period there were 58,000 deaths and 45,000 births.

Both the birth and death rates changed between 1901 and 2101. Perhaps this was because a lot of people did not want to have children.

(105 words)

ASSESSMENT

This is a weak answer which would score a low IELTS band. Problems:

- underlength
- introduction is copied from task
- no comparison between figures
- no focus on general trends
- no reference to the future (see projection on graph)
- conclusion tries to explain information rather than summarise it
- poor linking of ideas (only done by time markers)
- limited range of grammar and vocabulary

SAMPLE ANSWER B

> The graph shows changes in the birth and death rates in New Zealand since 1901, and forecasts trends up until 2101.
>
> Between 1901 and the present day, the birth rate has been consistently higher than the death rate. It stood at 20,000 at the start of this period and increased to a peak of 66,000 in 1961. Since then the rate has fluctuated between 65 and 50 thousand and it is expected to decline slowly to around 45,000 births by the end of the century.
>
> In contrast, the death rate started below 10,000 and has increased steadily until the present time. This increase is expected to be more rapid between 2021 and 2051 when the rate will probably level off at around 60,000, before dropping slightly in 2101.
>
> Overall, these opposing trends mean that the death rate will probably overtake the birth rate in around 2041 and the large gap between the two levels will be reversed in the later part of this century.

(166 words)

ASSESSMENT

This is a strong answer which would score a high IELTS band: Good points:

- fulfils criteria for length
- introduction is paraphrased.
- main sets of data are compared and contrasted
- clear focus on the different trends.
- important features of the graph, (e.g. cross-over point) included
- information summarised in conclusion
- well organised information
- range of linkers and referencing expressions
- good range of vocabulary and structures, used accurately

Task 2

Look at the Writing Task 2 in Module J on page 131. Compare the two sample answers below.

SAMPLE ANSWER A

> I agree that the image is becoming a more powerful way of communicating than the written word in the modern world. Firstly, pictures are beautiful and can make us pay attention. Everybody likes to look at images and they make our world colourful. And images can show things clearly. We can see the evidence for something with our own eyes. So images can tell us the truth. We can remember images more easily than we can remember words. And this is important for advertisers, for example. They like to use strong images to make people remember their products. In conclusion, there are images everywhere in our lives today and I agree that in the modern world the image is becoming a more powerful way of communicating then the written word.

(130 words)

ASSESSMENT

This is a weak answer which would score a low IELTS band. Problems:

- underlength
- introduction and conclusion are both copied
- power of the written word not considered
- ideas insufficiently organised, developed or supported
- no clear structure to the argument
- no paragraphing or signalling of stages
- limited range of linkers
- limited range of vocabulary and grammar

SAMPLE ANSWER B

In today's world, images in the form of photographs, films and pictures are used everywhere as a means of communicating with the public. I certainly agree that such images have become a very powerful means of communication and they are used in many different sectors to influence, inform and entertain the public.

The media, for example, use images to give detailed information and immediate impact to their news coverage. Similarly, advertising industries constantly use images to influence, persuade and make people identify with what they see. The powerful attraction of images is also evident in the entertainment industry and even in the growth in mobile phones that can send photos as part of a regular personal 'conversation'.

However, while it is evident that the image has certainly become a very powerful way of communicating, that it not to say that it has become more powerful than either the written or spoken word. Images can be interpreted in a range of different ways, and because of this they are rarely used alone. Captions, headlines and written explanations or spoken commentaries almost always accompany the use of images, whether they are used in advertising or the media. Used alone, the message of a picture can be notoriously misleading, and is less effective as a result.

In conclusion, therefore, I only partly agree with the statement. While it is true that images can send very powerful messages, they are only really effective as a means of communication when used together with either the written or spoken word.

(254 words)

ASSESSMENT

This is a good response which would score a high IELTS band. Good points:

- appropriate length
- relates the image to the written (and spoken) word
- clear opinion on the issues
- ideas well-supported and developed into an argument.
- clear summarising conclusion
- good organisation with clear paragraphing and logical links
- good range of vocabulary and grammar, accurately used

Now check your own written answers using the same criteria for assessment.

▶ Ideas for speaking and writing

The ideas and language in the reading and listening texts in this book can help you with other parts of the IELTS exam. Note down useful expressions from the texts and use them to help you answer the questions below, relating ideas from the text to what you already know about the subject.

S = Speaking. Use these questions for class disussion or to practise giving short talks on your own. Record yourself if possible.

W = Writing. Use these questions to practise writing. You could write a single paragraph or a full 250-word response.

MODULE B

Reading *Light years ahead*

S Why is solar power a good source of energy in countries like Uganda?

S W What are the drawbacks to using solar power as a source of energy in developing countries?

W What are fossil fuels and what problems are associated with them?

S What are the main sources of power in your country?

Listening *Wind-powered school*

S How is the school described in the listening similar to / different from your primary school?

S How enjoyable was your time at primary school? How useful was the education you received there?

S W How can children at primary school be made aware of global problems and issues such as pollution and energy sources?

MODULE C

Reading *Clocking cultures*

S W What variations are there in the way time is viewed in different cultures?

S W In what ways can different perceptions of time lead to misunderstandings between cultures?

S How can researchers find out about people's attitudes to time? What difficulties might they face?

S W In what ways do you think attitudes to time are changing in your country?

S Is there a difference in the pace of life in different parts of your country?

W What are the advantages and disadvantages for a society of living at a fast pace or a slow pace? (Think about efficiency, safety, health, etc.)

Listening *Sharing a flat*

S W What problems can there be when young people share accommodation? How can these problems be overcome?

MODULE D

Listening *Music course*

S W How is modern technology changing the way music is learned, played and enjoyed?

Reading *Fighting the dust*

S W What problems may be faced by those in charge of museums and historic buildings? How could scientists help with these problems?

S W What are the different functions that a museum can have (e.g. entertainment)? Do you think these functions are changing?

S W Museums, art galleries and other cultural institutions are expensive to set up and to run. How do you think they should be funded? Are they worth the money?

Listening *Art in Bali*

S W What is special about the attitude of the people of Bali to art and culture? How does this compare with your country?

S W How important do you think it is for great works of art or important buildings to be preserved in their original form?

MODULE E

Listening *Rotorua (New Zealand)*

S What is special about the area of Rotorua in New Zealand?

S W Which areas are the main tourist attractions in your country and why?

Reading *Eating up the* Titanic

S W What is unusual about the bacteria described in the reading text? In what ways are they harmful? How can they be useful?

S W Some people say that the *Titanic* should be left undisturbed as a memorial to those who died there. Others support the idea of raising the ship to the surface. What is your opinion?

MODULE F

Reading *The knowledge society*
S What is meant by the 'knowledge society'? How far does the situation described in the reading text apply to your country?
S W How far do you think that mental work will replace physical work in the next 20 years?
W 'Modern technology means that women can replace men in nearly all jobs.' How far do you agree? What does this mean for society?
S W What can be done to reduce stress in education and work?

Listening *Survey on computer facilities*
S What facilities do students need in order to study effectively? Which of these are most important? Which are most expensive?

MODULE G

Reading *Bridging the digital divide*
S W In what ways could providing computer training and equipment for the world's poor be more important than providing food?
S What types of technology do you use that your parents or grandparents were unfamiliar with?
S How is life in your country being affected by modern developments like mobile phones?
S W Some people say that older people are disadvantaged nowadays because they lack the ability to use technology confidently. How far do you agree? What could be done about this problem?

Listening *Radio broadcast*
S In what ways do animals (e.g. whales, elephants, dogs, monkeys, bees) communicate with one another or with people? Do you know of any research that has been done into animal communication?
S W Do you think that intelligent animals such as whales, elephants and chimpanzees should be treated differently from less intelligent ones?

MODULE H

Listening *Captive breeding*
S W What are the advantages and disadvantages of keeping animals in zoos?
S W Many scientists fear that large numbers of plant and animal species could become extinct in the near future. Why is this, and what can be done now to protect endangered species?

Reading *Genetically modified crops: accepting the inevitable?*
S W What are the main arguments for and against genetic modification of crops? What is your own opinion on this issue?
S Are genetically modified crops grown in your country? What do you think about this situation?
S W What other things can scientists do now that would have been considered unbelievable a hundred years ago? How far have these developments improved the quality of life for most people?
S W What developments do you expect to see in the next 50 years?

MODULE I

Reading *CUTE buses: a new direction for public transport*
S W Why is public transport so important? What is needed for a city's public transport system to be effective?
S W What other methods can be used to relieve congestion and pollution in city centres, apart from improving buses and bus services?
S W How might increases in traffic levels affect rural regions?
W People now expect easy and cheap transport for themselves and for the goods they consume. How can this be achieved? Is it a positive development?

Listening *Effects of tourism*
S How far does the model of tourism in the listening match the situation in your own country, or in other countries you know?
S Would you like to work in the tourism industry? Why/Why not?
S W In what ways can tourists have a positive or negative impact on the places they visit?
S W What responsibilities do tourists have in choosing a place to visit and in the way they behave when they arrive?

MODULE J

Listening *The first portraits*

S W Why do you think the first portraits were painted?

S W Some people say that photographs have replaced paintings as a way of portraying people. How far do you agree?

S W The remains of people who lived thousands of years ago may now be shown in museums around the world. How far do you think this is acceptable?

Reading *Getting the picture from DNA*

S How could the research described in the reading passage help in tracking down criminals? Are there any dangers in the way this research could be used?

S W In what other ways can science and technology help to control crime or catch criminals?

S Would you be interested in a career in forensics? Why/Why not?

S W Which of the following types of research do you think are most valuable? Which are least valuable? Why?

- sending people to other planets
- finding ways to allow people to live longer
- finding faster ways of travelling
- slowing down global warming
- discovering how the mind works
- finding a way of communicating with animals

Module E page 64, Focus on reading Exercise 2

a) .... an organisation that finds and gets back things which were lost or damaged, e.g. in a disaster

b) .... to eat or drink something

c) .... easily attacked or affected by something

d) .... the main part or body of a ship, made of wood or metal

e) .... easily broken

f) .... to go through something (e.g. the blood vessels permeate the body)

g) .... very small living creatures, such as bacteria and fungi

h) .... groups of bacteria that live together

i) .... metal pins used to fasten other pieces of metal together

j) .... the reddish-brown substance that forms on iron and steel when they get wet

▶ Answer keys

Focus on reading   page 8

1 a 1 Text 2   2 Text 1

2 a Text 1: Important words: *obesity* (*too much fat*) and
insulin (*a hormone which enables the body to store extra
calories as fat*)
Text 2: Important words: *convenience seekers* (*happy
heating up meals in the microwave*) and *casual diners*
(*people who skip breakfast and eat out … because they
can't be bothered to cook*)

b Text 1: Less important: *doughnuts* (no definition, but
context suggests this is an unhealthy snack food)
Text 2 Less important: *roast* (no definition, but context
suggests this is a traditional way of cooking meat in
Britain)

3 a 1 Just over one third of the total population of the <u>US</u> is
overweight.
2 <u>Asia</u> and <u>Europe</u> have an equal proportion of obese
children.
3 It is forecast that the proportion of overweight or
obese children in <u>China</u> will reach 20% in ten years'
time.
4 There is a downward trend in childhood obesity in
some <u>African towns and cities</u>.
5 <u>Insulin</u> levels rise sharply when foods with high levels
of starch, sugar and fat are eaten.
6 <u>Parents</u> play the most important role in improving
eating habits.

b 1, 2, 3, 4: A   5: B   6: C

c 1 NG (we are only given information about children
and adolescents)
2 F (Asia *lags behind* Europe in its obesity statistics)
3 T (10% are obese now, that percentage is expected to
have doubled in a decade)
4 F There is a (less marked) trend (i.e. rise in childhood
obesity) in urbanised areas of Africa.
5 T (fat … combined with sugars and starches can cause
surges in insulin levels)
6 NG (schools, health professionals, parents and
children have to work together)

4 b 1 b) a past participle   2 b) a change

c risen, remained constant, fallen

d 1 Spending on these foods has gone up by only six per
cent
2 Spending on

e 8 past participle   9 adjective   10–12 proportion/
fraction   13 infinitive   14 adjective

EXAM TASK
7 risen   8 remained constant   9 fewer   10 half
11 a quarter   12 a third   13 increase   14 smaller

Focus on writing 1   page 11

1 1 started a
2 fluctuated c
3 reached a peak b

4 increased, levelled off a
5 declined f
6 dipped, recovered d
7 stood c
8 overtook e

2

Movement upwards	Movement downwards	More than one movement	No movement
increase *Others:* rise, grow	decline *Others:* fall, drop, decrease	reach a peak, fluctuate, level off, dip, recover, overtake	start, stand *Others:* remain constant, finish

3 1 to   2 by   3 of   4 at   5 between   6 at

4 1 There has been a sharp fall in meat consumption.
2 Share prices dipped briefly at the start of the year.
3 There was a dramatic improvement in her fitness level.
4 Share prices will recover rapidly next year.
5 There has been a steady growth in the use of GM foods
in some countries.

Focus on writing 2   page 12

1 1 20 years, from 1983 to 2003
2 The percentage of club members who participated in the
different activities
3 Participation in swimming, team sports and gym
activities in the sports club.
4 Past tense: the period of time is finished
5 Most people did swimming in 1983, but team sports,
then gym were most popular in 2003. Participation in
gym and in team sports overtook participation in
swimming.

2 1 decreased   2 remained constant   3 reached a peak of
4 dropping   5 overtook   6 stood at   7 grew
8 levelling off at   9 dropped   10 rose

3 1 five
2 Paragraph 1 Introduction; Paragraph 2 Description of
participation in swimming, Paragraph 3 Team sports and
Paragraph 4 gym activities; Paragraph 5 Summary of the
trends
3 In contrast, Finally, Overall

4 a 1 Wrong tense   (3)
2 Active/passive verb confused   (2)
3 Agreement: single subject with plural verb   (1)
4 Preposition error   (3)
5 Article (*a, the*) missing   (1)

b The graph *shows* changes in participation *in* different
activities at a sports club.
Firstly, participation in swimming *decreased from* 1983 to
2003. In 1983 50% of club members *did* swimming but
only 15% *participated* in this in 2003. Secondly, the
percentage who *did* team sports *remained* constant
during that period.
Participation reached *a* peak in 1998. Finally, gym
activities *grew* from 1983 to 2003.

Focus on listening page 14

1 1 a student (Janet) and the manager of a sports centre
2 on the phone
3 a job
4 five

Audio script

You will hear a student called Janet talking on the phone to the manager of a sports centre about a job.
First you have some time to look at questions 1–5.

2 a three words
b a) a number: 6, maybe 7, 8
b) a time: 5
c) days of the week: 4

3 1 Days   2 Job responsibilities   3 Steve's direct line
4 Remember to bring   5 Job available

4 1 pool attendant
2 (the) equipment
3 water quality tests
4 Monday(s), Wednesday(s)
5 6 (p.m.), 10 (p.m.)
6 $19
7 Farndon Avenue
8 053210
9, 10 (*in either order*) application form, certificates

Audio script

You will hear a student called Janet talking on the phone to the manager of a sports centre about a job.
First you have some time to look at questions 1–5.
You will see that there is an example which has been done for you. On this occasion only, the conversation relating to this will be played first.

V1: Hello, White Water Sports Centre.
Janet: Hello, er, I wanted to enquire about a job at the centre.
V1: Right, I'll just put you through to the manager.
Steve: Hello, Steve Thompson speaking.

The manager's name is Steve Thompson, so *Steve Thompson* has been written in the space.
Now we shall begin. You should answer the questions as you listen because you will not hear the recording a second time. Listen carefully and answer questions 1–5.

V1: Hello, White Water Sports Centre.
Janet: Hello, er, I wanted to enquire about a job at the centre.
V1: Right, I'll just put you through to the manager.
Steve: Hello, Steve Thompson speaking.
Janet: Hello, er, my name's Janet Willis. Er, I'm looking for a part-time job and I saw an ad saying that you have some vacancies. I was wondering what sort of people you were looking for.
Steve: Well at present we're looking for a part-time pool

Janet: Oh, yes, I've spent the last three summers working for a children's summer camp, so I did a lot of pool supervision, and I'm actually a sports student – water sports is my special area.
Steve: OK, well no need to ask if you can swim then …
Janet: No, I'm certainly not afraid of the water. So what does the job at the pool involve?
Steve: You'd mainly be responsible for supervising the swimmers – we have to watch them all the time, obviously, in case of accidents, so you'd have regular shifts there.
Janet: OK.
Steve: Then as well as that, you'd have to look after the equipment that's used by the beginners' classes.
Janet: Right – and would I be involved in teaching them at all? I'd be quite interested in that.
Steve: Well, they have their own instructor, so that's not really part of the job. The attendant's job does involve taking regular water quality tests … but you wouldn't be involved in cleaning the pool or anything like that.
Janet: OK. And the ad said you wanted someone just twice a week.
Steve: Yes, that's right.
Janet: Can I choose which days?
Steve: Erm, well if you'd rung up earlier you could have done but I'm afraid it's got to be Mondays and Wednesdays – we've got someone for Tuesdays and Thursdays, and the weekends are already fully staffed. Is that going to be a problem for you?
Janet: No, that should be alright. And the ad said it was evening work, right?
Steve: Yes, you start at 6, and the pool closes at 9.30, but you wouldn't get away until 10 by the time you've checked the lockers and changing rooms.
Janet: Fine.

Before you hear the rest of the conversation, you have some time to look at questions 6–10.
Now listen and answer questions 6–10.

Janet: And how much do you pay?
Steve: The basic hourly rate is $15, but we'd go up to $19 for someone with the right qualifications.
Janet: Well I've got life-saving certificates and first aid qualifications.
Steve: Oh, with that and your experience you'd probably get the maximum rate then. Obviously, you'd have to come along for an interview, if you're interested?
Janet: Oh it sounds just the job I'm looking for. Shall we fix a time for the interview now?
Steve: OK … er, it's Janet, isn't it?
Janet: Yeah, Janet Willis.
Steve: How about Friday morning, Janet? Around 11.00.
Janet: Oh sorry – I have lectures, but I could make the afternoon.
Steve: 2 p.m.?
Janet: Fine. And can I just check on where you are … is it Findon Avenue?
Steve: No, it's 23 – 27 *Farndon* Avenue, that's FARNDON, it's off East Gate.
Janet: East Gate … Fine. I'll look forward to meeting you, then.

Steve: Ok, so if you need to phone me before then, you can get through to me directly on 053210.

Janet: Is there anything I need to bring along to the interview?

Steve: Well, you do need to fill in an application form – I'll put one in the post for you, so can you fill that in and bring it along.

Janet: You don't want me to post it back to you?

Steve: No, just remember to bring it along with you.

Janet: What about references? Should I bring any?

Steve: No, but do have your certificates with you when you come, we need to see those.

Janet: Great. Thanks very much then, I'll see you on Friday. Bye.

Steve: Bye.

Focus on speaking page 16

1 a 1 What do you like to watch on TV?
   2 What do you do to keep fit?
   3 What do you like to cook?
   4 What kind of clothes do you like to wear?
  b Speaker A: 3 Speaker B: 2 Speaker C: 4 Speaker D: 1

Audio script

A: Nowadays I don't actually do much cooking. I nearly always eat in the student canteen. I hardly ever cook for myself these days. But when I was living at home, I used to help my mother with the cooking. I always used to make the salad and cook the pasta and so on.

B: Nothing special, I'm afraid. I mean, when I was younger I used to do quite a lot of running and things. When I was at school I did a bit of sport. But to be honest, now I just don't have the time.

C: I suppose I like to wear casual clothes. I hardly ever wear smart clothes in the evenings or at weekends – I have to wear smart things for work, so it's good to change into casual things. When I was at school, I always used to wear a uniform and I hated that.

D: It all depends. I always try to watch the news, and I like watching movies. I always used to watch the soaps, but now I find them really boring.

2 *Speaker A*
   1 Nowadays
   2 nearly always
   3 hardly ever, these days
   4 used to help
   5 always used to
   Speaker B
   1 I'm afraid
   2 used to do
   3 When I was at school

3 a a) I'm afraid
     b) I mean
     c) actually
     d) to be honest
     e) and so on
     f) Well, I suppose
  b *Possible answers*
     1 I'm afraid 2 to be honest 3 actually 4 and so on

Audio script

A: What do you do to keep fit?
B: Not much, I'm afraid. I don't really like doing any kind of exercise, to be honest. Of course, I had to do some when I was at school, and I used to be quite good at football, actually. But these days, I'd rather spend my time studying or reading and so on.

Language review A page 18

1 a 1 sports centre 2 energy expenditure 3 physical exercise 4 training programme 5 competitive sports 6 intake of fat and sugar 7 a balanced diet 8 dairy products 9 fruit and vegetable consumption 10 sensible eating habits 11 a global epidemic 12 long-term benefits 13 insulin levels 14 childhood obesity 15 heart disease
  b 1 physical exercise 2 sports centre 3 training programme 4 competitive sports 5 sensible eating habits 6 balanced diet 7 fat and sugar 8 fruit and vegetable consumption 9 dairy products 10 insulin levels 11 heart disease 12 childhood obesity 13 global epidemic

2 1 events (football matches and horse races)
   2 responsibilities (answering the phone and dealing with customer queries)
   3 activities (housework, gardening)
   4 factors (exercise and diet)
   5 trends (the move towards ready-made meals and the increasing popularity of snack foods)
   6 functions (breathing and digestion)
   7 benefits (physical fitness and social contacts)
   8 developments (changes in transport and the nature of work)
   9 products (televisions and cars)
   10 sectors (fast food and specialist food)

3 a 1 The graph shows changes in the amount of fresh fruit, sugar and ice-cream eaten per person per week in Britain between 1975 and 2000.
     2 People consumed more fresh fruit than either sugar or ice-cream throughout the period.
     3 In 1975, the consumption of fresh fruit stood at 500 grams, then increased to 600 grams in 1980.
     4 Although it dipped in 1985, it then rose steadily and reached 750 grams in 2000.
     5 In contrast, there was a consistent drop in sugar consumption.
     6 The amount consumed decreased steadily from almost 400 grams per person to only 100 grams by 2000.
     7 The amount of ice-cream consumed weekly started at about 50 grams.
     8 However, this gradually increased throughout the period.
     9 By 2000 it was at the same level as the consumption of sugar.
     10 From the graph we can see that overall, the consumption of fruit rose, while the consumption of sugar fell.
     11 In addition, the consumption of ice-cream, while at a relatively low level, rose significantly during this period.

b The graph shows changes in the amount of fresh fruit, sugar and ice-cream eaten per person per week in Britain between 1975 and 2000.

People consumed more fresh fruit than either sugar or ice-cream throughout the period. In 1975, the consumption of fresh fruit stood at 500 grams, then increased to 600 grams in 1980. Although it dipped in 1985, it then rose steadily and reached 750 grams in 2000.

In contrast, there was a consistent drop in sugar consumption. The amount consumed decreased steadily from almost 400 grams per person to only 100 grams by 2000.

The amount of ice-cream consumed weekly started at about 50 grams. However, this gradually increased throughout the period. By 2000 it was at the same level as the consumption of sugar.

From the graph we can see that overall, the consumption of fruit rose, while the consumption of sugar fell. In addition, the consumption of ice-cream, while at a relatively low level, rose significantly during this period.

c 1 Although there was a dip in 1985, this was followed by a steady rise to 750 grams in 2000.
2 However, there was then a gradual increase …
3 Overall, there was a rise in the consumption of fruit, while the consumption of sugar fell.
4 There was a steady decrease in the amount consumed from almost 400 grams per person to only 100 grams by 2000.

4 1 ✓ 2 ✓ 3 ✓ 4 growth 5 ✓ 6 ✓ 7 fluctuation
8 recovery 9 ✓ 10 ✓

MODULE B

Focus on reading page 20

1 a 1 a power shortage 2 in Uganda 3 cheap solar panels 4 they are 'a hard sell' (i.e. they are difficult to sell)

c Paragraph B: Sunshine Solutions – Mr Kajubi's company
Paragraph C: BioDesign – British company set up by Graham Knight (retired inventor)
Paragraph E: Andrew Simms – expert from New Economics Foundation, London
Paragraph F: World Bank – often involved in large-scale projects (+ World Bank representative)

2 a 1 Paragraph C 2 Paragraph C 3 Paragraph D
4 Paragraph D 5 Paragraph E 6 Paragraph E
b 1 E 2 B 3 G 4 C 5 A 6 H

3 1 better
2 cheaper
3 the majority
4 in the long term
5 small-scale projects
6 enterprises
7 are more successful
8 damage to the environment

4 a A: B, D, H B: C C: E, G D: F
b 7 A 8 C 9 A 10 D 11 B 12 C 13 A

Focus on listening page 23

1 *Key words:*
1 School, first opened
2 fewer pupils, now, past
3 teacher, proud, energy
4 teacher believes, primary pupils, study problems
5 meals, unusual

2 1 – question 1 (first opened) 2 – question 2 (fewer pupils in the school now) 3 – question 3 (provided with energy from) 4 – question 5 (meals at school)
5 – question 5 (unusual)

3 1 B 2 C 3 A 4 B 5 A

Audio script

You will hear the head teacher of an English primary school talking about the school to a group of parents and visitors. First you have some time to look at questions 1–5.
Now listen carefully and answer questions 1–5.

Good morning everyone and as the Head Teacher of Cranley Hill Primary School I'm very happy to welcome you to our Open Day. Today the school is open not just to parents of our pupils, but also to anyone else interested in seeing the school. I'll start by telling you about the school, and after that you can walk round and see it for yourselves. We take most of our pupils from the two nearby villages of Seaborne and Milthorpe. These were once coal mining villages – there have been coal mines here since the 1830s. When the school was originally established, way back in 1899, almost every child's father worked in the mines. However, the coal mines were closed in 1983, and many people left the area as a result. Nowadays most of the remaining inhabitants tend to commute to work in the city rather than working locally. At present, the number of students on our rolls is just 90, compared to almost 200 in 1985, due to the decline in the population of the mining villages, and the staff see this as a big bonus because we know each student personally.
The school is very involved in the local community and we are especially proud of our status as Great Britain's first school to be entirely powered by wind energy. This project began several years ago when it was decided that a wind power turbine should be installed in the school field. This now supplies the school with all the electricity we need and there is also power left over for the villages near by – the opposite situation to that in the past, when it was the villages which supplied the school with power in the form of coal from the mines.
The project has been of enormous benefit to the school in other ways as well. It has allowed exciting learning opportunities about electricity generation and the turbine has also inspired poetry, art and even our own song. It also allows teachers to introduce global issues such as CO_2 emissions and global warming to the students. I feel it may be irresponsible to burden young children with worries about global issues which are insoluble – but by actually using wind power as a nonpolluting, renewable source of energy, instead of using fossil fuels such as oil or gas, we are offering practical solutions to our pupils in their own environment.

The school is also extremely involved in other environmental issues. In the last few years we have developed our school field into what we now call our 'secret garden', which you will have a chance to explore shortly. Here the pupils have their own organic vegetable patch, and another special feature of the school is that the vegetables grown here are used in the school kitchens for school lunches, with any extra ones being taken home by the children to share with the community.

4 1 north   2 Number 6   3 Number 7   4 play area
5 vegetable patch   6 Number 10   7 wind turbine

5 6 F   7 E   8 H   9 D   10 G

Audio script

Before you hear the rest of the talk, you have some time to look at questions 6–10.
Now listen and answer questions 6–10.

Now, I'd just like to tell you some of the things to look out for as you go round the school site. At present we're standing just at the front entrance to the school, facing north, and as you can see the ground slopes up quite steeply behind the school. To our right we have the car park, OK? And to our left we have our sports field – this is just for training and informal games, we use the village football field for our under-eleven matches. At the far end of the car park is our recycling centre; this is for things like paper, glass and so on and everyone is very welcome to make use of it. Immediately behind the school, to the north, we have the play area – unfortunately we had to remove the play equipment, the climbing frame and so on, because it didn't conform to safety regulations. But we do have the tree house in the middle of that area – that's very popular. Then at the top end of the play area, you'll find the entrance to the secret garden. The vegetable patch is in the bottom corner, and beyond it, hidden in the trees, we have a pond. The children love this because it attracts all sorts of wildlife: frogs, fish and lots of birds. I should just mention the trees; there are over 30 different species, all planted by the children. In the middle of the garden we have what we call the storyteller's chair, and this is where the children come with their teachers and sit on the grass to listen to stories. And finally, at the top end of the secret garden, to the left, is our wind turbine – and as you go round the classrooms you'll find lots of work done by the children explaining all about how it works and how proud they are of it.
Right, now before we …

Focus on writing   page 25

1 1 *Horizontal axis:* three different employment sectors
Bars: three different countries (Japan, Brazil and India)
2 percentage of the workforce employed
3 differences – no time progression
4 No – this is the language of change, but no changes are shown in the data
5 Japan and Brazil have similar patterns, whereas India is very different with a more important agricultural sector.
6 comparatives and superlatives

2 1 highest/largest   2 more, fewer   3 as many, as
4 most   5 majority   6 lowest proportion
7 largest/highest   8 more developed, a larger percentage

3 1 the largest percentage of, the majority of
2 the workforce, the working population
3 the same number of
4 the lowest percentage of, the fewest

4 1 compares (*presents* is less appropriate here; *gives information about* is the same as the rubric)
2 proportion of the workforce (the first option is in the rubric; *majority of workers* is less accurate)
3 agricultural, industrial and service sectors (the first option is same as the rubric; *different industrial sectors* is misleading as 'industrial' is a separate sector)
4 three economically different countries (contains most accurate information)

5 1 highest proportion/largest percentage   2 the fewest
3 equal number   4 the majority   5 lowest percentage / smallest proportion

6 A (not B because this tries to explain the data, rather than describing it)

7 First of all   But while …   In contrast   Overall / In conclusion

8 1 introduction
2 trends
3 tenses
4 summarising
5 150

9 a Figures must be part of a sentence grammatically, so they can be attached with the preposition *with*. Otherwise, they must be added in brackets to show they are outside the sentence.
b 1 Brazil has the same proportion of workers in the agricultural and industrial sectors, *with* 25% in each. / Brazil has the same proportion of workers in the agricultural and industrial sectors *(25% in each)*.
2 In Brazil and Japan the majority of workers *(50% and 61%, respectively)* work in the service sector.
3 Japan has the most workers in the industrial sector and the fewest in the agricultural sector *with* 32% and 7%, *respectively*.
4 India has the fewest workers in the service sector *with* 27%.
5 The lowest proportion of Indian workers *(11%)* are in the industrial sector.

10 a 1 Misuse of comparative/superlative forms (3)
2 Active/passive verb confused (1)
3 Incorrect punctuation (1)
b India has *the* highest proportion of workers in the agricultural sector and Brazil has more workers in this sector *than* Japan.
India has the fewest workers in the industrial sector, *while* Japan has the most.
61% of Japanese workers *are* employed in the service sector. Brazil has fewer employees in this sector, and the proportion in India is *the* lowest of all three countries.

Focus on speaking page 28

2 a The speaker uses 1, 3, 4, 6, 7, 9, 10 and 11

Audio script

Well I'd prefer to live in a city because I think it's much more exciting. There are more shops, and the streets are busier. There's more to do in the evenings, so you can have much more fun. On the other hand, I think living in a village is probably much healthier. There's less pollution – and life is much quieter, of course.

b 1 well, I'd prefer to 2 because 3 on the other hand

4 1 completely different 2 much bigger 3 a lot more 4 as high as 5 far less 6 much smaller 7 a lot warmer

Audio script

Yes they're completely different. People in the past used to live in much bigger houses because a lot more people lived together then. They weren't as high as buildings are now, of course, and they were far less comfortable to live in. Nowadays people tend to live in flats which are much smaller, but they're a lot warmer, with central heating and running water and so on …

5 1 ~~a lot~~ 2 ~~completely~~ 3 ~~totally~~ 4 ~~far~~ 5 ~~much~~ 6 ~~very~~ 7 ~~a lot~~

Audio script

I think that probably a lot of buildings were more or less the same in my grandparents' day – except they looked a great deal newer then, of course! Maybe the older ones looked much darker – you know, because the cities were really polluted with smoke and things then. But I think the high rise buildings are very different. They are far higher than anything in the past, and they're built with totally new materials now …

Language review B page 30

1 a 1 urban 2 densely 3 financial 4 congestion 5 rural 6 land 7 agriculture 8 crops 9 irrigation 10 standard 11 developed 12 wages 13 literacy 14 prosperity 15 developing 16 expectancy 17 poverty 18 facilities 19 birth

b 1 agriculture 2 crops 3 fertile land 4 irrigation 5 densely populated 6 urban areas 7 good wages 8 living 9 literacy 10 expectancy

2 1 enterprises, schemes 2 built, constructed 3 obstacles, stumbling blocks 4 low-tech, unambitious 5 associations, organisations 6 abandon, desert 7 a high proportion of, the majority of

3 a 1 far higher 2 much more 3 more or less the same as 4 slightly more 5 significantly greater 6 rather less 7 far more 8 far larger 9 significantly higher 10 rather better

b quantity, figures, proportion, amount, percentage

4 a *Money and business:* budget, costs, distribution, trade, investment, loan, marketing, sales, subsidies, profit, cash
Energy and resources: clockwork, coal, fossil fuels, gas, oil, renewable, solar power, electricity, wind power

b 1 loans, profit
2 oil, fossil fuels
3 cash, costs
4 renewable
5 subsidies (the word *subsidy* is often used to refer to monetary assistance from a government)
6 solar power, wind power

c *Setting up a business:* Sentences 3, 5, 1
Energy resources: Sentences 4, 2, 6

PROGRESS CHECK 1 (MODULES A AND B)

1 1 ✓ 2 ✗ (*fluctuated* = several changes, *slight dip* = one change) 3 ✗ (*recovered* suggests they regained an earlier level, *peak* suggests this was the highest point they reached) 4 ✓ 5 ✓ 6 ✗ (40 % is under/almost half) 7 ✗ (*setting up* does not include running costs)
8 ✗ (*low intensity* is the opposite of *vigorous/high intensity*) 9 ✓ 10 ✗ (*supervising* means watching, not cooking)

2 a 1 T 2 NG 3 F 4 NG 5 NG 6 F
b 1 a 2 b 3 b 4 a

3 1 while 2 In contrast 3 compared with 4 higher 5 lower 6 smallest 7 Overall 8 indicates 9 main 10 but 11 higher 12 than

4 1 c 2 d 3 b 4 a

MODULE C

Focus on reading page 34

1 b a) according to researchers and their findings

2 a Paragraph A Sentence 2 reflects the main idea;
Paragraph B Sentence 1 reflects the main idea
b *Suggested answers*
C … pace-of-life studies; … he concluded that the five fastest-paced countries are …
D … time perceptions in Trinidad; … the connections between power and waiting time …
E The complex nature of time makes it hard for anthropologists and social psychologists to investigate.
F … the ideas of associating time with money …
G … differences in how they visualise it from a more theoretical perspective

3 a 1 but
2 a) tells us b) personal
b 1 B – iii
2 C – vi
3 D – viii
4 E – ii
5 F – v
6 G – ix

4 a 1 Edward Hall Paragraph B
2 Robert Levine Paragraph C
3 Kevin Birth Paragraphs D, E, F, G
4 Trinidad Paragraphs D, F (Trinidadians)

149

b 1 parallel
2 different (*fulfil a request* means actually doing something)
3 parallel
4 parallel
5 different (*surveying* means asking questions of some sort)
6 parallel
c 7 C 8 B 9 A 10 A 11 B

5 12 arrow 13, 14 pattern, wheel (*in either order*)

Focus on listening page 38

1 1 Spurrock 2 North 3 freshfood@adders.co.uk
4 45 Castle Hill 5 Serena 6 Cliffe House 7 Glenn Ledbeatter 8 33 9 0234 735 733 10 14th May

Audio script
1 **A:** I live on Spurrock Street.
B: Could you spell that for me?
A: Yes, that's SPURROCK Street.
2 **A:** The house is in North Drive.
B: Northern …?
A: No, *North* Drive.
3 The e-mail address is freshfood – that's all one word – at adders – spelled ADDERS – dot co dot uk.
4 **A:** The address is 45, Castle Hill.
B: Was that 54, Castle Hill?
A: No, 45.
5 **A:** My name's Serena Jones.
B: Salina Jones?
A: No, my first name's spelled SERENA.
6 The company is based in Cliffe House – that's Cliffe with an e at the end.
7 **A:** Could you give me your name, please?
B: Certainly, it's Glenn – that's spelled with a double n – Ledbeatter, that's LEDBEATTER.
8 The total cost is $38 – oh, sorry, I can't read my own writing – it's $33.
9 The number's 0234 735788 – oh, sorry, that's 733 at the end.
10 **A:** I'll be arriving next Tuesday – that's the 13th of May, isn't it?
B: No, it's the 14th actually.

2 **a** three
b 1 people interested in sharing the flat
2 three
3 row by row
c 1 Description
2 Special requirements
3 Description
4 Description
5 Special requirements
6 Job

3 1 (a) sports 2 energetic 3 (a) big room 4 Spencer
5 hardworking 6 (an) engineer 7 competitive, stressed
8 bicycle 9 0777 687 2433 10 28th September / September 28th

Audio script
You will hear a conversation between two flatmates, Craig and Don, who are looking for a third person to share their flat.
First you have some time to look at questions 1–5.
You will see that there is an example which has been done for you. On this occasion only, the conversation relating to this will be played first.

Don: Hi, Craig. Been home long?
Craig: Yeah, quite a time.
Don: Did anyone phone about renting the spare room?
Craig: Yeah, we've had three phone calls about it.
Don: Really?
Craig: Yeah, do you want to hear about them?
Don: Sure.
Craig: Right. The first one was called Phil Parrott.

The name of the first person who phoned was Phil Parrott so *Parrott* has been written in the space.
Now we shall begin. You should answer the questions as you listen because you will not hear the recording a second time. Listen carefully and answer questions 1–5.

Don: Hi, Craig. Been home long?
Craig: Yeah, quite a time.
Don: Did anyone phone about renting the spare room?
Craig: Yeah, we've had three phone calls about it.
Don: Really?
Craig: Yeah, do you want to hear about them?
Don: Sure.
Craig: Right. The first one was called Phil Parrott.
Don: Uh-huh.
Craig: He's a teacher; he's just qualified, and he teaches sports.
Don: OK.
Craig: Actually I'm not sure about him. He certainly sounded energetic, but he asked lots of questions about whether we smoked, and what sort of food we cooked.
Don: Yeah, I mean we don't exactly live on pizza and chips and takeaways, well, not quite, but …
Craig: … but he might be a bit too health-conscious to really fit in with the sort of life we lead. Yeah. And he asked a lot of questions about the room … he said he needs a big room because he's got lots of sports equipment.
Don: Well, that's OK, the room's quite big but I'm not so sure about him … what about the second one?
Craig: He was called David Spencer.
Don: Spender?
Craig: No, Spencer – cer. He works at Cooper-Long – you know, the big company on Broad Street. He said he was a lawyer …
Don: Oh, I'd have thought in that case he'd be earning enough to rent his own place. I wonder why he wants to share a flat.
Craig: Well, he didn't say. He's quite a bit older than us. He did say he's just moved down here from the north of England. He seemed very quiet, actually. Maybe he wants to meet some new people. I got the impression he was a hardworking kind of person who doesn't go out all that much …

Don: Right.

Craig: But he sounded OK. Oh, one thing though, he said he wouldn't be staying in the flat at the weekends so he wants to pay reduced costs for gas and electricity … because he's only here five days out of seven.

Don: Oh, I'm not sure about that … what do you think?

Craig: Well, I suppose it's fair but it all sounds a bit complicated.

Before you hear the rest of the talk you have some time to look at questions 6–10.

Now listen and answer questions 6–10.

Craig: Anyway, there was a third person, Leo Norris.

Don: Yes.

Craig: He's an engineer.

Don: Oh, yeah?

Craig: And he's about our age.

Don: Right. What did he sound like?

Craig: Well, actually he was really funny, I couldn't stop laughing when I was talking to him. He *said* he was very lazy and never got up until noon at weekends and I said that wouldn't be a problem here …

Don: No, certainly not.

Craig: But actually I suspect he was joking when he said he was lazy … I think he lives life as it comes, he's certainly not competitive or stressed, but he likes cycling and things like that. He sounds like an outdoor type. Anyway, I thought he sounded as if he'd fit in. He wanted to check if there was somewhere safe for his bicycle … that's not a problem …

Don: No, he can leave it in the garage with my car. So did you get his contact details?

Craig: Yes, he left his mobile number, it's 0777 687 2433.

Don: And does he want to move in straight away?

Craig: Well, he's paid his rent in his present place up to the 31st of September, but he said that if possible he'd like to move in a bit before then – he said the 28th of September.

Don: And he was OK about the rent?

Craig: Yeah, he said it was fine.

Don: Right. So shall we give him a ring and see if he wants to come round and …

Focus on speaking page 39

1 a 1 shy 2 funny 3 calm 4 selfish 5 hardworking
6 supportive 7 noisy 8 warm

b 1 *Positive meanings:* caring, sociable, funny, calm, considerate, hardworking, *quiet, warm, supportive

2 *Negative meanings:* stressed, *serious, selfish, lazy, noisy, shy, excitable, unfriendly, competitive
* Could be positive or negative depending on context.

c 1 a little, rather (*too* is also used, but this emphasises rather than softens the criticism)

2 really

2 1 Describe a person who is popular in your neighbourhood; explain why he/she is popular.

2 three others

3 1, 3 and 4 in present tense; 2 in past tense

3 a

Prompt 1	Prompt 2	Prompt 3	Prompt 4
Local doctor friend	Met him about 6 yrs ago at local health centre	Calm; quiet, gentle way of speaking; small person, big brown eyes; supportive great sense of humour: makes people laugh	Good doctor; appreciated; very kind, caring person; they all trust him

b 1 Yes

2 Yes

3 No – only two features (not required by the task)

4 Yes

5 Yes – she used a clear signal: *The reason why I think he is so popular is because …*

6 No – usually present simple, but also past simple for where/when they met; present simple for description

Audio script

Well, the person I'm going to tell you about is our local doctor. In fact, he's, um, also a friend of mine – quite a good friend, in fact. I met him in the very first week we moved to the area … 'cos we'd been living in the north before and had to move because of our jobs … and that's about six years ago … and well, I went along to register at the health centre, and he happened to be there, so he introduced himself as the doctor and we started chatting … and well, we became good friends straight away, really.

Um, I think what I liked about him in the first place was his calm. He's, um, quite a small person, with big brown eyes … and he has this wonderfully quiet, gentle way of speaking. I think this is really why he is such a good doctor, and he's very supportive when you're ill and things, which is very important of course, but he also has this great sense of humour … he can always make people laugh … even when they're not feeling well … so they start to feel better right away.

So, um, I suppose the reason why I think he is so popular is because he's a really good doctor, and he's appreciated for it, in the whole neighbourhood, really. I think everybody knows he's a very kind, caring person, so they all trust him – and feel lucky to have him as their doctor; like I do, really.

Focus on writing page 42

1 1 c

2 Whether you think the changes in lifestyles have been positive or negative.

2 a 1 It introduces the topic.

2 In paragraph 2 it introduces positive changes; in Paragraph 3 it introduces negative changes.

3 That changes have been positive; in the conclusion

b *Addition:* Furthermore, In addition
Contrast: On the other hand
Introducing examples: As evidence of this, For example
Concession: Nevertheless
Summing up: In conclusion, But overall
Cause and effect One reason for, as a result

c *Changes have been positive*
Evidence: improvements in healthcare, education, standard of living, less physical labour, large leisure industries
Changes have been negative
Evidence: impact on environment, stress from pressure in schools/workplaces, loss of social relationships, reduced family life, increased crime/divorce, loss of sense of community

3 1 *Subjective:* I think, I feel
  2 *Objective:* It is undeniable that, Some people believe that, it can also be argued that, there is evidence to suggest that, it is clear that

4 a 1 of 2 on 3 for 4 to 5 for 6 in
  b The impact of computers *on* working conditions has been good.
  In terms of the environment, however, the changes have been negative.
  Such changes have affected our world *in* a negative way.
  And even higher salaries cannot compensate *for* long working hours.
  There is no need *for* physical labour anymore, and people have more access *to* different activities than before.

Language review C page 44

1 a *Work:* patterns, conditions, to delegate, overworked, sick pay, workload, efficiency, pressure, multi-tasking, salaries
  Beliefs and opinions: values, priorities, attitudes, notions, expectations, perceptions, awareness, views

  b 1 higher standard of living 2 economic development 3 more leisure facilities 4 better living conditions 5 improved healthcare 6 modern technology 7 faster pace of life 8 family breakdown 9 higher stress levels 10 time pressure 11 tight schedules 12 lost sense of community

  c 1 perceptions 2 attitudes 3 expectations 4 values 5 notions/views 6 priorities 7 overworked 8 modern technology 9 time pressure 10 tight schedules 11 workload 12 delegate 13 efficiency 14 family breakdown 15 sense of community

2 1 a link 2 Dillon's argument 3 a connection between stress and heart disease 4 combination of 5 discovery of a new law of physics 6 a suspicion 7 Cartwright's findings

3 1 get to 2 show up late 3 come up with 4 wind down 5 take up 6 not a big deal 7 deal with 8 strikes me 9 sort out

4 1 their 2 which 3 This 4 that 5 it is 6 they 7 like 8 These 9 who 10 their 11 this

MODULE D

Focus on listening 1 page 46

1 1 Computer equipment Questions 7–8
  2 Knowledge or skills needed for the course Questions 1–3
  3 Assessment Question 10
  4 Dates of course Question 9

2 a three
  b 1 a 2 b 3 a 4 b 5 a 6 a

3 1 Questions 7 and 8
  2 7 a number 8 part of a computer 9 a date 10 a number

4 1–3 C, E, F (*in any order*)
  4–6 B, E, G (*in any order*)
  7 64/sixty-four
  8 (a) sound card
  9 (in/next/this) January
  10 6/six

Audio script

You will hear two university students talking about a music course. First you have some time to look at questions 1–3. Now listen and answer questions 1–3.

Graham: Josie, come in. How are you?
Josie: I'm good.
Graham: Can I get you a coffee or anything?
Josie: No, that's OK. I can't stay long, but you said you wanted to talk to me about that course I'm doing this semester. Music 103?
Graham: That's right. Actually I was a bit confused because I thought you were majoring in maths.
Josie: That's right, I am. I'm doing four maths modules this year. But it's an optional course – you just choose it if you're interested. And you can do it whatever department you're in. Why? Are you thinking about doing it?
Graham: Well, I'm not sure. What are the requirements?
Josie: What?
Graham: The course requirements … I mean, what do I need to know about music to be accepted on it? I do listen to a lot of music, everything from hip-hop and rap to classical, and I can sing, sort of …
Josie: Well, for a start, one special thing about this course is that it's distance learning – you don't actually have to be at the university to do it, and you don't have lectures. So you've got to be able to work on your own without someone telling you what to do all the time.
Graham: (surprised) Oh? Oh … no, that should be OK, I reckon. I'm more worried about the actual musical stuff. Like, I don't know how to read music.
Josie: That doesn't matter, they don't assume that. You'll learn as you go along. How's your maths?
Graham: Not too bad …
Josie: Right. Some of it's quite mathematical, so you really need to be strong there.
Graham: But you play the violin, don't you? I don't play anything.
Josie: You don't need to. What about computer skills? You're OK there?
Graham: Yes, reasonably. Does that matter?

Josie: Yes, I'd say they're essential. Like I said, it's all distance learning, so it's computer-based.

Before you hear the rest of the talk you have some time to look at questions 4–10.
Now listen and answer questions 4–10.

Graham: But what about lectures?

Josie: You don't attend any. It's all online. So lots of the students aren't here in Canada at all – they're studying from home all over the world – we've got someone from my group in Jamaica, and a couple from Taiwan … oh and some from Hong Kong as well.

Graham: So how does it work?

Josie: Oh, well there's a multimedia course website on the internet where you can listen … you can listen and watch at the same time, and of course you can do it at your own pace, so if you don't understand something you just go back, or if you want some more examples of the music, there are links there to things that you can listen to. There's quite a lot of theory, but it's all done through musical examples, so it's practical at the same time. Like in the last module I did, we looked at a bit of the music from the movie *Star Wars* – the Darth Vader theme, you know …

Graham: Oh, yeah …

Josie: Then we looked at a theme from Wagner's *Tristan and Isolde*. Do you know it? Written in the 1850s – and we could see there were all sorts of parallels between them. And that's a feature of the course: we often look at modern Hollywood themes to illustrate concepts in classical music.

Graham: Mmm, it sounds really interesting? Do you have a coursebook?

Josie: No, we don't use one. We're given a software programme called NotaAbilityLite and what it does is it presents what we write, the music we write, really clearly and it also allows us to play back any piece of music on our computer at home. But that's not all, we can write our own music, quite complex stuff for various instruments, and the programme plays it back to us.

Graham: Plays the actual music?

Josie: Yes, so it means that your computer is actually your own musical instrument! And we can even submit our finished pieces to our tutor by e-mail.

Graham: So you do need your own computer, obviously.

Josie: Yes, with at least 64 Megabytes of RAM.

Graham: That's OK. I've got 128.

Josie: And a CD-ROM, and a sound card, of course.

Graham: No problem. So how long is the course?

Josie: It's six months. There are two a year, so you could actually enrol for the next one if you wanted. It starts in January. I started last September and I finish in February.

Graham: And how many credits is it?

Josie: Three. In order to pass, you've got to do six assignments – I'm just doing my fourth one now – and take a final examination. Anyway, why don't you call round sometime and I'll show you the sort of things we do. You can even listen to some of my music!

Graham: That would be great. Well, thanks, Josie. Now, are you sure you don't have time for that coffee?

5 1 majoring, modules
   2 optional
   3 distance learning, lectures
   4 skills
   5 theory
   6 credits
   7 assignments, examination

Focus on speaking   page 48

1 1 e 2 h 3 g 4 f 5 i 6 d 7 a 8 c 9 b

2 **a** 1 b 2 c 3 a
   b Speaker A 5   Speaker B 2   Speaker C 6   Speaker D 3
        Speaker E 1   Speaker F 4

Audio script

A: I think I'd prefer to have a photograph of someone I know because paintings of people can be really different – more how the artist sees them.

B: About two weeks ago, actually. I went to one in London – showing a group of modern painters. I liked some of it, but not all.

C: Well, if it's a good one, then I'd much rather have a painting – I love landscapes, especially if they're colourful.

D: Oh, we have some great galleries and museums, but they're mainly in the big cities.

E: All kinds, I think. I suppose I like ceramics best – mainly because of their feel and texture.

F: It all depends. If you mean artwork for public places, then I think the local government should pay … but local people should have a choice about it.

3 1 I suppose I like ceramics best – <u>mainly because of their feel and texture</u>.
   2 I'd prefer to have a photograph of someone I know <u>because paintings of people can be really different</u> …
      In 1 *because of* is followed by a noun (*because of* + noun).
      In 2 *because* is followed by a clause (*because* + subject + verb, etc.).

Focus on reading   page 49

1 **a** B
   b 1 Paragraphs A–B
        2 Paragraphs C–E
        3 Paragraphs F–I

2 **a** Question 2: keeping historical items clean; time, expense
        Paragraph B: cleaning exhibits; time and money
        Question 3: small pieces broken from; Roskilde; vacuum cleaner bags
        Paragraph B: fragments; Roskilde; the vacuum cleaner bag
        Question 4: Ryhl-Svendsen; breakages; lost
        Paragraph B: Ryhl-Svendsen; breakage; disappearance
        Question 5: Brimblecombe; London's Tate Gallery; does not support the idea
        Paragraph C: Brimblecombe; London's Tate Gallery; is beginning to overturn that idea
        Question 6: Brimblecombe and Ryhl-Svendsen; microscope slides; analysis
        Paragraph C: Brimblecombe; microscope slides; analysed
        Paragraph D: Ryhl-Svendsen; analysed

Question 7: research findings; levels of dust; visitor; exhibits

Paragraph E: both studies indicated; dust levels; objects; visitors

Question 8: the most serious threat

Paragraph E: the biggest menace

Question 9: a significant component; Viking ships; visitors' jeans

Paragraph E: Viking ships; a noticeable proportion; visitors' jeans

b The word does not fit grammatically in the sentence.

c 1 (systematic) research
2 damage
3 (Viking) ships (not *1000-year-old ships* as this repeats information given by *ancient*.)
4 information
5 (the) outside
6 sticky patches
7 numbers
8 clothes
9 fibres

3 a Paragraphs G–I (Paragraph F also deals with solutions, but not those suggested by the researchers.)

b 10–13 A, C, F, G (Answers can be written on the answer sheet in any order.)

Focus on listening 2 page 52

1 a 1 Art in Bali
2 *First part:* historical events and their importance for art; *second part:* characteristics of Balinese art today

b a)

2 1 China   2 (the) ruling families   3 colonisation
4 tourism   5 everyday life   6 formal training
7 (the) fertility/rich soil   8 (the) religion   9 group
10 permanent

Audio script

You will hear part of a lecture on art and culture in the Indonesian island of Bali.

First you have some time to look at questions 1–10.

Now listen carefully and answer questions 1–10.

Last week we looked at the traditional art of Japan. In this week's lecture we're going to move south and look at the very special way in which art has developed in the beautiful island of Bali, which is now part of Indonesia. I'll begin by giving you a brief historical overview.

It's thought that the first inhabitants of Bali were farmers who arrived around 3000 BC … at the beginning of the Iron Age. They probably originally came from China, and in Bali they cultivated rice and built temples ornamented with wood and stone carvings and statues. The Hindu religion was introduced in the14th century AD, and this has remained the main religion on the island. This was an important period in the artistic development of the island, when sculptors, poets, priests and painters worked together in the service of the ruling families. Rather than painting everyday scenes, artists concentrated on narrative paintings illustrating the epic stories of Hinduism. Bali's rich natural resources have always made it an alluring goal for merchants, and from the 17th century onwards, Dutch ships visited the island to trade in spices and luxury goods. Gradually the old royal families lost their power, and eventually in 1906 the Dutch East Indies Company was founded and the island became a colony. In the 20th century, art then took on a very different role: as a tool accessible to everyone in the fight of the Balinese people against colonisation rather than as the property of a minority. Shortly after this, in the 1920s, stories of the beauty of the island of Bali began to spread around the world, and Balinese art underwent another vast transformation with the advent of tourism to the island. At first, this was only on a small scale, but it had important effects. Expatriate artists from Holland and Germany settled on the island bringing paper, Chinese ink and other new materials with them. They worked with local artists, encouraging them to experiment with concepts like naturalism, expressionism, light and perspective, as well as to move away from the traditional focus on narrative painting towards something closer to their own experience. When independence came in 1945, this desire for an art to match a new national identity became stronger and the traditional narrative paintings started to give way to scenes showing the everyday life of the Balinese people – harvests, market scenes and daily tasks – as well as the myths and legends of their history.

Many of the features that give this art its special place in the world today can be traced back to these historical roots. One feature that is rooted in the events of the last century is that today in Bali the production and the appreciation of art is not restricted to a minority – in fact there is a famous saying that in Bali, everyone is an artist. And it's not considered that to make art, or talk about art, any formal training is needed. Art is just produced as part of Balinese life. Even fruit salad is served with flowers strewn on top. One factor which has contributed to this productivity is Bali's fertility – over the centuries the rich soil and the fact that food and shelter are readily available has given the islanders the leisure to develop their arts. While painting, sculpture, carving and music have traditionally been the province of men, women have channeled their creative energy into making lavish offerings to the gods with spectacular pyramids of flowers, fruit and cakes offered at the temples on festival days and celebrations. All these kinds of art still have close links with the religion of the people, and are something that people do on a daily basis. Another special characteristic of art in Bali is that it is not generally seen as an individual pursuit. In the West, art is often carried out by the artist on his own, reflecting his own individual world view, in the hope of achieving personal wealth and fame. For Balinese artists, art is something that's done as a group and many artists may participate in one piece of work. And Balinese art is not restricted to temples and offerings – it decorates objects such as jackets, motorcycles, hotel menus and so on.

But perhaps the most significant characteristic of Balinese art, and one that distinguishes it most from the art of the West, is to do with its expected lifespan. Carvings are made in soft stone, which is gradually destroyed over the years. The humid climate rots paper and cloth paintings; the magnificent offerings of fruit and sweets are eaten; wooden statues are destroyed by insects. But Balinese artists accept that their work is ephemeral, not permanent, and instead of

slavishly preserving the originals, they produce new art …
and all this rebuilding, renovating and replacing means that
the island's art continually evolves and perpetuates itself.

Focus on writing page 53

1 1 c

2 Problems and solutions

3 a Suggested paragraph plan:
Paragraph 1: introduction to topic
Paragraph 2: identifying problems
Paragraph 3: suggested measures/action
Paragraph 4: conclusion: summarising main points and
opinions

b *Sample answer*

> *The increasing amount of violence that is shown regularly in
> films has been a cause of concern for some time. Such films
> make violence appear entertaining, exciting and even
> something to be copied. However, it seems to be increasingly
> clear that this development is causing problems in our
> society.*
>
> *First of all, those who enjoy such films eventually stop
> associating the violence with any real consequences. They
> therefore lose their sense of reality and no longer take violence
> seriously or have any sympathy with the victims. This is bad
> for both individuals and for our whole society. Another
> worrying trend is that in these films the heroes are shown as
> people to be admired, even though they are very violent
> characters. This leads impressionable people to believe that
> they can gain respect and admiration by copying this
> aggressive behaviour, and so the levels of violence increase,
> especially in major cities throughout the world.*
>
> *What is needed to combat these problems is definite
> action. The government should regulate the film industry on
> the one hand, and provide better education on the other.
> Producers must be prevented from showing meaningless
> violence as 'fun' in their films. Instead, films could emphasise
> the tragic consequences of violent acts and this would educate
> people, especially young people, to realise that violence is real.*
>
> *To conclude, I think that viewing violence as entertainment
> may indeed cause serious social problems and that the only
> way to improve this situation is by regulating the industry
> and educating the public about the real human suffering that
> such violence brings.*

c 1 two problems: 1 don't see real consequences of
violence; 2 violent 'heroes' are copied

2 (expressions used to introduce problems) First of all,
Another worrying trend is …

3 1 lose sense of reality, don't take violence seriously, no
sympathy for victims, bad for society and individuals;
2 levels of violence increase

4 (expressions used to introduce effects) therefore, no
longer, bad for both …, and so, this leads to …

5 two: 1 regulate industry; 2 educate public

6 (expressions used to link the ideas) What is needed to
combat these problems is …, on the one hand … on
the other

7 To conclude

4 a 1 The government <u>should</u> regulate the film industry.

2 Producers <u>must</u> be prevented from showing
meaningless violence as 'fun'.

3 Instead, films <u>could</u> emphasise the tragic consequences
of violence.

a) must   b) could   c) should

b must
have to
need to
should
could
may be able to

c 1 d   2 c   3 e   4 b   5 a

5 a 1 b   2 b   3 a   4 b   5 a   6 a

Language review D page 56

1 a *Visual arts:* 1 art gallery   2 catalogue   3 exhibit
4 paintings   5 statues   6 sculptures   7 carvings
8 ceramics

Performing arts: 1 programme   2 performance
3 conductor   4 instrument   5 orchestra   6 concert
7 screen   8 sound track   9 subtitles   10 on location
11 special effects   12 cinema   13 dress rehearsal
14 scenery   15 stage   16 theatre

b 1 subtitles   2 special effects   3 on location
4 paintings   5 statues   6 ceramics   7 catalogue
8 conductor   9 theatre   10 scenery

2 1 exhibits (objects on display)   2 technique (method)
3 exhibition (display)   4 fragments (small pieces)
5 threat (menace)   6 Competence (ability)   7 emotions
(feelings)   8 qualities (features)

3 a 1 S   2 S   3 P   4 S   5 P   6 S   7 S   8 P

b 1 it is a cause for concern that
2 causes many problems
3 another worrying trend is
4 is needed to combat these problems
5 One thing that would improve the situation is
6 the government should take measures to solve these
problems, for example by

4 1 and yet   2 However   3 after all

5 1 c   2 f   3 b   4 e   5 a   6 g   7 d

> ### PROGRESS CHECK 2 (MODULES C AND D)
>
> 1 1 are closely linked   2 objects in the exhibition
> 3 have different attitudes   4 has broken down
> completely / has completely broken down   5 of their
> research   6 to come up with   7 caused by stress
> 8 carried out a study
>
> 2 a 1 B   2 D
> b 1 a stone's throw from   2 thus far   3 have sparked
> calls   4 cast their eyes on   5 swallowed
> 3 a b)
> b Paragraph 2: f, c, a
> Paragraph 3: e, d, b
>
> 4 1 d   2 b   3 g   4 e   5 h   6 a   7 f   8 c

MODULE E

Focus on listening page 60

1 1 B 2 B 3 A 4 A 5 B 6 B 7 A

2 1 F 2 T 3 F 4 T 5 F 6 T 7 F 8 F

3 1 B 2 E 3 H 4 G 5 active 6 40 7 carving(s)
   8 1886 9 $25 10 stone(s)

Audio script

You hear a tour guide speaking to a group of tourists who are visiting a part of New Zealand called Rotorua.
First, you have some time to look at questions 1–4.
Now listen carefully, and answer questions 1–4.

Hello, everyone, and I'd like to welcome you all to Rotorua, one of the most famous destinations in New Zealand, where we have a long history of welcoming visitors. I'd like to explain a bit about the geography of this amazing region, famous for its geothermal activity, and tell you what we've planned for your stay.

Well, if you'd like to have a look at the map of the region that's in your welcome pack, if you find Lake Rotorua on the top left … the big triangular lake? We've just driven down along State Highway 5, SH 5, down the western side of the lake and then we turned off through the town, and we're here at the Lakes Motel, just around the southern tip of the lake. OK? Now, tomorrow we'll be heading off along SH 30 in the opposite direction from the town, towards Lake Rotoiti, where we'll be visiting the Hell's Gate Thermal Reserve. This is the area between the SH 30 road and the lake, and I'll be telling you more about this in a minute. We'll then be returning to the motel and in the afternoon we'll be visiting the town of Rotorua itself, and also the Arts and Crafts Institute which is just along the SH 30 from the motel where it meets the SH 5 outside the town.

Now if you look directly out of the motel towards the south east, in the opposite direction to Lake Rotorua, you can just see the peak of Mount Tarawera, and the day after tomorrow we'll be visiting the volcanic valley which was formed when this last erupted.

We'll drive down the SH 5 and then head off towards Lake Rotomahana – the valley's on the opposite side of the lake from the mountain, so you can see what a powerful effect the eruption had. There's also an interesting archaeological site – a village buried by the same eruption – on the western shores of Lake Tarawera, just to the north, but I'm afraid we won't have time to visit that as a group although you may wish to go there on your own. However, on the way back towards Rotorua along the SH 5 we'll be stopping at Tamaki Village, which is on the main road about 12 kilometres outside town.

Before you hear the rest of the talk you have some time to look at questions 5–10.
Now listen and answer questions 5–10.

So now let me tell you a bit more about these attractions. Just driving past the lake and through the town, I'm sure you've realised this is somewhere quite different from anywhere else in the world.

So tomorrow we'll start by visiting Hell's Gate Thermal Reserve. This is the most active area of the region volcanically, and you'll see New Zealand's largest boiling whirlpool, where the water is actually 100°C, together with the largest hot waterfall in the Southern hemisphere, where it's a more comfortable 40°C – just right for a hot shower. Entry is just $12 for adults, and $6 for children. We'll come back to the motel for lunch, after which we'll visit the Arts and Crafts Institute, where you can learn about the Maori people, who lived here before the Europeans came. There's a display of Maori carving, showing this traditional skill at its most impressive, and exhibitions where you can learn about the use of geothermal waters for cooking food and for medicinal purposes. Entry is free, and you'll find plenty to do there for the whole afternoon.

The following day we'll be visiting another highlight of the region, the volcanic valley. This is a very new part of New Zealand – the valley was formed less than 150 years ago in 1886, when Mount Tarawera erupted violently, completely destroying the beautiful pink and white terraces that used to attract tourists to the region. After lunch you can take a boat trip to see the volcanic activity at the edge of the lake, that's $25 for adults and $5 for children. We'll then be spending the afternoon learning more about traditional Maori life and pre-European New Zealand at Tamaki Village. As you walk around this recreated village, your Maori guide will tell you more about this traditional culture, and as the sun sets, you can enjoy a traditionally-cooked feast known as the hangi – that's H A N G I – consisting of meat and vegetables cooked over hot stones, which are placed in a hole in the ground and covered with earth. And there's no extra charge for this – it's all included in the basic cost of your holiday.
Now, does anyone have any questions?

Focus on speaking 1 page 62

1 1 a rural place
   2 3 = past tense; 1, 2, 4 = present
   3 4 (*explain why*)

2 a

Where it is located	What it looks like	When speaker first went there	Why it is especially beautiful
Crete, southwest of island	beautiful: mountains in the background and sea in front	when a student – a long time ago, by accident	unspoilt because so wild doesn't attract tourists

b 1 Well, the place I'd like to talk about is …
   2 What attracted me to it was …
   3 The first time I went there was when …
   4 And the reason why …

Audio script

Well, the place I'd like to talk about is in Crete – you know, the big island that belongs to Greece. And this is a small village, it's located in the southwest of the island … um … and it's surrounded by mountains. The whole landscape is very mountainous. If you stand in the village and look around, you can see the White Mountains in the background and the sea in front – that's the Libyan Sea, stretching out in front of you. The very first time I went, I loved this place, and what attracted me to it was how beautiful it is – it gets good weather practically all the year round, and the mountains look fantastic – you know, changing colours all the time according to the time of day and the season and so on. The hillsides look quite dry, but they always have lots of wild flowers and herbs for a lot of the year, and, er, it's one of my favourite places, actually. The first time I went there was when I was a college student, a long time ago now, and, er, I was with a friend and we were travelling around the island and went there by accident, really. But we just fell in love with it.

And the reason why I think this place is especially beautiful is, um, because it is so unspoilt. It must have hardly changed over the last hundred years. I suppose, it's so wild that it doesn't attract many tourists, so the natural environment is still very special.

4 b 1 Do you <u>often</u> go to this place? No, I've only been <u>once before</u>. No, but I wish I <u>could</u>. Yes, as often as I <u>can</u>.
2 Would you <u>recommend</u> this place to <u>other people</u>? No, that would <u>spoil</u> it. Yes, <u>definitely</u>! I <u>suppose</u> so.
3 Do you think you'll go to this place <u>again</u>? Probably <u>not</u>, it's too hard to <u>get</u> to. I'll <u>certainly try</u>. I <u>hope</u> so.

Focus on speaking 2 page 63

1 b Problem: biggest problem is pressure on *natural areas*
Cause: population is *expanding*, forests being *cut down* for agriculture, *housing and factories, etc.*
Result: loss of *trees and wildlife*
Solution: government should
– introduce *strict regulations*
– offer *alternative places to new farmers …*
schools have to *educate children about looking after the environment*
Future: If action taken, *we can reduce these problems.* Otherwise *the problems are going to get worse for whole world*

Audio script

Examiner: What do you think is the main environmental problem in your country?
Candidate: Well, um, I suppose the biggest problem in my country is the pressure on natural areas. You know, the population is expanding, so the forests are being cut down for agriculture or for housing and factories, and so on … And of course, this affects the wildlife very badly … so we're losing both the trees and the wildlife …
Examiner: And what do you think could be done to deal with this problem?
Candidate: Well, I think the government should protect the forests. They should have very strict regulations … and of course, they need to offer alternative places to new farmers … and schools have to educate children about looking after the environment.
Examiner: So do you think this problem will get better or worse in the future?
Candidate: Well, if action is taken, then I think we can reduce these problems. But otherwise, I think the problems are going to get worse … for the whole world.

Focus on reading page 65

1 a 1 False (but it was the biggest of its time)
2 True
3 False (it sank when it hit an iceberg)
4 False (1,523 died)
5 True
6 True (the director, James Cameron, went down to the wreck in a submersible and filmed it; some of these shots were used in the film)
b 1 They look like underwater icicles.
2 bacteria, fungi and other microbes
3 They are removing iron from it.
4 Yes.

2 b 1 d 2 j 3 a 4 e 5 g 6 h 7 f 8 c 9 i 10 b

3 1 Paragraph C (the structure of a rusticle)
2 Paragraphs A and B
3 Paragraphs E–H

4 1 T 2 NG 3 F (he investigated the deterioration of the wreck) 4 T 5 NG (we're only told it was the largest of the rusticles brought up by *Nautile*) 6 layered
7 communities 8 task 9 (the) surface
10 iron compounds 11, 12 (*in either order*) C, G
13, 14 (*in either order*) A, D

Focus on writing page 68

1 a 1 El Niño is a warm ocean current that affects weather patterns on both sides of the Pacific Ocean.
2 The diagrams compare normal and El Niño conditions in the Pacific Ocean.
b 1 from the east
2 They blow it westwards.
3 It brings rain to Australia.
4 It rises in the east.
5 Fish numbers increase and the weather is good.
c 1 Strong winds blow from the west.
2 They push the warm water eastwards.
3 It is dry and sunny.
4 It stays at the bottom of the sea.
5 There are fewer nutrients so fish stocks reduce and the weather is bad.

2 b 1 The warm water builds up in the west, *allowing* cool water to rise to the surface in the east.
2 The cool water brings rich nutrients to the surface, *enabling* the numbers of fish to increase near Peru.
3 In El Niño conditions, warm surface water flows eastwards, *bringing* rain to Peru.
4 Storm clouds are formed in the eastern Pacific, reducing rainfall in Australia.
5 The warm water forms a layer on top of the cool water, *preventing* the cool water from rising to the surface.

3 a Paragraph 1 Introduce information
Paragraph 2 Describe normal conditions
Paragraph 3 Describe El Niño conditions
Paragraph 4 Give an overview of the key information
b 1 The first 2 Consequently 3 while at the same time
4 also 5 The second 6 In these conditions 7 while
8 so

4 Sentence b

5 1 present
2 ocean currents are changed, rainfall is greatly reduced. NB: the passive is not used very much here because the diagrams show the active **agents** of what happens: the winds, etc.
3 blowing, bringing, allowing, enabling, bringing

6 a 1 Wrong spelling (1)
2 Active/passive verbs confused (1)
3 Agreement (3)
4 Wrong word form (2)
5 Wrong word or expression (3)
b The *diagrams* give information about the El Niño current in the Pacific Ocean.
Firstly, in normal conditions we can see that the wind *blows* the warm water to the west *causing* cool water to rise up to the *surface* in the east. This *brings* rich nutrients, *enabling* the number of fish to increase. In *these* conditions Peru *gets* sunshine and Australia gets rain.
However, in El Niño conditions the weather is different.

Language review E page 71

a 1 quality   2 table   3 shortage   4 vapour   5 level
6 treatment   7 fresh   8 drinking   9 waste   10 rain
11 ground   12 salt   13 sea
b 1 drainage system   2 recycling plant   3 domestic use
4 scarce resource   5 piped water supply   6 daily consumption   7 vehicle emissions   8 air pollution
9 illegal dumping   10 greenhouse effect   11 health risks
c 1 water shortage   2 recycling plant   3 waste water
4 treatment   5 domestic use   6 scarce resource
7 daily consumption   8 air pollution   9 health risks
10 vehicle emissions

MODULE F

Focus on reading page 72

1 B

2 1 a century ago, these days
2 knowledge workers, by putting it in quotation marks
3 knowledge technologists
4 education
5 role of women
6 F 2   G 3   H 1

3 1 C   2 A   3 D   4 A   5 B

4 c 6 N   7 Y   8 NG (no information on becoming successful by accident)   9 Y (*the upward mobility* = good point; *comes at a high price* introduces bad points)
10 NG (writer does not give his opinion)
11 N (*viciously competitive* suggests it is **not** right)
12 Y   13 NG (no statement made about helping people)

5 1 manual   2 knowledge workers   3 knowledge technologists   4 continuing   5 role of women
6 psychological pressures

Focus on listening page 76

1 1 Sami, Irene (students) and their tutor
2 a survey about access to computer facilities

2 1 the percentage of students recommending a booking system
2 about 70%
3 about 77%

3 1 C   2 B   3 A   4 A   5 C

Audio script

You will hear part of a tutorial between two students and their tutor. The students are doing a research project to do with computer use.
First, you have some time to look at questions 1–5.
Now listen carefully and answer questions 1–5.

Sami: Dr Barrett?
Tutor: Sami, come in. Is Irene with you?
Irene: Yes.
Tutor: Good. Sit down. Right, we're looking at how far you've got with your research project since we last met. You decided to do a survey about computer facilities at the university, didn't you?
Irene: That's right. We decided to investigate the university's open access centres, and in particular the computer facilities. Lots of the students are having trouble getting access to a computer when they need one, so we thought it would be a useful area to research.
Tutor: Good. Fine. It's not a topic anyone has looked at before, as far as I know, so it's a good choice. So what background reading did you do?
Sami: Well, we looked in the catalogues in the library but we couldn't find much that was useful – it's such a specialised subject, hardly anything seems to have been published about it …
Irene: And as well as that, the technology is all changing so quickly.
Sami: But the open access centre has an online questionnaire on computer use that it asks all the students to do at the end of their first year, and the supervisor gave us access to that data, so we used it as a starting point for our research. It wasn't exactly what we needed, but it gave us an idea of what we wanted to find out in our survey. Then we designed our own questionnaire.
Tutor: And how did you use it?
Irene: We approached students individually and went through our questionnaire with them on a one-to-one basis.
Tutor: So you actually asked them the questions?
Irene: That's right. We made notes of the answers as we went along, and actually we found we got a bit of extra information that way as well – about the underlying attitudes of the people we were interviewing – by observing the body language and things like that.
Tutor: How big was your sample?
Sami: Well, altogether we interviewed a random sample of 65 students, 55% male and 45% female.
Tutor: And what about the locations and times of the survey?

Sami: We went to the five open access computer centres at the university, and we got about equal amounts of data at each one. It took us three weeks. We did it during the week, in the day and in the evenings.

Tutor: Not the weekends?

Sami: No.

Tutor: So presumably your respondents were mostly full-time students?

Sami: Yes … oh, you mean we should have collected some data at the weekends, from the part-time students? We didn't think of that.

Tutor: OK. It's just an example of how difficult it is to get a truly random sample. So how far have you got with the analysis of results?

Irene: Well everyone agreed there was a problem, but we're more interested in what they think should be done about it. The most popular suggestion was for some sort of booking system. About 77% of the students thought that would be best. But there were other suggestions; for example, about 65% of people thought it would help if the opening hours were longer, like 24 hours a day.

4 a Problems and disadvantages
   b A problem related to *different rooms for educational and recreational use*
   c 6 B 7 D 8 F 9 E 10 G

Audio script

Before you hear the rest of the talk you have some time to look at questions 6–10.

Now listen and answer questions 6–10.

Tutor: So what other suggestions did people come up with?

Irene: Well, actually the main reason why people can't get to a computer is because so many students are using them for personal e-mails or just surfing the web, so one solution would be to have some computer rooms for recreational use, and some for people to do serious work in. The trouble is, quite often people do their work, then they want to check their e-mails, and it would be a nuisance if you had to get up and go to another room and log on again just for that.

Sami: Another problem is that during the day, tutors book whole blocks of computers for complete sessions. So several people said there should be restrictions on block bookings; but the trouble is the classes need the computers – there's nothing else they can use. Some people said the whole problem would be solved if the university would just buy more computers, but other people said it might make things better for a bit, but it wouldn't really solve the problem permanently; you can't just solve the problem by throwing money at it.

Irene: And with the suggestion that the computer rooms should stay open round the clock, some people did point out that there'd have to be someone around all the time to make sure the equipment didn't get stolen, especially at night.

Tutor: So a booking system seems to be the best suggestion?

Irene: Yes, apparently some universities have a sort of queueing system … it means the staff at the open access

centres have to organise it, but people say it works quite well … you go along and if there isn't a computer free just then, you're given a numbered ticket and then when your number is called out, you have the next available computer … or it can be done electronically as well, but that's more complicated and it isn't really necessary.

Tutor: Good. So now let's discuss …

5 a, b
   1 nuisance (B)
   2 nothing, use (D)
   3 solve, permanently (F)
   4 someone, stolen (E)
   5 staff, organise (G)

Focus on speaking 1   page 78

1 1 what the event was
   2 what happened during it
   3 who was there
   4 explain why you remember this event so well

2 a) a party, a special dinner
   b) a debate, a guest lecture, a graduation, a prize-giving ceremony
   c) a championship final, a tournament, a sports match

3 Speaker A school graduation (ceremony, head teacher, speech, Minister, certificates, leaving school, last time … to be together)
   Speaker B championship final (supporters, team, their biggest chance, players)
   Speaker C party (decorations, music, students had organised everything, food, masses to eat and drink)

Audio script

A: At the beginning of the ceremony, the head teacher gave a speech, but it wasn't too long or anything. And then the Minister got up to give out the certificates, but before she did that, she told us about how *she* had felt about leaving school. And at the end, we all realised that this might be the last time for us all to be together …

B: On the big day, all the supporters felt really nervous – I mean, we all knew the team were really good, but because this was their biggest chance, everybody seemed very stressed, apart from the players, that is. They all seemed amazingly calm and confident.

C: In terms of the decorations, the music and stuff, the students had organised everything themselves, except for the food. The college provided that, and there was masses to eat and drink – except for alcohol, that is. According to the college, that wasn't appropriate.

4 a Extract A

Focus on speaking 2 page 79

2 a 1 Personally 2 Clearly 3 Obviously 4 Generally
5 Inevitably 6 Frankly 7 Surprisingly
8 Predictably

b a) personally
b) frankly
c) generally, typically
d) obviously, clearly
e) predictably, inevitably
f) surprisingly

3 b

> ### Audio script
>
> 1 Personally, I don't think organised social events are very important because students often prefer to have a separate social life, outside college.
> 2 Well, clearly, there should be some role for sport in schools because it's so important for a child's development.
> 3 But obviously the first aim of primary education is to teach students basic literacy skills, because they're the tools for all other types of learning, aren't they?
> 4 Generally, it's hard to get a job these days with no qualifications, though it's always possible, as that's the first thing employers look for. And there's always lots of competition for jobs.
> 5 Inevitably, ability is usually judged by exam results because it's the easiest way for schools to assess their students.
> 6 Frankly, I don't believe exams are necessarily the best way to assess a person. That's because they usually test what you remember, don't they? Rather than what you can actually use.
> 7 Surprisingly, weak students sometimes get pretty good exam results because they just memorise stuff. Then they forget it all afterwards.
> 8 Predictably, most people find exams are stressful and they can never perform at their best when they're too stressed out.

Focus on writing page 80

1 1 University education
2 Who should have access? A large proportion of young people, or only a few?
3 To what extent do you agree or disagree?

2 *Possible answers*
Access should be restricted because:
a) not appropriate for economy – technicians needed more than graduates
b) graduate unemployment will rise and create dissatisfaction
c) better to create vocational further education programmes
Access should be widened because:
a) individuals need technological skills and knowledge
b) societies need educated citizens in order to develop
c) everyone should have a chance to fulfil their potential, and university is part of that

3 a 1 Introduce the topic
2 State your thesis/point of view
3 Justify your opinion
4 Summarise your thesis/point of view

4 a 1 disagree
2 three (*Firstly, Furthermore, Finally*)
3 Firstly, Futhermore, Finally

b B Underlength answer – if you write fewer than 250 words you will lose marks.
E The conclusion does not answer the question – you should ensure that yours does.
F Ideas are not developed – you must develop, clarify and support your ideas in order to write a good argument.
G No paragraphing – this means the argument is not properly structured and is difficult for the reader to follow.

c Language in the introduction is copied from the task – should be paraphrased.

5 1 tertiary 2 limited 3 the most academic
4 many more

6 b A 2 B 3 C 1

7 *Sample answer*

In the past, tertiary education was limited to a small proportion of people who were the most academic students. Today, however, many more young people have the opportunity of going to university, and I think that this is a much better situation for several reasons.

Firstly, individuals today need much higher level skills and technical knowledge. For example, many professionals require advanced computer skills and an ability to adapt to a rapidly changing workplace. Schools do not have the resources to equip students with these skills, so universities have to fulfil this role.

Furthermore, societies cannot continue to develop unless more citizens are educated. In order to progress and compete in the modern world, each country needs people who can develop modern technologies further and apply them in new fields.

Finally, it is only fair that anyone who could benefit from a university education should have access to one. Therefore, there should be equal opportunities for everyone to realise their full potential. Going to university is part of this.

In conclusion, I totally disagree with the statement because I believe that the increasing availability of tertiary education is vital both for the individual and for society as a whole. Individuals need as high a level of education as possible to achieve their full potential, and in the same way, society in the 21st century cannot function unless it has large numbers of highly educated people to cope with the changes to our living and working environment that are likely to occur in the coming decades.

(255 words)

Language review F   page 82

1 1 Department   2 lectures   3 seminars   4 tutorials
5 class   6 self-access centre   7 subjects   8 full-time, part-time   9 undergraduates   10 Faculty   11 lecturers
12 professors   13 stimulation   14 learning capacity
15 mental   16 nerve fibres

2 a 1 active   2 beneficial   3 dominant   4 ludicrous
5 substantial   6 adequate   7 domestic   8 efficient
9 overwhelming   10 systematic
b 1 ludicrous   2 overwhelming   3 domestic
4 beneficial   5 substantial   6 systematic   7 adequate
8 dominant   9 active   10 efficient
c 1 seemed a ludicrous idea
2 the overwhelming majority of people
3 domestic service
4 The beneficial effects of
5 make a substantial contribution to
6 some kind of systematic preparation
7 an adequate level of education
8 a dominant force in society
9 play an active part in
10 the most efficient machine

3 1 We had to do a lot of background *reading*. before we began.
2 We decided we wanted to observe the *behaviour* of students in language classes.
3 We carried out a *survey* to discover student attitudes to language learning.
4 We designed a *questionnaire* and asked all the students to complete it.
5 We also selected a random *sample* of students to interview.
6 We then conducted face-to-face *interviews* with these students.
7 We compared the *performance* of the students in the final exam with their *level* of motivation.
8 We found that the *majority* of the successful students were highly motivated.

4 a 1 Most people go to study at university immediately after leaving school.
2 But for some of them it might be better to take a break from education for a year or two, and get a job instead.
3 Even though they would have relatively few qualifications, they would gain valuable work experience.
4 On the other hand, they might find that it was difficult to readapt to life as a student when the time came for them to return to their studies.
5 They might even decide not to do a university course at all, despite the problem that lack of qualifications might cause them later on.

PROGRESS CHECK 3 (MODULES E AND F)

1 1 ✓   2 ✗ (*restricted to* means not open to anyone else, this information is not given in a)   3 ✗ (*contributions* and *achievements* are not the same)   4 ✓   5 ✗ (*a growing body of evidence* is not the same as *all the evidence*)   6 ✓   7 ✓   8 ✗ (*an important influence* is beneficial, *unnecessary pressure* is not)

2 a 1 habitats   2 environmental problems   3 repair (damaged) soil   4 complex root network
5 harvesting   6 produces more oxygen
7 atmosphere   8 durability
b 1 adaptable   2 adverse effects   3 potentially crucial
4 an astonishing variety   5 eco-friendly

3 1 Well, first I started classes in kindergarten.
2 And after that, when I was still a little kid, my family moved to the US for a while.
3 So during that time I learnt a lot – and had a really good accent of course.
4 But eventually we came back home and I started to forget everything.
5 At that stage being back at my old school in my home town seemed a bit boring, so I kind of lost interest.
6 But later I started to get into pop music and English bands …
7 and from then on I started to work hard again.
8 Now it's one of my main ambitions – to speak English really well.

4 1 also   2 First of all   3 while/whereas   4 for instance
5 6.4c   6 whereas/while   7 0.85c   8 both   9 5.7%
10 3.2%   11 respectively   12 however   13 0.013%
14 0.006%   15 despite   16 1.1%   17 Overall

MODULE G

Focus on speaking 1   page 86

1 a Ways of communicating
b a) personal preferences: 1, 2, 6
b) general public preferences: 3, 4, 5
c four questions: 2, 3, 4 and 6

Audio script

Examiner: Now let's talk about ways of communicating. Do you prefer making calls on a land line or a mobile phone?

Candidate: Well, obviously a mobile can be used anywhere, so that's a big advantage. But given the option, I'd rather use a land line, mainly because the quality of the line tends to be better, and, um, there's more privacy.

Examiner: How popular is text-messaging compared to talking on the phone?

Candidate: It's hard to say. I mean, young people where I live are definitely texting more, rather than making calls. But I guess that's because it's much cheaper. I think maybe older people would still prefer to make calls 'cos they might not like to change … but I don't honestly know for sure.

Examiner: Do people in your country prefer to write letters or e-mails?

Candidate: Oh I think nowadays, the preference is for e-mails, especially for work or just keeping in touch with friends. They're so easy and fast … and letter-writing takes too long these days. Mind you, I think letters can be more personal, and definitely more private, so perhaps some people would still choose to write letters in some situations.

Examiner: Would you rather get a letter or an e-mail?

Candidate: It depends. If it's just routine stuff, then I like e-mails better, but I'd sooner get a letter if it's about something more important … e-mails seem a bit too informal for that, somehow.

Examiner: Well, now let's move on to talk about …

2 a 1 given the option   2 rather than   3 would still prefer
     4 the preference   5 would still choose   6 I'd sooner
  b 1 Mainly because the quality of the line tends to be better and there's more privacy.
     2 Because it's much cheaper.
     3 Because they might not like to change.
     4 They're easy and fast.
     5 Letters can be more personal and are definitely more private.
     6 E-mails seem a bit too informal.

Focus on listening 1   page 87

1 1 Drive   2 Avenue   3 Way   4 Hill   5 Lane   6 Square

2 1 Douglass
  2 135 Park Hill Avenue
  3 765482
  4 low volume / volume (is) low
  5 (a) power cut
  6 Schneider SVV5002
  7 7 years (old) (not *ago*)
  8 B
  9 C
  10 A

Audio script

You will hear a woman phoning an electrical repair company about a problem with a piece of household equipment.

First you have some time to look at questions 1–7.

You will see that there is an example that has been done for you. On this occasion only, the conversation relating to this will be played first.

Kevin: Hello. Sinclair Electrical Services. Kevin speaking.

Molly: Oh, good morning. Er, I believe you do television repairs?

Kevin: That's right, we do.

The woman is calling about her television, so *television* has been written in the space.

Now we shall begin. You should answer the questions as you listen because you will not hear the recording a second time.

Listen carefully and answer questions 1–7.

Kevin: Hello. Sinclair Electrical Services. Kevin speaking.

Molly: Oh, good morning. Er, I believe you do television repairs?

Kevin: That's right, we do.

Molly: Well, my television's not working, but I don't have a car, … can you come round to see it?

Kevin: That shouldn't be a problem.

Molly: Good.

Kevin: Can I just take a few details, then?

Molly: Certainly.

Kevin: So if I could start with your name?

Molly: Yes, it's Mrs Douglass.

Kevin: DOUGLAS?

Molly: It's double S at the end, actually.

Kevin: OK. And the address?

Molly: 135 Park Hill Avenue.

Kevin: In Sommerton?

Molly: That's right. And would you like my phone number?

Kevin: Yes, please.

Molly: It's 765 482.

Kevin: 428?

Molly: No, 82.

Kevin: OK. Right, so what's the problem with the television?

Molly: Er, low volume. Even when you turn it up to maximum, it doesn't seem to make much difference. I mean, it's quite an old TV but it's always worked perfectly well, up to now. And the picture's OK.

Kevin: Mmmm.

Molly: I did wonder … we had a power cut a couple of days ago, and it's not been right since then. I don't know if that could have affected it?

Kevin: It certainly might have something to do with it. Anyway, I'll come over and have a look. Er, can you tell me the make and model number by any chance … the number'll be on the back of the TV.

Molly: Yes, it's a Schneider –that's SCHNEIDER – and the model number's … let me see, yes it's SVV5002.

Kevin: Right. Is that a fairly recent model?

Molly: Not really … I got it seven years ago. I remember the date because it was the year after I moved into this house and that was eight years ago. I hope you can fix it … I really don't want to buy another one.

Before you hear the rest of the talk you have some time to look at questions 8–10.

Now listen and answer questions 8–10.

Kevin: Well I'll see what I can do when I come round to the house to look at it. I think I know your road. Is it the one that's off the High Street?

Molly: That's right. The house is on the left if you're coming from the High Street, just before the road bends to the right. I'm afraid it's getting harder and harder to park on the road but if you drive on round the bend, you can usually find somewhere.

Kevin: That's all right. Now, let's see, when would it be convenient for me to come round?

Molly: Well as soon as possible really.

Kevin: Well, what's today … Friday. I'm booked up today and then we've got the weekend so I'm afraid it looks like Monday morning's the earliest.

Molly: You can't come tomorrow?

Kevin: Well, Saturday morning I'm in the showroom, and I don't work Saturday afternoon and Sunday.

Molly: OK. I'll make sure I'm in.

> **Kevin:** Oh, and one last thing … I wonder if you'd mind telling me how you heard about us. We've just opened a new webpage and we're interested to see how effective it is.
>
> **Molly:** No, I actually heard about you from the woman next door. She couldn't remember your number but I looked it up in the phone book.
>
> **Molly:** Oh, right. It's always the best advertising, word of mouth. Right, OK, thank you, Mrs Douglass.
>
> **Molly:** Thank you. Goodbye.

3 a 4 spelling mistake (*volume*)
　　5 incorrect insertion of present tense verb (*is*)
　　6 overlength answer (verb + article not needed)
　　7 insertion of *ago* means that this does not answer the question *How old …?*

Focus on reading page 88

1 a 1 Yes, he does.
　　2 e-mail and the World Wide Web
　 b 1 In what concrete ways can information and communication technologies (ICTs) benefit the two-thirds of humanity who are more concerned about their next meal than about e-mail or eBay?
　　　But how can those people who need ICT capabilities most, be best helped to bridge the Digital Divide?
　　2 benefits of information technology for economics, health, education and government
　　3 Information Village Project and Simputer

2 1 costs 2 epidemics 3 distance learning
　 4 (government) information 5 confidence

3 a Information Village Project, Simputer
　　Paragraphs G and H
　 b 6 C
　 c 7 B 8 D 9 A 10 D 11 C

4 a call centres, Indian economy
　 b the first and last paragraphs
　 c 12 B 13 D 14 A

Focus on writing page 91

1 1 The advantages and disadvantages of using e-mail for social and professional communication

2 a *Advantages:* 1, 4, 6
　　Disadvantages: 2, 3, 5
　 b 2 and 6 (1, 3 and 5 can all be used for both contexts; 4 is social only.)

3 1 b 2 a

4 a argument-led
　 b 1 The overall length is only 89 words instead of 250. This would lose marks.
　　2 The introduction is copied. This would lose marks.
　　3 The argument is not developed; points are simply listed.
　　4 The link words are only used to add information; other relationships are not signalled.
　　5 There is no conclusion, so it does not answer the question.
　　6 The range of language is repetitive, e.g. *disadvantage, advantage.*

5 It is certainly true that the use of e-mail has greatly changed the way we communicate at work as well as socially. But it is also true that not all the effects of this innovation have been positive.

7 *Advantages:* an obvious benefit, a good point, an argument in favour of, a positive aspect
　Disadvantages: a drawback, a negative effect, the downside, a frequent/common criticism, an objection

8 a *Adddition:* Another objection to … is that
　　Introducing examples: A common example of this is when
　　Cause and effect: This is because, so
　　Clarification: In other words
　 b 3 (it signals a new section of the response; 2 is also possible, but this only contrasts with preceding information, so does not introduce the new section effectively)

9 Conclusion 1. This is because it summarises the argument and answers the question. Conclusion 2 does not answer the question.

10 *Sample answer*

> It is certainly true that the use of e-mail has greatly changed the way we communicate with each other at work as well as socially. But it is also true that not all the effects of this innovation have been positive, although there are certainly some advantages.
>
> A common criticism of e-mail in the workplace is that it causes extra work and stress. This is because employees receive more messages than they can answer every day and since e-mail writers expect a quick response, this further increases pressure on employees. Other objections to e-mail for both social and professional users include the way it encourages people to spend even longer at their computers and also the danger of incoming messages allowing viruses into your computer system.
>
> In spite of these negative effects, however, e-mail has brought important benefits as well. One such advantage of using e-mail is that it is a fast and easy way to communicate with family, friends and work colleagues wherever they are in the world. It not only allows people to stay in touch with each other, but it also allows them to send all kinds of information (such as pictures, photos, diagrams, texts, etc.) very quickly, cheaply and with a very good quality of reproduction. This is a huge advance on earlier communication systems, and the low cost of e-mail means it is very widely used.
>
> To sum up, while there are some obvious drawbacks to using e-mail, this fast and user-friendly technology has greatly improved our ability to communicate both professionally and socially. Therefore, I think e-mail has brought us many more benefits than disadvantages.

(271 words)

Focus on listening 2 page 94

1 1 7.50   2 Park Square   3 media   4 News and weather
  5 first letter

2 **b** *Social bonds* comes before *strong*
  c 6 social bonds   7 brains   8 sound   9 silent singing
    10 feet

Audio script

You will hear a radio announcer giving details of the evening's broadcast programmes. First you have some time to look at questions 1–5.
Now listen carefully and answer questions 1–5.

The time is 6.55 on Thursday October 15th, and now here is a brief review of this evening's programmes on Radio 6. Starting in just a few minutes, at seven o'clock, we have the first programme in our new series 'Animal Talk', a documentary with Laura Martins and Jeff Burns. And I'll be telling you some more about that in a minute. Then at 7.50 there will be a broadcast on behalf of the Rare Species Protection Group, telling you about some of the work they're doing to preserve endangered species. This will be followed at 8 o'clock by today's episode of 'Park Square', our drama series following the fortunes of a close-knit community in North London, in which Sunita begins to wonder if Carl has been telling her the truth … and Carl gets into trouble when a private e-mail is read by the wrong person. At 8.30 we have our phone-in programme 'What's your view'. Today's topic is the impact of the media, and you are invited to call in with your own views and questions on this topic. If you have a question for the panel, the number to call is 0207 815 4222. This will be followed at 9.00 by news and weather, and then at the new time of 9.20 we have our 'Book of the Week' read by Graham Stannish. This week's book is a collection of Rudyard Kipling's *Just-so Stories*, which the author wrote for his children at the beginning of the 20th century, and which are now enjoyed by children and adults alike. This evening's story, entitled 'How the first letter was written', is an imaginary account of the events that led to the invention of writing, involving a young girl called Taffy and a series of misunderstandings that arise when Taffy sends the first written message in the history of the world.

Before you hear the rest of the talk you have some time to look at questions 6–10.
Now listen and answer questions 6–10.

And now some more information about our major new documentary series 'Animal Talk', which explores the fascinating area of animal communication. Tonight's programme compares the communication systems used by two of the world's largest creatures, the killer whale and the elephant. Although these might seem like very different creatures, in fact there are a lot of similarities between them. They're both mammals, they both live in groups, and the social bonds they form are extremely strong. For example, when a new elephant is born, the others in the group will all gather round to greet it. They also live for a long time – like humans – and their brains are very large, which means that there may be room for something in there that allows them to process some type of language.

In the programme, Laura Martins, who has spent many years studying the communication systems of whales, describes how although whales do have very good sight, like humans they mostly use *sound* to communicate – in the case of whales this is because this travels well in water, where visibility may be limited. In the programme you'll hear underwater recordings of the whale calls, but what we don't know yet is whether the whales are talking to one another or whether the sounds are just to allow them to identify one another.

Also speaking on the programme is Dr Jeff Burns, who has made a special study of elephant communication. Elephants use all their senses to communicate, but as Dr Jeff Burns explains, one way we are only just beginning to find out about is what has been referred to as 'silent singing' – sounds produced by elephants which are too low for humans to hear but can be heard by other elephants. And did you know that another way in which elephants can 'hear' is with their feet? So when one elephant stamps on the ground, maybe to warn about danger, the sound travels though the ground, and another elephant up to 30 kilometres away may pick it up. To find out more about exactly how they do this, stay tuned to Radio 6 for 'Animal Talk'.

Focus on speaking 2 page 95

1 1 what it was about
  2 where you read it
  3 how it made you feel
  4 why you found this article interesting.

2 **a** 1 Basically it was about the ways that *kids today have been affected by the technology they use.*
    2 I read this article in a *popular magazine.*
    3 Anyway, the article actually made me feel *a bit worried.*
    4 And the reason I found this article interesting was because *of my little brother.*
  b 1 it was based on   2 it suggested that
    3 it really described   4 the article explained
    5 it also gave some advice about

Audio script

Well, I read a very interesting article last week. Basically it was about how, er, the ways that kids have been affected by all the technology they use.

Erm, I read this article in a magazine – it's quite a popular one in my country – for the general public, not specialists or anything … it was quite short and it was based on some surveys they carried out last year.

Anyway, the article actually made me feel a bit worried because it suggested that all of these electronic devices – you know, all the computer games and mobile phones that kids use all the time – are making them much less sociable than they used to be … So I think that's quite a worrying trend …

And the reason I found this article interesting was because it really described the changes I've seen in my little brother. He used to play outside all the time, had lots of friends and so on. But now he just sits in front of his computer and doesn't go out much at all. So it was interesting that the article explained this as quite a common trend for teenagers these days. It also gave some advice about how to encourage kids to be more sociable, to spend more time with friends and family … so I found it an interesting read.

3 a Several countries, including the UK, have recently implemented measures to <u>ban the use of hand-held cell phones by drivers.</u> Researchers claim that the <u>risk of accident</u> during or just after a cell-phone conversation is <u>four times higher</u> than would be expected in normal driving conditions. Studies have shown that <u>calls are much more distracting</u> for the driver than listening to the radio or talking to passengers. The problem is that <u>drivers</u> are not aware of this and as a result are <u>not aware of the real dangers</u> that this activity poses.

Language review G page 96

1 a 1 information technology 2 global access 3 a smart card 4 computer model and make 5 a digital operating system 6 means of communication 7 yearly per capita income 8 business transactions 9 goods and services 10 a call centre 11 informed decisions 12 reduced costs 13 latest developments 14 news headlines 15 weekly edition 16 final episode 17 current affairs 18 drama series 19 radio broadcast 20 media coverage

   b 1 information technology 2 global access 3 means of communication 4 latest developments 5 business transactions 6 reduced costs 7 per capita income 8 good and services 9 drama series 10 final episode 11 current affairs 12 news headlines

2 a 1 c user-friendly 2 e labour-saving 3 b/g built-in 4 j long-lasting 5 a hand-held 6 i high-tech 7 d battery-operated 8 f touch-sensitive 9 g/b phone-in 10 h short-term

   b 1 high-tech 2 short-term 3 user-friendly 4 hand-held 5 built-in 6 long-lasting 7 touch-sensitive 8 phone-in 9 labour-saving 10 battery-operated

3 1 Currently, exciting innovations are occurring in the field of communication technology.
   2 Some people think that one of the most significant features of contemporary life is the availability of information.
   3 Although scientists first had the notion of linking separate computers to produce a network many years ago, they had no idea of the long-term implications.
   4 However, it is essential that governments consider several major questions concerning electronic media.
   5 People are showing growing anxiety about the way that technology can violate their privacy, for example.
   6 The potential impact of technology on businesses such as the entertainment industry could also be catastrophic.

4 1 odd one out 2 left out 3 loads of 4 cheap and cheerful 5 high on the list 6 quite far down 7 a lot in common 8 in depth 9 keep in touch 10 why bother

MODULE H

Focus on speaking 1 page 98

1 1 likely 2 a strong chance 3 probably 4 quite possible 5 almost certainly 6 unlikely 7 might possibly 8 not much likelihood

Audio script

Examiner: Now let's consider space exploration in the future. Do you think there will be more space exploration or less in the next few decades?

Candidate: Well, I suppose it's still a bit of a race at the moment, so in the short term I think there will definitely be more research and investment. And I think this is likely to continue in the long term.

Examiner: Why do you say that?

Candidate: Because I think there's a strong chance that the Earth won't be able to support the growing population, so we'll probably need to look for somewhere else to go.

Examiner: I see. So what future developments might take place in space exploration, do you think?

Candidate: Mmmm, it's hard to say. I think it's quite possible that people will land on Mars in the not too distant future. And I think we'll almost certainly discover new planets and maybe even new galaxies. But I think it's unlikely that we'll find any aliens.

Examiner: So how do you think the technology from the space industry will affect our lives?

Candidate: I think we might possibly see big developments in transport, but there's not much likelihood of us all having our own spaceship or anything like that.

2 a

99% sure	75% sure	Not very sure
definitely almost certainly	(*positive*) likely a strong chance probably (*negative*) unlikely not much likelihood	quite possible might possibly

   b 1 impersonal subjects (*there/it*): definitely, likely, a strong chance, quite possible, unlikely, not much likelihood
      2 personal subjects (*we*): probably, almost certainly, might possibly

3 b

Audio script

1 Well, er, I think that if there are rapid changes in technology, then older people will probably find it very hard to adapt.
2 I suppose if more and more people work from home, then workplaces will possibly disappear altogether.
3 I'm sure that provided we have sufficient food and healthcare, people will definitely live longer in the future.
4 I think that unless we find alternative energy sources, it's clear that fossil fuels will certainly run out.
5 Well, if more and more people do all of their shopping online, shopping malls will probably disappear altogether.
6 Unless we make some efforts to save minority languages, they'll probably just die out.

Focus on listening   page 99

1 1 To discuss an essay (and his problems with it)
   2 captive breeding / breeding animals in captivity
   3 Its purpose is to prevent species of animals from becoming extinct, and to allow them to be reintroduced into the wild. However, there are some associated disadvantages and problems. This process probably takes place in zoos.

2 1 B and E (in either order; both answers needed for one mark) 2 definition 3 zoos 4 expensive 5 disease

Audio script

You will hear Eliot, an environmental science student, talking to his tutor about an essay he is writing on captive breeding programmes.
First you have some time to look at questions 1–5.
Now listen carefully and answer questions 1–5.

Eliot: Dr Ran?
Dr Ran: Oh, come in, Eliot. Thanks for sending me the draft of your extended essay. Now, you're writing about captive breeding of endangered species, aren't you.
Eliot: Yes.
Dr Ran: OK. Well, this isn't a bad first draft, but there are some issues I think we need to discuss.
Eliot: Yes. I wasn't sure if I'd done enough research before I started writing.
Dr Ran: I'd say you've got plenty here – too much in places. You've got this very long introduction on factors threatening the survival of species now and in the future for instance, it's interesting, but it doesn't address the main issue of this essay.
Eliot: Oh … I thought I needed to give supporting evidence for my ideas.
Dr Ran: Yes, but only for key ideas. You can't cover everything – you've got to focus on the area you've chosen, which is the breeding of endangered species in captivity. Now you have lots of relevant material about that, but I think you need to look at the planning of your central section again; at present it's all rather a jumble.
Eliot: Oh, you mean I need to write it all out again?
Dr Ran: Well, it's just a matter of moving the things around a bit. Your introduction needs a rethink, as I said. Why don't you just begin by saying what captive breeding *is*?
Eliot: Give a definition?
Dr Ran: That's right. Then you should make it clear which are positive points and which are negative ones, For example, you start with the fact that breeding endangered species in captivity may be the only way we have of preserving some from extinction in the years to come, which is clearly an advantage. Now what other advantages did you mention?
Eliot: Er, well, the whole thing about zoos … that since they're the obvious places for captive breeding to take place, this could justify their role in the future: they're not just a place for people to go and stare at animals for fun. And then there's the point that captive breeding eventually allows the animals to be reintroduced to the wild again … in theory at least.
Dr Ran: Right. So put those points together. Then the disadvantages.

Eliot: Well, the point that these programmes are very expensive, obviously. Then thinking about the animals themselves, the psychological effects of captivity.
Dr Ran: Yes, and you also had a good section on the problem of disease for animals in captivity. But maybe you could have mentioned the poor success rate when they are eventually reintroduced into the wild.
Eliot: Right.

3 a b
   b 1 C 2 B 3 A
   c 6 A 7 B 8 C 9 B 10 A

Audio script

Before you hear the rest of the talk you have some time to look at questions 6–10.
Now listen and answer questions 6–10.

Dr Ran: Now your next section's on requirements for successful release of these animals into the wild. I think you need some evaluation here – which of these requirements are more important and which are less important, according to the available data.
Eliot: I had some information about that, but I wasn't sure if I needed to put it in ….
Dr Ran: Yes, definitely.
Eliot: My first point, for example, that's to do with the fact that animals bred in captivity have to be taught how to survive before they're released. All the data shows that's absolutely essential. Unfortunately, if they're just released without training, they won't know how to hunt, and how to avoid predators and so on. Some articles suggest that it's necessary actually to provide food and shelter for the animals after they've been released, at least for the first few months, but the research suggests that this is less crucial to the successful reintegration of the animals.
Dr Ran: Right. You also mentioned the idea of providing employment for local people in the areas where the animals were being re-released – and education so that they'll see the return of the animals into their habitats as a positive thing.
Eliot: Yes, that sounds important to me, but I couldn't actually find any statistics or information about it. And I'd have thought it was really important to screen the animals to be sure they were healthy before they were returned to the wild, but the figures show that actually it doesn't make much difference.
Dr Ran: That's surprising, yes. Did you get any data on the effects of acclimatisation?
Eliot: Yes … it showed that if animals are kept on the site where they were to be released for a time in order to acclimatise, they have a far better survival rate than those released directly into the wild.
Dr Ran: OK, well you've got some good information there. Have you thought at all about your final section?
Eliot: Well, I think I'll be looking at the whole question of habitat protection, and whether in fact captive breeding is the answer, or whether we can protect endangered species within their natural habitat.
Dr Ran: That sounds fine. So I think if you go away and make those changes, that sounds quite promising.
Eliot: Thank you …

Focus on writing 1 page 101

1 1 It is used for generating electricity.
2 It is built onto the side of a sea wall or cliff.
3 It consists of a main chamber, which opens to the sea at one end, and a closed vertical column at the other end. A turbine is located inside the column.
4 Air is pushed into the column; it drives the turbine to produce electricity.
5 The same happens in reverse: air is sucked out of the column and turns the turbine.

2 a Five paragraphs.
Paragraph 1: Introduction to diagrams
Paragraph 2: Description of structure
Paragraph 3: Process shown in first diagram
Paragraph 4: Process shown in second diagram
Paragraph 5: Conclusion

3 1 be produced   2 is built   3 consists   4 is positioned
5 is used   6 enters   7 is forced   8 turns   9 is sucked
10 generates

4 Conclusion b)

Focus on reading page 103

1 b Summary A
c to involve the reader and provide a concrete example of how ordinary people are involved in national/international affairs

2 c 1 B   2 A   3 F   4 G   5 C   6 A   7 E   8 C

3 a 1 arguments against/for GM technology
2 three, four
3 They are *indented* (placed further to the right) to make it easy to see they all apply to point b.
b The relevant part of the text begins at paragraph D and continues to paragraph G. The arguments against are given first.
c 9 pollen   10 chemical pollution   11 herbicide
12 disease(s)   13 cassava

4 14 A

Focus on writing 2 page 106

1 1 Three: the two opposing views given and the writer's own opinion
2 The argument-led approach because this follows the instruction and focuses on discussion of opposing views.

2 a Paragraph 1: *GM food products* to end of gap 5 sentence
Paragraph 2: beginning of gap 6
Paragraph 3: beginning of gap 10

1 a) against GM crops = paragraph 2   b) in favour of GM crops = paragraph 1
2 The writer is against GM crops; this opinion is given in paragraph 3.
3 The writer recommends more research before any more crops are planted.
b 1 First of all   2 Secondly   3 for example   4 also
5 This means that   6 However / On the other hand
7 not only   8 but also   9 For instance
10 In conclusion   11 while/whereas   12 overall

c *Positive:* many advantages, massively increased, more resistant, improved by adding vitamins, removing problem genes, last much longer, stored longer, less waste, obvious benefits
Negative: oppose, worry that, long-term negative effects, concerned, not been able to prove, how safe, contaminate, concerns, potential dangers, irreversible

Focus on speaking 2 page 107

1 a 1 c   2 a   3 b
b a) it would have, I would choose, I could hang, I'd love to ask, perhaps he could explain
b) I've always loved, I've always liked, I've always admired

2 Describe the sport or physical activity you would like to be good at.
You should say:
what the sport or activity is
what skills you would need
where you would do it
And explain why you would choose this sport or activity.

3 1, 4, 6, 2, 7, 5, 3

Audio script
Well, the sport or activity I'd really like to be good at is mountain climbing. Um, and that would mean I'd have to develop a lot of skills, you know, specialist skills to do with, um, climbing in rocky places and under snowy conditions. I'd also need to develop lots of physical fitness, um, I'd probably have to do a lot of work on my, er, determination … and, you know, my, sort of, desire to actually achieve an objective …
And I'd also have to develop my map-reading skills because that's something you obviously need in mountain climbing. The places I'd like to do it in are … I'd choose those vanishing places in the world, you know, um, like the Himalayas, obviously, but also I'd want to climb in the Andes in South America. And I'd love to be able to climb some of those great peaks in the Alps.
Um, and why would I choose this activity? Well, partly because, em, it's something I've always wanted to do … and I've got enormous admiration for some of the great climbers in history. But also because in the world, I think, in the future we're going to find that isolated, beautiful places will become fewer and fewer, and I'd love to be able to visit those places and explore them before they get spoilt, really …

Language review H page 108

1 a 2 space ship   3 space flight   4 space shuttle   5 space mission   6 space exploration   7 space station
b 1 artificial satellite   2 Earth's atmosphere   3 rocket launch   4 alien civilisation   5 astronaut   6 solar radiation   7 in orbit   8 nuclear technology
9 alternative energy   10 genetic engineering
11 bio-tech industry   12 GM crops   13 scientific advances   14 supporting evidence   15 relevant material   16 statistical data   17 accepted definition
18 poor success rate   19 first draft   20 key points

c 1 space exploration   2 astronaut   3 space mission
4 Earth's atmosphere   5 in orbit   6 scientific
advances   7 nuclear technology   8 alternative energy
9 genetic engineering   10 GM crops   11 bio-tech
industry
12 key points   13 supporting evidence   14 statistical
data   15 relevant material

2 a 1 ✓ 2 ✗ (it is highly unlikely, it's quite possible) 3 ✓
4 ✗ (I doubt whether, It's quite likely) 5 ✗ (will
definitely, are likely to)

3 1 The satellite is designed to monitor *not only*
environmental change *but also* pollution.
2 Envisat, *which* has taken 14 years to develop, will
transmit environmental data *as well as* specific data on
greenhouse gases and ozone levels.
3 The satellite, *which* cost £1.4 billion, is equipped with ten
different instruments *and* will have a ten-year lifespan.
4 It will register minute surface movements *in order to* give
advance warning of natural disasters, *such as* mud-slides,
floods and hurricanes.
5 The satellite, *which* is the size of a large lorry, will be
launched on an Ariane rocket.
6 Envisat will orbit the earth 14 times a day *at a height of*
800 kilometres.
7 It will be guided by a team of 50, based in the European
Space Operations Centre in Germany.
8 The satellite, *moving* in a 35-day cycle, will take just three
days to draw a complete map of the world.

PROGRESS CHECK 4 (MODULES G AND H)

1 1 more endangered species   2 It is crucial   3 people
are worried about pollution   4 a very controversial
topic   5 undermined his confidence   6 has a large/
wide/big circulation   7 gave the go-ahead
8 is still prohibited

2 a 1 D 2 A 3 C 4 B 5 C 6 A
b 1 belt out, bellowing, cacophony
2 ballad, serenade
3 call, banter

3 a A 3 B 4 C 2 D 1
b 1 for instance, 2 Similarly 3 Examples
4 However, 5 Yet 6 Instead of
c 1 We are becoming more and more dependent on
machines in the modern world. (In fact, machines
have brought benefits …; I certainly agree about
our overall dependence.)
2 This is a very negative development. (But this does
not necessarily mean that the effects of our
dependence are negative; It is hard to find reasons
why our dependence on machines is negative; We
should appreciate the many benefits that machines
bring.)

4 1 d 2 a 3 b 4 e 5 f 6 c

MODULE I

Focus on reading   page 112

1 a 1 An experiment involving a new type of bus which is
non polluting and uses renewable energy sources
b 1 Europe
2 nine
3 the means of hydrogen production, organisation of
infrastructure, the operating conditions for the buses

2 *fuel cell:* the place where hydrogen molecules are split and
power is produced as a result
zero emission: a situation where no polluting by-products
are given off at any stage in a process

3 1 T   2 NG   3 T   4 NG   5 F   6 C   7 F   8 A   9
D

4 a Paragraphs C, D and E contain the necessary
information
b 10 wind power   11 natural gas   12 on-site
13 congested traffic   14 geographical conditions

5 1 the average speed of traffic at peak times
2 in the fuel cells
3 the nine participating cities
4 hydrogen
5 wind power (not renewable sources)
6 cities using renewable energy sources, i.e. Amsterdam,
Hamburg, Stockholm and Barcelona
7 (the transportation) of hydrogen
8 on-site production of hydrogen
9 congested traffic
10 it has extreme geological conditions

Focus on speaking 1   page 115

1 1 what the problem is
2 what the causes are
3 how it affects you
4 explain how you think it might be solved

2 a 1 poor bus service
2 traffic jams so buses don't come on time;
overcrowded; overstretched service at peak times
3 usually late for college
4 invest more; bigger, cleaner buses; extra buses; make
bus lanes
b 1 one of the biggest transport problems
2 the service is so poor
3 depend on the buses
4 of solving these problems

Audio script
Well, in my city I think one of the biggest transport
problems is the poor bus service, especially during rush
hours ….
… I think the reason why the service is so poor is because –
like everywhere – we have a lot of traffic jams, so the buses
don't come on time. And they are really overcrowded when
they do come … I think the service gets completely
overstretched at peak times …
… I depend on the buses, so it means that I have to leave
home early to get to college, but I'm still usually late …
… In terms of solving these problems, well, I know it's not

easy. But I think we need to invest more in the buses … buy bigger – and cleaner – vehicles, and perhaps we could have extra buses in the rush hours. And the city authorities should make special bus lanes, so that buses don't get stuck in traffic, I think …

Focus on speaking 2   page 116

2

Audio script

Examiner: Do you think everybody has the right to have their own private transport?

Candidate A: Well, it all depends on the kind of private transport we're talking about … you know, in the case of bicycles, or even motorbikes, then I think yes, everybody does have that right. But obviously, in the case of private cars, there are lots of problems involved …

Examiner: Do you think everybody has the right to have their own private transport?

Candidate B: I'm not sure there's an easy answer to that … I mean, there are lots of mixed messages today. Like, on the one hand, the car industries persuade everybody that they want their own car, but on the other hand, we say not everybody can have one, 'cos it'll damage the planet. It's a complex issue, isn't it? Obviously I'm no expert, but I suppose in the short term everybody has the right, but in the long term, this is really not … you know… sustainable.

3 It all depends (on the situation) ✓ (first candidate)
Obviously I'm no expert, but … ✓ (second candidate)
I'm not sure there's an easy answer … ✓ (second candidate)

4 1 It's a confusing situation: *on the one hand,* advertisers persuade everybody to buy their own car, *but on the other,* we're told that private transport is bad.
2 I think everybody does have the right to private vehicles *in the case of* bicycles, *but in the case of* cars there are a lot more problems.
3 *In the short term* I think everybody should be able to have their own transport, but *in the long term* that situation can't be sustained.

Focus on listening   page 117

1 b)

2 3 As tourist development begins to increase …
1 Doxey identifies four stages.
4 If development continues to increase, …
2 He calls the first stage …
5 … in the final stage of the model …

3 1 novelty   2 economic benefit(s)   3 commercial
4 congestion   5 lifestyle(s)   6 (very) negative
7 (the) relationships   8 traditional crafts/skills
9 women   10 (new) languages (NOT language)

Audio script

You will hear part of a lecture about tourism and the leisure industry. First you have some time to look at questions 1–10. Now listen carefully and answer questions 1–10.

In today's lecture we'll begin with an overview of the impact of tourism on the societies and cultures of the host area, then we'll look at some case studies.

One model for the socio-cultural impact of tourism has been provided by Doxey – you'll find a reference in your reading list. He called his model the 'Irridex' – that's a contraction of 'irritation index' and it attempts to show how the attitudes of local people to tourists and tourism change over the years. Doxey identifies four stages.

He calls the first stage *Euphoria* – happiness – because initially the tourists are regarded as a novelty, and because of this they're welcomed by everyone in the host area. But as well as that, there's another reason for the people in the host community to welcome tourists: local people realise that tourism brings scope for economic benefits.

As tourist development begins to increase, however, local interest in the visitors becomes sectionalised. That means that some sections of the local population become involved with tourists while others don't, and it is increasingly the case that commercial rather than social factors are influencing relationships between tourists and the host community; people are less interested in the tourists for their own sake. Doxey calls this stage *Apathy.*

If development continues to increase, apathy may change to *Annoyance.* What's causing this? Well, development of the tourist area may start to spiral up out of control, and this is often accompanied by congestion, which is going to make life difficult for local people. So the policy makers, the government, the local authorities, and so on, provide more infrastructure for the area – more roads, more car parks and so on – to try to help cope with the influx of tourists. But the lives of the local people are made increasingly difficult and in the final stage of the model, annoyance has turned to *Antagonism* and open hostility to the tourists, and now all the detrimental changes to lifestyles in the host area are, fairly or unfairly, seen as due to the tourists.

Well, this sort of pathway is certainly a fairly good reflection of what happens in some tourist destinations, but Doxey's model has drawn a number of criticisms. The most significant is that it suggests a very negative attitude to the socio-cultural effects of tourism – the fact that the model is unidirectional, that it only works in one direction, seems to suggest that decline in the host–visitor relationship is inevitable. Now in practice, fortunately, things aren't always quite like that. If you look at real situations, you'll see that the relationships between local people and tourists are rather more complicated, and prone to greater variation, than this model suggests. So the model is really rather oversimplified. In fact, studies have highlighted quite a few positive effects of tourism. For example, Doxey's model doesn't look at the effects on the tourists themselves – they may well benefit from increased understanding of the host society and culture. Then, traditional crafts in the host area may be revitalised because tourism provides new markets such as the souvenir trade, for example, so instead of these traditional skills being lost, local people are encouraged to develop them. There may also be more long-lasting changes, which actually lead to the empowerment of both groups and individuals in the host area. For example, tourism creates openings for employment for women, and through giving them a chance to have a personal income, it allows them to become more independent. In addition, because tourism tends to work through a very few languages that have world-wide usage, those working in the tourist industry may be encouraged to acquire new languages, and this will empower them through providing wider access to globalised media, and improving their job prospects in a wider context.

Right, now we'll take a short break there and then we'll look at a couple of case studies and see how far the points we've discussed so far apply to them.

4 1 unidirectional   2 complex   3 increased   4 the host community   5 revitalisation   6 creating

Focus on writing page 119

1 1 applications and acceptances
   2 First area into men and women; second area into men, women + % of total applications accepted
   3 more men than women
   4 three
   5 applications decrease and acceptances increase
   6 language of change and comparison

2 Paragraph 2: Describe figures and trends related to applications
   Paragraph 3: Describe figures and trends related to acceptances
   Paragraph 4: Overview: summarise information

3 1 related to   2 changes   3 numbers   4 male and female students   5 between

4 a 1 men, women, fell/declined/decreased/went down, 2,750
     2 applications, men, fell/declined/decreased/went down
     3 fell/declined/decreased/went down
     4 men, women
     5 percentage, rose/grew/increased/went up, 21%, rose/grew/increased/went up
     6 men, women
     7 fell/declined/decreased/went down, percentage, rose/grew/increased/went up
   b Paragraph 2: Sentences 1–3
     Paragraph 3: Sentences 4 and 5
     Paragraph 4: Sentences 6 and 7
   c Paragraph 1 (start of introduction): The table shows
     Paragraph 2: Firstly, we can see that with regard to applications,
     Paragraph 3: In terms of acceptances,
     Paragraph 4: Overall,

5 1 courses in tourism, transport and travel
   2 numbers of male applicants
   3 female applicants
   4 between 2000 and 2002
   5 in tourism, transport and travel
   6 2000, 2001 and 2002
   7 applications
   8 2000, 2001 and 2002
   9 the applications

6 *Sample answer*

> The table predicts changes in the types of transport used in Shanghai between 1996 and 2020.
>
> The figures show that in 1996 the most popular form of transport was public bus, accounting for 39% of passenger kilometres. This was followed by bicycles with 27% whereas cars and scooters were used less, representing only 15% and 12% of passenger travel respectively. Predictably, walking made up the smallest percentage.
>
> It is expected that in 2020 the use of cars will increase dramatically and account for over half of all distance travelled (52%). In addition, trains will probably account for 13% of passenger kilometres, while the use of all other means of transport will decrease. Bus journeys, for example, will only represent 22% of distances travelled, while bicycle trips will drop to as little as 3%, similar to the figure for walking.
>
> Overall, the table predicts a massive increase in the use of cars by 2020, at the expense of other forms of transport.

Language review I page 122

1 a 1, 2 bicycle, truck (*either order*)   3, 4 helicopter, steamship (*either order*)   5 vehicles   6 exhaust fumes   7 increasing levels of congestion   8 traffic jams   9 dangerous driving, e.g. speeding   10 overstretched public transport systems   11 danger to pedestrians   12 bus lanes   13 construction of more roads   14 zero emission fuels   15 efficient public transport   16 the impact of tourism   17 the host community   18 an influx of tourists   19 traditional crafts   20 the souvenir trade   21 long-distance travel   22 the tourist season
   c 1 exhaust   2 vehicles   3 jams   4 congestion   5 helicopter   6 construction   7 efficient   8 season   9 traditional   10 souvenir   11 long-distance   12 community   13 impact

2 a, b Example: b geographical and climatic
       1 j innovative and sustainable
       2 h government and industry
       3 d performance and costs
       4 f needs and expectations
       5 c terms and conditions
       6 e planning and design
       7 a views and behaviour
       8 i environmental and social
       9 g groups and individuals

3 a 1 local trains   2 practical solution   3 theoretical model   4 commercial scale   5 chemical reaction   6 environmental issues   7 initial collection
   b 1 They all end in -*al*.
     2 1 local: location, locality
       2 practical: practice, practicality
       3 theoretical: theory
       4 commercial: commerce, commercialisation
       5 chemical: chemical, chemistry, chemist
       6 environmental: environment
       7 initial: initial, initiation

4 1 hard d   2 depends on b   3 expert a   4 easy answer c

MODULE J

Focus on listening page 124

1 a 1 For example, bigger eyes in portraits, and the man's beard.

2 Students may think they're just done from the portraits.

b It covers the history of the portraits and the creation of the reconstructions.

2 b 1 gap 1

2 gap 5

3 gaps 2, 4 and 6

3 1 Greece **2** over the face **3** wax **4** in/during the life/ lifetime **5** (more) realistic **6** in/inside the houses **7** B **8** A **9** C **10** A

Audio script

You will hear part of a lecture on art history. First you have some time to look at questions 1–10.

Now listen carefully and answer questions 1–10.

In the last lectures, we looked at the art of the ancient Egyptians, and then considered the art of other ancient Mediterranean civilisations, in particular Greece and Rome. We're now going to return to Egypt to consider a set of very unusual pictures known as the Fayum portraits.

The Fayum is a lush green area about 100 kilometres west of Cairo. Following the conquest of Egypt by the Greek warrior Alexander the Great in 332 BC, large numbers of businessmen and officials who had come over from Greece settled in this fertile region with their families. They gradually adopted some features of Egyptian culture, including the practice of mummification, embalming the bodies of their dead and wrapping them in linen bandages in order to preserve them as mummies (the name actually comes from an Arabic word meaning 'an embalmed body'). These newcomers made one distinctive innovation, though: after binding the mummy, they laid over the face a picture representing the person inside.

The portraits look like oil on canvas, but they were actually produced using a technique called encaustic, where the artist applies pigmented wax to a wooden board with a small spatula. The Egyptologist William Petrie, who discovered many of these mummies with their accompanying portraits at the end of the nineteenth century, was convinced that they were actually done in the lifetime of the subject, rather than being painted after the person's death, as had been the case with older Egyptian paintings. He felt they were very different from the traditional stylised images that had been used on Egyptian mummy casings in previous centuries, and was convinced that they were actually portraits, giving a realistic depiction of the person. He pointed out that the boards on which they were painted showed signs of having been cut down to size to fit within the mummy bandages. To him this suggested that they may have originally been larger and been hung in the houses of the owners during their lifetimes.

But, more than a century after they came to light, nobody knew how far they were really depictions of real people, as against idealised portraits. Then a team from Manchester University decided to find out, by recreating the faces of Fayum mummies in clay, and then comparing the reconstructions with the portraits. The team was provided with skulls from two Fayum mummies from the British Museum, and given the information, based on X-rays and other evidence, that one of the mummies was of a 50-year-old man, and the other was a woman in her early twenties. Armed only with this information, they set to work.

First, they created copies of the skulls. Then they used clay to build up the facial muscles in order to reconstruct what the person looked like. After weeks of painstaking labour, two faces emerged. Only then were the two portraits revealed, so that the match between the reconstructions and the portraits could be examined.

In the case of the man, both model and portrait showed a broad flat face with a slightly hooked nose and a fleshy mouth, with broad lips, but the man in the portrait was noticeable for his 'five o'clock shadow', the beard beginning to grow around his chin and on his cheeks. This would have been quite a recognisable feature of the man in real life, and an easy thing for the painter to copy. However, it wasn't something that the makers of the model could know about. In the reconstruction, the right eye was slightly higher than the left – and this was the same on the portrait. But on the portrait, the eyes were very large, which is standard with many of the Fayum portraits, while in the model they were longer and narrower.

The portrait of the woman appeared to be even more of a standard type, with her large eyes, straight nose and small mouth. These pretty, feminine features suggested this could be an idealised woman's face, and yet it proved to match the reconstruction surprisingly closely. The proportions of the lower face corresponded, and so did those of the forehead, though in the portrait the eyes were closer together and larger than in the reconstruction. And in both cases, the head was set on a solid neck, suggesting a more powerful physique than you might have expected from these delicate features.

So overall, the similarities between the portraits and the models are too close to be accidental. The artists may have started from a standard picture, but attempts were made to modify this to reflect the characteristics of the subject – what gave the face its personal qualities. Obviously this isn't much of a sample upon which to judge an entire genre of portraiture, but the researchers are convinced that, on the whole, the artists aimed to represent their subjects as they appeared in real life, whether this was flattering to them or not.

4 1 three (although one word is often possible)

2 the letters of the answers **only**

Focus on reading page 126

1 a 1 a) DNA   b) forensics
  2 DNA can be matched to suspects or to the DNA
    information on other criminals held in archives
  3 information about the appearance of a criminal

  b 1 Paragraphs C and E   2 Paragraphs F, G and H
  3 Paragraphs C and D

  c Forensic Science Service (FSS), based in Britain,
    DNAPrint Genomics of Florida, USA, biotechnology
    firm
    University College London (UCL), based in Britain,
    University of Konstanz, based in Germany
    'Liberty', UK-based human rights group

2 1 D 2 B 3 A

3 a 1 the title: Research into the genetic basis of eye colour
    (a title is often given)
  2 six
  3 paragraph D
  b 4 mice 5 correlation(s) 6 50 7 4

4 a a) question 9 b) questions 8, 10 and 12
  c) question 11
  b 8 DNAPrint Genomics 9 three/3 10 University
    College London 11 Germany 12 'Liberty'
    13 playing rugby

Focus on writing 1 page 129

1 1 The diagram illustrates the process of producing black
    and white photographs.
  2 a dark room
  3 Four main pieces: a camera, a development tank, an
    enlarger and a chemical bath

2 1 The diagram shows that in order to produce black and
    white photographs, a dark room and *four main pieces of
    equipment* are needed, namely *a camera, a development
    tank, an enlarger and a chemical bath.*
  2 The flow chart shows that the process of producing black
    and white photos is carried out in a dark room and
    involves the use of *a camera, a development tank, an
    enlarger and a chemical bath.*
  3 The flow chart indicates that *four main pieces of
    equipment* are used in the process of producing black
    and white photographs: *a camera, a development tank, an
    enlarger and a chemical bath.*

3 1 are captured, (are) recorded
  2 is removed
  3 is developed
  4 are produced
  5 are viewed, be enlarged, edited
  6 are printed
  7 are developed, fixed, washed and dried.
  8 be removed (As this does not necessarily happen in the
    process, the modal is more appropriate here.)

4 *In the first stage,* images are captured by the camera and
  recorded onto film. *Once* this film *has been* removed from
  the camera, it is developed in a development tank in the
  dark room and negatives are produced. The negatives are
  then viewed in an enlarger, where they can be enlarged and
  edited. *Next* they are printed onto sheets of photographic
  paper. *After this* the prints are developed, fixed, washed and
  dried. *Finally,* the photographs can be removed from the
  dark room.

5 a At the editing stage, the image <u>can be</u> changed <u>either</u> by
    cropping <u>or</u> by focusing on one enlarged section.
    <u>Alternatively,</u> the image <u>may be</u> printed without editing.
  b Black and white photographs can be developed either at
    a pharmacy or by a professional photographer.
    Alternatively, they may be developed at home.

6 *Sample answer*

> In order to produce photographs from a digital camera, three
> main pieces of equipment are needed: the camera, a computer
> and a printer.
>
> In the first part of the process, the image is recorded by the
> digital camera using a smart card. The image is then
> downloaded onto a computer. Here the image can be shown on
> the screen and edited. The picture may be cut so that less
> interesting parts are removed, and the quality of the picture can
> be improved. In addition, the sizing of the picture can be
> changed so that it is larger or smaller.
>
> When the editing has been completed, the picture can be
> transmitted in three different ways. It could be sent to other
> people electronically in an e-mail, or it could be stored on the
> computer itself or on a CD. Alternatively, the image can be sent
> to a printer for printing on photographic paper. The image may
> be printed either in colour or in black and white in order to
> produce the finished photograph on paper.
>
> Overall, the diagram shows that this process is carried out
> in three main stages, using the camera, the computer and
> the printer.

Focus on writing 2 page 131

1 *Notes for sample answer*
  1 Images – photos/films/ pictures = used everywhere to
    communicate – hard to escape
  2 Agree: image = powerful way to communicate
    used to inform, e.g. in the media
    used to influence, e.g. in advertising
    used to entertain, e.g. cinema, TV
  3 Disagree: NOT better means of communication than
    writing
    image alone = misleading = less effective
    Used WITH either written word /spoken commentary =
    most powerful comm.
  4 Overall: Partly agree – image = powerful way to
    communicate, but most effective with writing/speaking
  For a sample answer see page 140.

Focus on speaking page 133

1 b The best performance was Speaker C because Speaker C
    – answered the question
    – communicated relevant information, giving full
    responses
    – used a range of vocabulary and structures
    – used fluency markers
    – kept going – no long pauses
    – engaged with the questions and the interviewer

Note: All of the speakers had clear pronunciation and none made grammar mistakes. But two still did not perform well because of the way they answered the questions.

Speaker A failed to communicate effectively, used very little language and did not focus on the questions. He needs to answer the questions asked, give longer responses using a range of language, try to keep going rather than make long pauses, engage with the questions and the examiner.

Speaker B failed to communicate effectively because his responses were obviously memorised and did not answer the questions. This speaker was very unprepared for taking part in a live conversation. He needs to change strategies, from memorisation to engaging in spontaneous conversation, engage with the examiner and the questions, use the language he knows and try to keep going.

Audio script

Examiner: Now let's talk about clothes. How do you feel about shopping for clothes?

Speaker A: OK.

Examiner: How do you feel about shopping for clothes?

Speaker A: … Yeah, I like it.

Examiner: … Would you prefer to have a lot of clothes or only a few, better-quality ones?

Speaker A: … I always wear jeans, so it's OK.

Interviewer: … Why?

Speaker A: Yeah … because I always wear jeans.

Examiner: Now let's talk about clothes. How do you feel about shopping for clothes?

Speaker B: I always wear casual clothes because I like to feel relaxed, and actually I prefer sportswear, especially the clothes of famous manufacturers like Nike or Adidas. I don't like to wear formal clothes because …

Interviewer: How do you feel about *shopping* for clothes?

Speaker B: Um … Yes, … I like it.

Interviewer: Would you prefer to have a lot of clothes or only a few, better-quality ones?

Speaker B: … I prefer sportswear, especially the clothes of famous manufacturers like Nike or … Adidas …

Examiner: Now let's talk about clothes. How do you feel about shopping for clothes?

Speaker C : To be honest, I don't like it very much. Of course, when I was in my teens I used to love shopping, and especially for clothes. But now I don't have the time … and I certainly don't like spending too much money on clothes.

Examiner: Would you prefer to have a lot of clothes or only a few, better-quality ones?

Speaker C: Well, personally I'd much rather have fewer clothes that are really good quality. That way, I would choose them more carefully – they wouldn't just be the fashion of the moment … and it would be easier to decide what to wear every day.

d

Audio script

Examiner: Now let's talk about photographs. How popular is photography in your country?

Examiner: On what occasions do people like to take photographs?

Examiner: Why do you think some people prefer to have home movies or videos?

Examiner: What kind of photographs do you like to keep?

2 a C = more effective to talk from; covers all points of task; key vocabulary prepared
A = whole sentences; for reading aloud **not** talking; few points covered
B = in mother tongue, so speaker must translate as well as talk; no vocabulary or language prepared; no real preparation for speaking in English

b The best performance is by Speaker B.
Speaker A: This speaker has not prepared well. The long turn is difficult to follow because it is not organised. The ideas are not linked and the speaker does not talk fluently.
Speaker B: The long turn is clear, well-organised and deals with the prompts in the task. There are clear signals to the listener and the ideas are well linked.
Speaker C: This candidate just uses the language from the task to deliver a long introduction. This is inappropriate to the task and more suitable for a very long piece of writing. The part where the task is addressed is undeveloped and uses a very limited range of language.

Audio script

Speaker A: I remember seeing this fantastic image of huge waves in the sea, you know, um, white and, um, foaming … and as the waves break and curl over, they turn into, er, white horses, um, leaping in the water. But it happens slowly … and it's hard to, um, see at first … I loved it. It was, um, sort of magical and exciting … and, um, all my friends liked it too … and it was, um, …

Speaker B: Well, the advert I want to talk about used the image of the sea and, um, these fantastic huge waves. I saw it both on TV and in the cinema, so it was shown quite often for a time. Um, it was actually advertising a beer – and I suppose that's why it had the image of foaming, white waves because, um, this particular beer was famous for having white froth. But what was particularly effective about the ad was that it showed …

Speaker C: In this talk I'm going to tell you about an advertising image that I think was effective. I will tell you about where I saw this advertising image and what it was advertising. Then I am going to tell you about what it showed, and finally I am going to explain why I thought it was effective. Firstly, I saw this advertisement on the TV. Secondly, it was advertising a drink. Thirdly the image showed some horses in the sea. And finally …

173

3 1 a 2 b 3 c

Audio script

Examiner: Did you ever buy this product?

Examiner: Will you buy this product in the future?

Examiner: Do you still see this advert?

4 b The candidate responds well, answering the questions directly, while focusing on the wider issues and extending the responses with clarifications and reasons. A good range of language is used, and the speaker uses pronunciation to help emphasise the main points. A good performance.

Audio script

1 **Examiner:** Some people think advertising can be dangerous. Would you agree or disagree with that?
   Candidate: Yes, I think I'd agree, advertising can be dangerous. I mean, it's designed to persuade us to buy things, isn't it? Even to buy things that aren't necessarily good for us … and it's a huge, rich industry these days, so it's obviously successful.
2 **Examiner:** Do you think that governments should use laws to protect people from advertising?
   Candidate: It's hard to say … just passing laws won't necessarily protect people. And that kind of measure raises all kinds of other issues about individual liberties. So, I don't really think that regulation's the answer.
3 **Examiner:** How will people be able to resist advertising in the future?
   Candidate: Well, I really don't think that there's an easy answer. But maybe in the future people will be better educated to resist the kind of mass persuasion that *is* dangerous … Everything else would only be a short-term measure, so I hope people will be able to, you know, be more aware of the influence … and, well, the *pressure* that the market puts on us.

d

Audio script

Examiner: Well, let's consider the values of our society. What effect does advertising have on our values, do you think?

Examiner: Some people think that adverts give people unrealistic expectations. Would you agree?

Examiner: What do you think about the way advertisers target children?

Language review J page 134

1 a 1 cheek 2 forehead 3 jaw 4 facial muscles 5 skull 6 features 7 biotechnology 8 DNA sample 9 DNA sequence 10 genetic difference 11 negative 12 print 13 focus 14 to edit 15 to enlarge 16 to develop 17 digital camera

  b 1 digital camera 2 developed 3 edit 4 enlarge 5 prints 6 Biotechnology 7 features 8 DNA sequences 9 DNA sample 10 forehead 11 skull 12 genetic differences

2 a, b
  1 A picture frame *consists* of three main parts: the frame itself, the glass and the backing.
  2 The glass fits inside the frame and *covers* the picture or photograph.
  3 The backing, which may be made of wood or cardboard, *is held* in place by two clips, one at the top and one at the bottom.
  4 The frame shown in diagram B is *rectangular* in shape.
  5 Its overall *height* is 30 cm, and its overall width is 20 cm.
  6 The frame itself *is* quite narrow, leaving a large space for the picture inside, and it is made of silver.
  7 The frame shown in diagram C is also rectangular, and it is *approximately* the same size, but it is made of wood instead of silver.
  8 However, this frame is *much wider* than the first one, so the space left inside for the picture is only a fraction of the size of that in diagram A.
  9 It is therefore clear that the first frame would be *used* for a large picture, while the second would be suitable for a small picture.

  c A picture frame consists of three main parts: the frame itself, the glass and the backing. The glass fits inside the frame and covers the picture or photograph. The backing, which may be made of wood or cardboard, is held in place by two clips, one at the top and one at the bottom.
  The frame shown in diagram B is rectangular in shape. Its overall height is 30 cm, and its overall width is 20 cm. The frame itself is quite narrow, leaving a large space for the picture inside, and it is made of silver.
  The frame shown in diagram C is also rectangular, and it is approximately the same size, but it is made of wood instead of silver. However, this frame is much wider than the first one, so the space left inside for the picture is only a fraction of the size of that in diagram A.
  It is therefore clear that the first frame would be used for a large picture, while the second would be suitable for a small picture.

3 a 1 gave 2 were applied 3 resulted 4 was investigated 5 were recorded 6 suggested 7 provided 8 sifted 9 was reflected
  b a) how the research was carried out: 2, 4, 5, 8
  b) what was found from the research: 1, 3, 6, 7, 9

PROGRESS CHECK 5 (MODULES I AND J)

1   1 ✗ (*wound down* does not mean the same as *completed*)
    2 ✗ (*diminishing* and *escalation* have opposite meanings)
    3 ✓   4 ✓   5 ✗ (*not conclusive* means the results weren't clear; *not completed* means the experiment was not finished)   6 ✓   7 ✓   8 ✗ (*anecdotal* evidence comes from what people say, not from actual *research*)
    9 ✓   10 ✗ (a cube (three-dimensional) and a square (two-dimensional) are not the same

2 **a** 1 principle   2 boundary   3 ambient   4 struggle to
   b 1 (the) software   2 high contrast   3 sizes and positions / positions and sizes   4 (known) criminals   5 (a) match

3   1 hard   2 example   3 idea/issue   4 obviously
    5 hand   6 taking   7 environment   8 aware
    9 sustainable   10 use

4   1 b   2 f   3 e   4 d   5 a   6 c

blishers are grateful to the following for their permission to reproduce
ht photographs:

mages for 28 bottom, 60 left, 73 and 89; Corbis for 8, 41, 42, 60 right,
8; DaimlerChrysler (www.fuel-cell-bus-club.com) for 112; Getty
or 28 top and 121; Jacqui Goddard for 104; NASA for 98; PhotoEdit
otolibrary.com for 50; Pearson Education for 86; Rex Features for 63;
eave/RD-DS Partnership for 124 top right and 124 bottom right;
oto Library for 126; Still Pictures for 21; The Trustees of the British
or 124 top left and 124 bottom left.

by Peter Lubach and Tech Type
© Stone
Linda Reed and Associates

from www.digitalopportunity.org; The Economist
an extract from 'Survey: The near future' by Peter Drucker published in
The Economist 1st November 2001; Fujita Research for the image 'Schematic of
an oscillating water column' published on the Australian Renewable Energy
website © Fujita Research; Geographical Magazine for extracts from 'A growing
concern' by Jacqui Goddard and 'Satellite to world-watch' by Chris Amodeo
published in *Geographical* Vol 74, No 3 March 2002 © Geographical, the
Magazine of the Royal Geographical Society; Guardian News Services Limited
for extracts from the following articles 'Light Years Ahead' by Charlotte Denny
published in *Guardian Weekly* 26th July 2001 © The Guardian, 'The Bear's
Necessity' by Keith Laidler published in *The Guardian* 20th March 2003
© Keith Laidler, and 'Roasts Off Menu as We Eat on the Go' by Jamie Doward
and Edward Gibbes published in *The Observer* 27th July 2003 © The Observer;
The Headteacher Mr Jim McManners and Cassop Primary School for an
extract about the Cassop Primary School wind turbine from www.
cassopschool.org.uk; The National Academies Press, Washington DC for the
table 'Appendix B: Case Study: Shanghai, China' by D Sperling, Lu Ximing and
Zhou Hongchang published in *Personal Cars and China* © 2003 The National
Academy of Sciences; New Scientist for the articles 'IstabFarming comes to
town to feed the world' published in *New Scientist* 15th June 1996,
Vol 150, 'If the face fits…' by Kate Douglas published in *New Scientist*
December 2001, Vol 172, 'Ready for your close-up?' by Clare Wilson published
in *New Scientist* July 2002, Vol 175, 'Grime fighters' by Alison Motluk and
'Iron rations' by Carolyn Fry published in *New Scientist* 26th July 2003,
Vol 179; Dr Schuckert and CUTE/ECTOS for a map published on
www.fuel-cell-bus-club.com © CUTE/ECTOS; Scientific American for the
extracts adapted from 'Does Class Size Matter?' by Ronald G. Ehrenberg,
Dominic J. Brewer, Adam Gamoran and J. Douglas Willm published in
Scientific American November 2001 © 2001 Scientific American, Inc. and
'Clocking Cultures' by Carol Ezzell published in *Scientific American* September
2002 © 2002 Scientific American, Inc. All rights reserved; Statistics New
Zealand for the table 'Births and deaths, series 4, 1901–2101' published on
www.stats.govt.nz; Taylor & Frances for an extract from *Tourism Geography* by
Stephen Williams published by Routledge; and UCAS for a table from 'The
Times Higher' by Gary Haslam published in *Focus Travel and Tourism* 8th
August 2003.